CAMBRIDGE Professional English

D0525879

English 365

Teacher's Book 3

Matt Smelt-Webb

CAMBRIDGE
UNIVERSITY PRESS

CAMBRIDGE UNIVERSITY PRESS
Cambridge, New York, Melbourne, Madrid, Cape Town, Singapore, São Paulo

Cambridge University Press
The Edinburgh Building, Cambridge CB2 2RU, UK

www.cambridge.org
Information on this title: www.cambridge.org/9780521549172

First published 2005

Printed in the United Kingdom at the University Press, Cambridge

A catalogue record for this book is available from the British Library

ISBN-13 978-0-521-54917-2 Teacher's Book 3
ISBN-10 0-521-54917-5 Teacher's Book 3

ISBN-13 978-0-521-54916-5 Student's Book 3
ISBN-10 0-521-54916-7 Student's Book 3

ISBN-13 978-0-521-54918-9 Personal Study Book 3
ISBN-10 0-521-54918-3 Personal Study Book 3

ISBN-13 978-0-521-54919-6 Student's Book 3 Audio CD Set
ISBN-10 0-521-54919-1 Student's Book 3 Audio CD Set

ISBN-13 978-0-521-54920-2 Student's Book 3 Audio Cassette Set
ISBN-10 0-521-54920-5 Student's Book 3 Audio Cassette Set

Thanks and acknowledgements

The authors of the course would like to thank:

- Will Capel and Sally Searby of Cambridge University Press for their unflinching support from start to finish;
- Alison Silver for her eagle eye for detail, for her good sense and good cheer throughout the editorial and proofreading process;
- Julie Moore for her help with the *Do it yourself* exercises, based on research from the Cambridge Learner Corpus;
- Helena Sharman for writing the worksheets for the Website;
- Sarah Hall for proofreading the Student's Book and Ruth Carim for proofreading the Teacher's Book and Personal Study Book;
- James Richardson for producing the recordings at Studio AVP, London;
- Sue Nicholas for the picture research;
- Hart McLeod for the design and page make-up;
- Sue Evans; Lorenza, Mathieu, Jérôme and Michael Flinders; and Lyn, Jude, Ruth and Neil Sweeney; Catherine Jarvis for their continuing patience;
- colleagues and friends at York Associates and in the School of Management, Community and Communication at York St John College and the EFL Unit, University of York for their tolerance of authorial distraction;
- and Chris Capper of Cambridge University Press for his immeasurable contribution to the project – it is above all his huge efforts which have made this book possible;
- Matt Smelt-Webb would also like to thank Caroline Smelt-Webb and Rob Shaw.

The authors and publishers would like to thank:

- Henri Baybaud, PY Gerbeau (X-Leisure), Vicky Stringer (Orient-Express magazine), Rachid Bouchaib (Norwich Union Life), Terje Kalheim (LO, Norwegian Confederation of Trade Unions), Gener Romeu (Rotecna), Adrian Strain (Leeds City Council), Dr Rosalind W. Picard (MIT), Maria Roques-Collins (Montex, Paris), Alan Ram (Top Coaching), Sue O'Boyle (TMSDI), Melly Still, Ameeta Munshi (Thomas Cook India Ltd), Nicky Proctor (Department of Management Studies, University of York), Ylva Andersson (Göteborgs-Posten), Kristina Keck (Lafarge Zement), Peter Harrington (QA Research), Harald Petersson (Statoil), Yoshihisa Togo (Japan Committee for UNICEF), Marcus van Hooff (Amigos sem Fronteiras), Dani Razmgah (FöreningsSparbanken), Aisha Rashid (Samanea PR, Malaysia), Barry Gibbons, Jitka Otmarová (Gide Loyrette Nouel, Prague);
- Paul Munden for technical support; Andy Hutchings, Wyatt-Hutchings Marketing, and Pete Zillessen for help with research;
- Desmond Rome, Cambridge University Press, Portugal, for providing the introduction to Marcus van Hooff;
- Andy Finlay, Rosemary Richey, Brian Schack, Helena Sharman and Chris Turner for reviewing the material in its early stages.

The authors and publishers are grateful to the following for permission to use copyright material. While every effort has been made, it has not been possible to identify the sources of all the material used and in such cases the publishers would welcome information from the copyright owners.

Background briefings
Martinique Tourist Board for the text on p. 18 and for the weblink; X-Leisure for the text on p. 21 and for the weblink; Orient-Express Hotels, Trains & Cruises for the text on p. 26 and for the weblink; Terje Kalheim and Bradford University for the text on p. 32 and for the weblink; Rotecna NA for the text on p. 32 and for the weblink; Chinapages for the text on p. 35 and for the weblink © 2005 Chinapages.cn. All Rights Reserved; Leeds City Council for the weblink; Guggenheim Museum, Bilbao for the text on p. 37 and for the weblink; MIT Media Laboratory for the text on p. 40 and for the weblink; Montex for the text on p. 43 © Montex; TMSDI for the text on p. 48 and for the weblink; The Royal National Theatre for the text on p. 50 and for the weblink © The Royal National Theatre; Lonely Planet Publications for the text about Jaisalmer on p. 56 and for the weblink © 2005 Lonely Planet Publications. Reproduced with permission; Thomas Cook India for the text on p. 56 and for the weblink; University of York for the text on p. 58 and for the weblink; Göteborgs-Posten for the text on p. 62 and for the weblink; Lafarge Zement for the text on p. 65 and for the weblink; QA Research for the text on p. 65 and for the weblink; The National Autistic Society for the text on p. 69 and the weblink; Statoil ASA for the text on p. 71 and for the weblink; UNICEF for the text on p. 73 and for the weblink; Amigos sem Fronteiras for the text on p. 77 and for the weblink; FöreningsSparbanken for the text on pp. 77–8 and for the weblink; Samanea PR for the text on p. 80 and for the weblink; CSA Speakers Ltd for the text on p. 85 and for the weblink.

Extra classroom activities
Dyson UK for the text on p. 105 and for the weblink; BBC News for the text on p. 110 'TV conquers remote Bhutan' taken from the website www.news.bbc.co.uk 10 March 2005, by permission of BBC News at bbcnews.com; Nielson BookScan for *The Observer* bestseller lists on p. 119 © Nielson BookScan 2005; Comic Relief and the BBC for the text on p.121 'Big Hair, Big Dosh' taken from the BBC website www.bbc.co.uk/tyne. By kind permission of Comic Relief and the BBC; BBC News Interactive for the adapted text on p.127 'Union claims £300m equal pay win', adapted from the BBC news website. By kind permission of the BBC.

Better learning activities on the Website
The Council of Europe for the weblink in the Teacher's notes for activity 2; University of Cambridge ESOL Examinations for the weblink in the Teacher's notes for activity 4.

Contents

You can access the following on the Website:

- ten Better learning activities with accompanying Teacher's notes
- a Teacher's diary
- two revision units
- a worksheet for every unit.

See www.cambridge.org/elt/english365.

Student's Book Contents

Welcome

Who is *English365* for?

This course is for working adults who want English for their working and personal lives. Students using Book 3:

- are at an intermediate level
- will have studied English in the past but need a new extensive course to refresh, practise and consolidate what they know as well as to learn new language
- need a supportive environment to build speaking skills by activating known language, which is largely passive at the moment, and by learning new language and communication and social skills.

How long is the course?

This course provides at least 60 hours of classroom teaching. The Student's Book contains:

- 30 units which each provide 90 minutes of classroom teaching material per lesson (45 hours).

The Teacher's Book provides:

- 30 Extra classroom activities linked to each unit. Each activity takes at least 15 minutes to complete and some of them can occupy 30 minutes or more (10–20 hours).

The Personal Study Book with Audio CD provides:

- 30 self-study practice exercises linked to each unit in the Student's Book (15 to 30 minutes each)
- 12 self-study listening exercises which develop the social and professional communication work done in the Student's Book
- the pronunciation work from the Student's Book
- learning diaries for students.

The Website provides:

- two revision units with up to 60 minutes of extra classroom or self-study exercises to work on (2 hours)
- a worksheet for every unit in the Student's Book
- ten Better learning activities with accompanying Teacher's notes.

What does *English365* give to the learner?

The course aims to provide:

- a balance between English for work, travel and leisure
- a balance between grammar, vocabulary, pronunciation and professional communication skills (at this level: writing, presenting, negotiating and communicating in meetings)
- a balance between the skills of speaking, listening, reading and writing
- clear and relevant learning aims in every unit
- stimulating content and activities to motivate adult learners
- sensitive support to students who have problems achieving the transition from passive to active use of English

- a strong emphasis on recycling and consolidation
- motivation to students to achieve a useful balance between classroom and self-study.

What about levels?

We have provided references to the Council of Europe Common European Framework levels as this can provide a useful point of reference for teachers gauging the three levels of *English365*. However, please note that these are not meant as exact comparisons due to the different purpose and nature of these coursebooks.

English365 Book 1 aims to take post-elementary students (students who have reached the end of Common European Framework level A2 approximately) up to lower-intermediate level (approximating to Common European Framework level B1).

English365 Book 2 aims to take lower-intermediate learners to intermediate level (approximately through level B1 to the beginning of level B2). So by the time they complete *English365* Book 2, having done sufficient exam preparation, students should be ready to sit the Cambridge Examinations Preliminary Business English Certificate (BEC Preliminary).

English365 Book 3 aims to take intermediate level learners to the beginning of upper-intermediate level (progressing part of the way through level B2).

How is it different?

1 **Authenticity** Much of the material is based on authentic interviews with real working people, many of them doing similar jobs and with similar personal and professional concerns as the people likely to be studying the book. Each unit focuses in part on a professional individual who provides the context for the subject matter. The original interviews have been rerecorded to make listening comprehension easier, but the texts still retain the original flavour which we believe will be motivating and involving for your students.

2 **Organisation** The units are divided into three types (see Organisation of the Student's Book on page 9). We think that working through cycles of three units provides the right balance between learners' dual need for variety and for a sense of security.

3 **Vocabulary** The book has an ambitious lexical syllabus: we believe students can learn vocabulary successfully if exposed to it in the right way and that vocabulary is an important key to better understanding, better communication, progress and motivation.

4 **Grammar** The book's approach to grammar is based less on traditional PPP (Presentation – Practice – Production) and more on TTT (Teach – Test – Teach). We think that the majority of adult students at this level have been subjected to the grammar features of our syllabus through PPP already; they do need to revise and extend

their existing knowledge but they don't want to be bored going through traditional presentations all over again.

5 **Self-study**
  - The Teacher's notes for each unit offer suggestions to pass on to students about how they can consolidate their classroom learning.
  - The Personal Study Book with Audio CD provides students with 15 to 30 minutes' worth of self-study material per unit and up to 15 minutes of listening material (recyclable) for each unit with a listening component.

6 **Learner training** Additional activities on the Website and in the Personal Study Book, as well as the Teacher's notes to the units in the Student's Book, encourage teachers and learners to focus on the learning process itself.

Course components

There are six components for this level:
1 Student's Book
2 Classroom Audio Cassettes/CDs
3 Personal Study Book
4 Personal Study CD
5 Teacher's Book
6 Website.

The **Student's Book** contains:
- an introduction to the student
- 30 classroom units
- file cards for pair and groupwork exercises
- a grammar reference section
- a tapescript of the Classroom Audio Cassettes/CDs
- the answer key to the exercises.

The **Classroom Audio Cassettes/CDs** contain:
- all the tracks relating to listening work in the Student's Book.

The **Teacher's Book** provides:
- an introduction to the course and how to work with it
- detailed notes on the units in the Student's Book
- 30 extra photocopiable classroom activities, each one linked to a unit in the Student's Book, supported by Teacher's notes.

The **Personal Study Book** contains:
- Language for language learning – two alphabetical lists of the grammatical and other terms used in the Student's Book together with definitions taken from the *Cambridge Learner's Dictionary*
- one page of self-study exercises per unit of the Student's Book for additional practice
- the answer key to the exercises
- learning diaries for the students
- a tapescript of the contents of the Personal Study CD.

The **Personal Study CD** contains:
- self-study listening exercises – these encourage students to practise talking about their job and personal life, communicating in meetings, presenting and negotiating, and are designed to support and consolidate the work in the Student's Book
- the listening material relating to pronunciation work in the Student's Book (type 1 units).

The **Website** provides:
- information about the course and the authors
- two revision units
- 30 worksheets, linked to the Student's Book units, for students to monitor their progress
- ten extra photocopiable activities for better learning, designed to improve the effectiveness of students' learning, also supported by Teacher's notes (see page 11)
- links to organisations referred to in the Background briefings in the Teacher's Book.

See www.cambridge.org/elt/english365.

Organisation of the Student's Book

The Student's Book has 30 units. They are clustered into ten groups of three, over which a full range of language items and communication elements are presented and practised.

Whilst the units are designed to be delivered sequentially, their flexibility is such that they may be dealt with out of sequence if a specific need or occasion arises.

Each type of unit is designed as follows. All units contain a section called 'It's time to talk' which provides opportunities for transfer and freer practice of the main learning points. See page 15 for teaching approaches to each type of unit.

Type 1 units (Units 1, 4, 7, 10, 13, 16, 19, 22, 25 and 28)
Type 1 units present and practise:
- Listening on a work-related theme
- Grammar
- Pronunciation
- Speaking.

Rationale
Type 1 units present and practise a grammar point, introduced first through the medium of a listening exercise. The theme is work-related and the listening text also permits the passive presentation of useful vocabulary. The grammar point is then formally presented and practised and there is also extrapolation to presentation and practice of a discrete pronunciation point. The unit finishes with a supported but freer speaking practice activity which enables students to gain fluency and confidence with the grammar, whilst expressing their ideas on relevant work-related topics.

Type 2 units (Units 2, 5, 8, 11, 14, 17, 20, 23, 26 and 29)
Type 2 units present and practise:
- Listening on a work-related theme
- Work-related vocabulary
- Speaking
- Communication skills for work.

Rationale
Every second unit in the cluster presents professional vocabulary through the medium of a listening exercise on a work-related theme. Students develop listening skills like listening for gist and listening for specific information and also have the opportunity (in 'What do you think?') to briefly discuss the issues raised in the text. There is explicit presentation and practice of vocabulary followed by a short fluency activity designed to enable students to use the

vocabulary in freer and realistic exchanges. The unit finishes with a focus on professional communication, with presentation and practice of key phrases and skills. These are often introduced by means of a short listening text. The professional communication skills targeted in *English365* Book 3 are:

- writing
- presentations
- language for meetings
- language for negotiations.

Type 3 units (Units 3, 6, 9, 12, 15, 18, 21, 24, 27 and 30)
Type 3 units present and practise:

- Social skills
- Reading on a general theme
- General vocabulary
- Speaking.

Rationale

Every third unit in the cluster begins with a focus on social skills. Students listen to two dialogues. The first is a poor version and the second an improvement. Students will consider how the dialogue has been improved. The listening is followed by practice exercises. The second part of each unit focuses on reading skills such as skimming and scanning. This then leads into work on vocabulary related to the topic of the reading text.

The unit finishes with a speaking activity designed to practise the vocabulary and to foster fluency and confidence when speaking about general topics.

Revision units

There are two revision units on the Website, one to follow Unit 15 and the other to follow Unit 30. These contain exercises summarising the work covered thus far. They can be used in a variety of ways, including:

- to test students' knowledge
- as supplementary classroom material
- as supplementary self-study material.

Students who have finished *English365* Books 1 and 2

Some or all of your students may have completed Book 1 and Book 2. If so, it is worth pointing out that Book 3 is organised along similar lines. The early units revise and recycle language that appeared in Book 2, so it may be necessary to ensure that students do not feel that they are simply looking at language that they have studied previously. Remind students of the importance of revision and that while looking at items of vocabulary that they may have seen before, you are going to focus on the students' accurate and active use of these words. Tell them that recognising and understanding a word is one step along the road to learning it, but the ultimate aim is to use the word accurately in appropriate situations.

Starting up the course

This section suggests different approaches to starting up a new course with *English365*. The first lesson of a new course is obviously important and can be handled in many different ways. Your aim should be not just to teach the language of Unit 1 but to create a positive attitude towards learning English in general in the mind of each student and to create a good group dynamic which will help this learning to take place. You want students to leave the lesson believing that this course is going to be:

- comprehensible
- coherent
- useful and
- enjoyable – or even fun!

Think about how you can achieve these goals. You should choose the way that you and (as far as you can anticipate this) your students feel most comfortable with. You may know everyone in your group very well or you may never have met them. They may know each other, they may not. However, you should know something about them so, as you prepare, think about the best way to start up. Once you have told them what you plan to do in this lesson, there are many possibilities. You can't take up all of the suggestions which follow but doing one or two for five to ten minutes at the start of the lesson may help to tailor the book to your style and the style of your group.

Talk to your students

Tell them that you are going to talk to them for a few minutes so that all they have to do is relax and listen. Speaking clearly, and avoiding difficult language, introduce yourself and tell your students a few things about yourself. Talking to students at the beginning of a course in language they can understand can help them relax and attune their ears to the sounds and meanings of English. Remember that they will be nervous too – some of them very much so. If you know the group, clearly it won't be necessary to introduce yourself, but there may be newcomers as it is the start of the course and so it is important to make them feel welcome and comfortable with their new classmates. You could get students to ask you questions about yourself. Give them time to prepare some questions, perhaps in pairs – this will also give you some initial indication of their level of English. You will find that they will respond to you better if they can see you are open and willing to talk about yourself.

Tell them how you work

You may also wish to talk about how you like to work, what your objectives are, and about creating a winning team, the members of which will work together to achieve individual and group objectives. Working together will give better results for everyone.

Talk about the book

Give students the chance to look through their copies of *English365* Book 3 – to see how long each unit is, how many units there are, to find the grammar reference, etc. at the back of the book, and so on. You may want to ask questions to guide them, e.g. *Where is the grammar reference?* Even if students have completed *English365* Books 1 and 2 and so will be familiar with the structure of the course, getting students to look through Book 3 is worthwhile. The book is a prime learning tool for them. It's important for them to be able to find their way around and have an idea of its organisational principles. In particular, point out, or remind them of the colour coding for the three different types of unit and explain briefly what these are. Tell them too about the other components, and show them in particular a copy of the Personal Study Book and accompanying CD. Stress also that the Website is a useful resource.

Do a needs analysis

Unless you have already had the chance to do so with the students themselves, do a needs analysis of the expectations and objectives of the group or of the learning backgrounds of the learners either at the beginning of this lesson or later on. If the group is continuing from *English365* Book 2, it is still a good idea to review their expectations and objectives as these can change over time. And, of course, you may have new students joining the group. You can use any or all of the first three of the Better learning activities to support this (see the Website). Unless you have received detailed briefing on your students, you will need to find out all this information in any case during the first two or three lessons.

Do the admin

You may have administrative business to get out of the way: registers to take, attendance sheets to get signed, etc. Decide when in the lesson you want to do this.

Define principles

Get students to agree to a set of class rules for the course. For example:
- We will help each other to speak better English.
- We will not speak our own language in the classroom.

Break the ice

Use your own ice-breaking technique for starting up with a new group of intermediate learners. If you don't have a favourite ice-breaking activity, try the following.

Get students to work in groups of three. Student A should interview Student B and Student C should take notes. Then B should interview C and A takes notes, and so on. The person who took notes can then introduce that student to the rest of the class. If the students already know each other, get them to find out some information that they didn't know before.

Choose the ways of breaking the ice which you feel are most appropriate to your teaching style and to the group, as far as you can tell.

Better learning activities

The Better learning activities are a key part of *English365*. You will find the activities which accompany Book 3 on the Website.

These learning to learn activities can be done in parallel to the main course, though you may want do the first three at the beginning of the course.

They do not necessarily take up a great deal of time, but they are important in getting students to think about how they learn and so learn better. Especially at this level, students should be taking on more responsibility for their learning and developing learner autonomy.

2 Introduction to the Teacher's Book

Getting ready

The language of the Teacher's notes

The 30 sets of notes in the next section are intended to provide you with ideas and support if you need them. They are not prescriptive. The imperative style (as in 'Ask', 'Check', 'Tell', etc.) is therefore only to keep the notes short and simple, not to tell you how best to do something. The less imperative style 'You could also ...', 'You may like to ...' signals additional ideas not directly found in the Student's Book.

Talking to students

While most students at this level will be able to understand you, there may be some variation in their profiles. Some students may not have studied English for some time, some may have continued on from another course. It is worth repeating that when we speak to our students, we should remember to:

- speak clearly and fairly slowly
- use vocabulary and structures (most of which) they can understand
- as far as possible, use intonation and pronunciation patterns which replicate speech at normal speed. So, for example, try to keep unstressed words and syllables unstressed even when you are speaking more slowly than usual.

It's your responsibility to make sure students understand what you say. You can help them maximise the usefulness of what language they already possess.

From passive to active

Some students may be happy to produce language straightaway – others may need more time. More confident students are given opportunities to talk in the Warm up right at the start. On the other hand, more hesitant students can focus on the objectives at this stage without having to say very much. Some students may have a relatively good knowledge of English and it is important to stress that though some of the vocabulary and grammar work, especially, might have been covered before, you want to activate that language and get them to use it accurately.

Classroom language

While most students will probably understand the metalanguage used in the Student's Book and the instructions you give them, it's worth remembering always to give instructions clearly – it is important, of course, that students know what you want them to do.

Classroom resources

The range of resources and equipment available to teachers ranges from the rudimentary, or worse, to the very sophisticated. If equipment is not so good, remember that in any case your best resources are your students and yourself.

Dictionaries

Students are recommended to buy a good learner's dictionary. *The Cambridge Learner's Dictionary* is excellent. See also www.dictionary.cambridge.org for online dictionaries. If students don't have their own dictionaries, it helps to have one or two available for them in class. At this level students should be using an English–English dictionary.

The whiteboard

The Teacher's notes often recommend you to use the whiteboard to build up sets of vocabulary and collocations during a lesson both to develop students' vocabulary and also because it's good for students' morale when they can see how many words they can recognise and use.

The electronic whiteboard

The advent of interactive whiteboards in the classroom creates exciting new opportunities for different ways of teaching. *English365* is at the forefront of this technology. For more information on interactive whiteboard software for the course, see www.cambridge.org/elt/english365.

The overhead projector

OHPs are especially useful for pairs or small groups reporting back work in writing after an activity. They can write directly onto a transparency and then show other students the results. If you write your feedback – for example for a pairwork activity – on a transparency, you can also project it straightaway to the whole group.

Computers

Computers are especially useful for writing in the classroom. Whether you have time to provide individual correction for all your students' work outside class time is another issue!

Doing written exercises and checking answers

Written exercises can be approached in a number of different ways and you should try to vary what you ask students to do. Be attentive to their mood and level of concentration. They may welcome the opportunity to do two or three exercises alone in order to assimilate input thus far in the lesson and take a rest from the requirements of active language manipulation and production. A quiet class does not mean that it is a boring one. Give them time to do one or more exercises on their own (although don't always wait for the last student to finish before moving on). Then check the answers by going round the class. However, you don't always have to say immediately whether the answer given is correct or not. Write a suggestion up on the board and ask the others to reach agreement on whether it is right; or ask students to lead this part of the lesson; or ask students to work in pairs.

Pair and groupwork

Pairwork is an opportunity not just for practice but also for students to develop support for each other and, potentially, for them to learn from each other in terms of language competence and learning style. Ensure that students work with different partners from lesson to lesson and within lessons. You may find that there is some resistance to pairwork from some students. It is, therefore, perhaps useful to stress that doing pairwork maximises the amount of time that they can spend speaking English, as they will not be able to talk to you the whole time.

Timing

Timing is important in pair and groupwork activities, especially more open ones as in *It's time to talk* sections. Decide how much time you want to spend on the activity. In many cases, ten minutes is plenty.

Procedure

A basic procedure for pairwork is as follows:

1 Present the activity and read through the relevant input to check understanding. Pre-teach difficult vocabulary and provide any grammatical or other models which you would like students to use.

2 Choose pairs. If you have an odd number, work with the odd person yourself, or make a group of three.

3 If there is a preparation phase before the activity, decide whether to put some or all of the Student As and Bs together in separate groups or whether preparation should be done alone; or ask students to decide.

4 During the activity itself, walk round and monitor. Make notes of good and not so good language. You can write good language on the board even while the activity is still going on. You may also like to make notes directly onto a transparency to save time later.

5 You may wish students to reverse roles later. Watch the time so that both get an equal chance in both roles.

6 After the activity itself, students usually report back. The form of this will depend on the nature of the activity. You may want to summarise the findings on a problem or question for the class as a whole (or ask students to do so). If students were set to solve a problem, find out which solution was preferred and why.

7 You may often invite selected pairs to perform the same activity in front of the others. Encourage the others to provide constructive criticism of these performances.

8 As the first stage in the debriefing, ask students what language or communication difficulties they had.

9 You will then provide feedback on the activity as a whole (see the section on feedback which follows). Be conscious of the balance between feedback on the language and communication aspects of the activity.

10 Summarise the main points you want students to take away with them. Encourage them to write them down or make some other effort to retain them.

Serial pairwork

The non-alcoholic cocktail party is a variation on basic pairwork except that students talk to two or three others in turn during the activity. You should certainly encourage students to get up and walk around for this: getting students up and about now and again is good for their energy levels and good for kinaesthetic learners – ones who like moving about, touching and handling things, and physical activity. They will need to have pen and paper – sometimes a photocopy of the activity – to note down the answers to their questions. Timing is again important here because you may need to tell them when partners should swap from asking to answering questions, and when students should swap partners each time.

Telephone pairwork

For pairwork on the telephone, you can suggest that students sit back-to-back, if you don't have telephone equipment for them. Some students may be surprised at this and perhaps resistant to the idea of sitting back-to-back, so it is a good idea to explain the rationale, i.e. on the telephone the speakers do not get non-verbal help and need to rely only on their listening skills, and so should not look at each other.

Groupwork

The Student's Book and Teacher's notes generally refer to pairwork, but you can vary things by putting students into groups of three and four. You can also put students into pairs and nominate one or two others as observers. One can provide feedback to the group, the other can provide language feedback to the pair after they have finished. Before the lesson, think about how you are going to divide the class up into groups.

File cards

If a lesson involves using the file cards at the back of the Student's Book, you should read the roles in advance so that you have a clear idea of what students will be required to do. Students will often need time to prepare questions for their partner. Either there is specific guidance on what questions to ask or they can prepare questions on the basis of the information on their own file cards. Once again, you could decide to put all the As together in one group and all the Bs in another at this stage.

Feedback and correction

In addition to all of the above:

• Be selective. Identify the main points you want to make.

• Be positive. Give feedback on good language as well as the not so good.

• Be constructive. Praise students for their efforts before suggesting ways of doing it better.

• Get them to be constructive with each other. This is part of building a team which will help all its members to achieve more. Create an environment of mutual support.

• Students will appreciate feedback on all the activities they do in class. It is easier to give immediate feedback and correction during grammar exercises, but it is no less important in freer speaking activities. One way of offering effective correction and feedback without hindering communication is to make a note of mistakes as you monitor so that you can go over them at the end of the activity with the whole group. Students will also appreciate it if you type up their mistakes and go through them in a subsequent lesson.

- When checking answers after activities, it may not always be necessary to go round the whole class to get their answers before you say if they are right or not. It is a good idea to vary the way you check answers. You could, for example, simply tell the students the answers, or, if you have a smaller group, check them yourself while you are monitoring.
- You may want to refer to Unit 27, where the social skills section focuses on giving feedback.

Raising learner awareness

As students improve their level of English, it is a good idea to foster increased learner awareness and autonomy. Encourage them to reflect on how well they performed during an activity and how they can improve for next time. See the Better learning activities on the Website and the learning diaries in the Personal Study Book for more on this.

Self-study, consolidating learning and making progress

Students are more likely to make progress if you build lots of recycling into the course and encourage students to work on their English outside the classroom. There are a variety of suggestions about how to achieve this in this book. In sum, we recommend you to:

1 revise the previous lesson of the same type at the start of every class
2 clearly state lesson objectives and remind students of these at the end of every lesson
3 make regular use of the Extra classroom activities at the back of this book and the Better learning activities on the Website.

We recommend you encourage students to:

1 reread the unit in the Student's Book which they have just done with you
2 do self-study exercises for the equivalent unit in the Personal Study Book and, where applicable, use the Personal Study Audio CD
3 do follow-up activities suggested in the Teacher's notes for each unit
4 start and maintain vocabulary notebooks
5 keep learner diaries (see below about the Learning diaries in the Personal Study Book).

Teacher's diary

The Teacher's diary (on the Website) aims to help you in your own professional development. We suggest that you make multiple photocopies of it and put the copies in a separate file. The page is self-explanatory. It is designed – realistically we hope for busy teachers – for you to spend three minutes completing one sheet for every lesson. By getting into the habit of doing this and reflecting on what you do, we hope it will encourage you to experiment, develop and communicate with other teachers about the issues which interest and involve you.

Learning diaries

At the back of the Personal Study Book there are six learning diaries for students to use on a regular basis as they study

with both the Student's Book and the Personal Study Book. Explain to students that writing down personal reflections on their English learning will allow them to:

- see areas where they have improved (this is important for their motivation)
- understand the learning methods which enabled them to improve (this is important to maximise their success as learners)
- identify areas which continue to give them difficulty (this is important to overcome troublesome areas)
- think about where they should place their priorities within the language learning process (this is important for setting clear objectives).

Students will require guidance on which diary (or diaries) to use. At the beginning of the course, it would be useful to suggest that students select one or two diaries to focus on their own individual learning interests. Encourage students to discuss their selections with you.

It would be useful to review students' learning diaries from time to time in order to encourage their use and prove their value.

Creating a dynamic group

Last, but perhaps most importantly, aim to help create a lively, energised group of learners, a group which is ready to:

- get up and walk round to refocus when concentration dips
- offer support and positive criticism to all its members
- openly discuss language without fear of losing face
- take the initiative to lead the class.

Common elements

This section offers guidance on how to handle the lesson stages which are common to every unit.

Why are we doing this?

Always make clear what the objectives of each lesson are. Follow these steps at the start of every lesson.

- Explain which type of unit you are working on today.
- Then tell students the objectives of this lesson (see On the agenda).
- Identify the main points and write up key words on the board or OHP (see Teacher's notes for each unit).
- Leave them there through the lesson so that students have a clear idea of the basic structure of the lesson and also of where they are at any particular stage.

Thinking about what you are doing and where you are going helps consolidate learning.

Background briefings

In the Teacher's Book, some units have extra information about the company, people, place or event covered (e.g. Martinique in Unit 1 and PY Gerbeau in Unit 2). These are intended as a brief introduction for teachers who are perhaps unfamiliar with the subjects or want further information. If you or your students want more information, you can go to their websites via the *English365* website: www.cambridge.org/elt/english365.

Warm up

As the name suggests, this is intended as a quick way into the unit, to help you and the students focus on the main objectives and to get them used to speaking the language. The Warm up is intended as a short activity involving answering or briefly discussing some questions, doing a simple matching exercise, etc. As a matter of course, draw students' attention to the photo of the unit personality and the information about him/her.

It's time to talk

This is the open practice section of each unit, designed to consolidate the learning which you are aiming for learners to achieve within a relevant and useful context: a transfer from closed to open and from a generic to a more specific contextualisation, although this varies from unit to unit. See also the notes on pair and groupwork above.

Remember

Check this section quickly with the whole class. Then ask: 'What did we do today?' If necessary, remind students of the objectives of the lesson (by referring to your key lesson structure words on the board or On the agenda).

Follow up

For you: use the Extra (photocopiable) classroom activity in this book which corresponds to the unit you are teaching. For students: encourage students to consolidate their learning by doing regular homework and self-study between lessons. Standard ways to do this are:

- to reread the unit in the Student's Book
- to read the corresponding unit in the Personal Study Book and do the exercises.

See the Teacher's notes for each unit for other suggestions.

Timing

The timings suggested in the following sections are based on a 90-minute lesson. They are intended to provide broad guidance only. Your timings will obviously depend enormously on the specific lesson, the kind of class you have and the kind of teacher you are. Be flexible. Over-rigidity can stop you listening to your students and can interfere with real communication.

Teaching type 1 units

Unit structure and timing

The structure of type 1 units, together with suggested approximate timings, is:

What did we do last time?	5–10 minutes
On the agenda: Why are we doing this?	5 minutes
Warm up	5 minutes
Listen to this	10 minutes
Check your grammar	10 minutes
Do it yourself	10 minutes
Sounds good	15 minutes
It's time to talk	20 minutes
Remember → What did we do today?	5 minutes
→ Follow up	

Listen to this

Introduce each track by saying in broad terms what students are going to hear and why. Make sure students have read the rubrics and that they understand what they have to do.

Listening for gist

The instruction to the teacher in the Teacher's notes is usually simply to 'Play track 1.1'. It is for you to decide whether to play the track or part of the track more than once or not, but only up to a maximum of three or four times; in some cases advice is given for this in the Teacher's notes. Tell students that very often it's best to listen for the main message and not to worry about not understanding every word. In real life, there are rarely more than one or two chances.

Listening tasks

Specific suggestions are made in the Student's Book or the Teacher's notes for individual units, but you can also ask them:

- if they can predict part of a track from what they know about it before they listen
- if they can reproduce parts of a track after they have listened to it
- to listen for examples of particular words or types of word or grammar examples.

Tapescripts

You can encourage students to make use of the tapescripts at the back of the Student's Book for reading at the same time as they listen; and for doing grammar and vocabulary searches of texts they have already heard.

Check your grammar

The syllabus

- The grammar points taught in the type 1 units have been identified as being those of most use to working people. The grammar syllabus is selective rather than comprehensive in order to achieve a good balance between this and the other components of the syllabus – work-related and general vocabulary, communication skills, and so on.
- For information about particular grammar points and how to handle them in class, we strongly recommend *Grammar for English Language Teachers* by Martin Parrott (Cambridge University Press).

Activating passive knowledge

For any given grammar point, you can ask students some basic questions to check the extent of their knowledge. They may have notions of the point in question and the listening will have jogged their memory. Otherwise, you can vary your approach from lesson to lesson. For example:

- first present the information given in a grammar section, then practise the points by filling the gaps; or
- ask students to elicit rules from the listening extract they have heard or from the tapescript of the listening, and then do the gap-filling exercise; or
- ask students to do the gap-filling exercise and then to formulate rules alone, in pairs or as a whole class.

Grammar reference

Always refer them to the Grammar reference section. Make sure students know where it is, and, if appropriate, go through it with them.

Sounds good

Tell students each time that this is the pronunciation part of the lesson. Pronunciation is important but it can also be fun and can appeal to a different kind of learner, some of whom may be less confident about other areas of language. Encourage students to identify what aspects of pronunciation they have problems with and to concentrate on them.

Teaching type 2 units

Unit structure and timing

The structure of type 2 units, together with suggested approximate timings, is:

What did we do last time?	5–10 minutes
On the agenda: Why are we doing this?	5 minutes
Warm up	5 minutes
Listen to this	10 minutes
The words you need	10 minutes
It's time to talk	15 minutes
Communicating at work	35 minutes
Remember → What did we do today?	5 minutes
→ Follow up	

Listen to this

Procedure

See the guidelines above (in Type 1 units) for the basic procedure for dealing with listening activities.

Note-taking

In some units (e.g. Unit 2), students are asked to take notes. Since note-taking may be a new skill for many students, it is worth spending some time on the basics. You could try to elicit and then highlight the following:

- stress that students should try to listen for and note down only the main points
- they should write in their own words – they should not attempt to write what they hear verbatim
- they should not write full sentences and should only record key content words – these are usually nouns and verbs; stress that students should try to minimise the time they spend writing and maximise the time they spend listening
- the notes should be clear and concise and easy to understand at a later date
- the notes should be organised – where appropriate, encourage students to use numbering, underlining and headings to structure their notes
- before asking them to make notes, make sure students have some paper or their notebook as there will not always be enough room in the Student's Book
- when giving feedback on notes, of course there is no one right answer – it is possible to write the same thing in a number of different ways; one way to approach this, if

you have time, is to build up a set on notes on the whiteboard or OHP by asking students for their input on what should be included and how it should be written

- explain the rationale for focusing on note-taking – it can be a useful skill during presentations, meetings and conferences, as well as in academic lectures.

The words you need

At this level students should be taking on more and more responsibility for their own learning. You can encourage this by getting students to look back through the tapescripts to identify words that are new to them. Advise students to look at 'chunks' of language rather than just single words – this will help them to activate the language more easily. Get them to look at prepositions that follow certain words, for example, and record whole phrases. Suggestions are provided in each set of Teacher's notes.

It's time to talk

Suggestions are provided in each set of Teacher's notes.

Communicating at work

Suggestions are provided in each set of Teacher's notes.

Teaching type 3 units

Unit structure and timing

The structure of type 3 units, together with suggested approximate timings, is:

What did we do last time?	5–10 minutes
On the agenda: Why are we doing this?	5 minutes
Warm up	5 minutes
Social skills	15 minutes
Have a go	10 minutes
Read on	10 minutes
The words you need	10 minutes
It's time to talk	20 minutes
Remember → What did we do today?	5 minutes
→ Follow up	

Social skills

The objective of this section is to develop students' communication skills in social and work situations and not just their language. Each social skills section has two dialogues based on the same subject. The first dialogue is a poor version and the second an improvement. The aim is for students to compare them and focus on exactly what the makes the second one better.

The standard procedure is as follows.

- Ask students to discuss the Warm up questions quickly in pairs or small groups. This introduces the theme of the social skills section.
- Get students to read the questions and check any vocabulary problems before you play the first track.
- Check the answers.
- Get the students to read the questions for the second dialogue and play the second track.
- Check the answers.
- Play the second track again and get students to complete

the sentences. This focuses students on the language and skills used to create a better dialogue. You may need to play the track more than once, pausing after each sentence in order to give students time to write.

- Students work in pairs to think of other language and expressions they can use in different situations. There is, of course, no one right answer for this, so write up students' suggestions on the board or on an OHP. There are possible answers listed in the relevant section of the Teacher's notes.
- Refer them to the Remember section at the end of the unit.

This formula can be varied, of course. For example, you can:
- listen to dialogue 1 and get students to tell you how it can be improved before listening to dialogue 2
- ask students to identify useful language in dialogue 2
- listen to dialogue 2 and get students to role-play the situation in pairs.

Use the standard procedure in the first one or two units (Units 3 and 6) and then vary the formula thereafter.

Have a go
This section leads straight on from the previous one and provides opportunities for less controlled practice of the social skills techniques and language. Once again you can adopt a standard procedure as follows.

- Set the scene and make sure that students are clear about their roles – give time for preparation. A few minutes should be enough for this.
- Remind students to use the social skills and language presented in the previous section.
- The first two students perform the role-play and the third acts as the observer.
- The observer should listen carefully to the dialogue and prepare to give feedback on the students' use of language and social skills. The observer can use the advice at the end of the unit as a checklist against which to measure the performance of Student A and B. You should tell observers to take notes so they can report back to the students at the end of the activity. This role is very important as it encourages students to reflect on the activity and think about their performance and how it can be improved. Students should be honest in the assessment but they should also be positive and sensitive and provide suggestions as to how to improve.
- The students take it in turns to play the different roles. It is important to ensure the first observer also takes part in the role-play, but you may not always have time for the dialogues to be performed three times.
- Do some whole class feedback. Ask students how they felt the role-plays went and how they could be improved.

Read on
The Read on sections of these units are designed to help students with their ability to predict, skim, scan and read for gist. The tasks for each reading section vary. Students may, for example, be asked to predict the topics from headlines and then match the headlines to stories before doing more detailed comprehension questions.

A standard procedure is as follows. There is further guidance in each set of Teacher's notes.
- Get students to discuss the introductory questions in pairs or small groups.
- Do the prediction task, if appropriate.
- Read the rubric and the questions.
- Ask students to skim the text before answering the questions.
- Check the answers.

You may encounter some resistance to reading in class so it is worth making the rationale clear: you want students to improve their reading skills (skimming, for example) and this means reading texts in different ways. Consequently, you will need to vary your approach to reading in class. What you do will depend to a large extent on your students, but here are some possible suggestions.
- Always set time limits. This ensures that the pace of the class is kept up.
- Assign different paragraphs for students to summarise to their partner or group.
- Introduce an element of competition. If you are doing a scanning exercise, for example, put students in groups and award points to the group which finds the answer first.
- Do the readings as jigsaws. Give partners in a pair different halves of the text to read and different questions to answer.
- Get students to write their own questions for different parts of the text and then put them to a partner.
- Stress what an important learning resource a text can be. The texts in Book 3 are extremely rich in vocabulary.
- Ultimately, remember that some students enjoy reading. If they are quietly reading a text it does not necessarily mean that they are bored. They may be grateful for the chance to take a break from 'communicating'.

Reading in other contexts in the Student's Book
More generally, the instruction 'Read' in the Teacher's notes for any unit can be handled in various ways.
- Students can read silently.
- Individual students can take turns reading aloud.
- You can read aloud to them.
- Students can read to each other in pairs.
If there is no specific suggestion, do different things at different times; and ask the students what they want to do.

The words you need
Suggestions are provided in each set of Teacher's notes. This section often focuses on the texts from the reading section and is a useful way of encouraging students to develop their vocabulary range from reading texts. You can encourage them to read as much as possible outside the classroom too, and to try and develop their vocabulary range independently.

It's time to talk
This is an extension of the theme of the unit and an opportunity to practise speaking in English and use the vocabulary presented in the earlier sections.

1 Martinique meets Paris

Starting up the course

Read the section on Starting up the course on page 10 and decide how you want to:
- introduce yourself
- introduce the students to each other
- introduce the material.

As a brief 'getting to know you' activity, you might want to ask pairs of students to interview each other and take notes. They can then introduce their partner to the rest of the class. Write the following prompts on the board:
- name
- job + what likes about his/her job
- main interests
- a future dream in life
- anything else.

On the agenda: Why are we doing this?

Read about Type 1 units on page 9 and Teaching type 1 units on page 15.
Explain that this is an example of the first of three types of unit. This type normally looks at grammar and pronunciation. Type 1 units also practise listening.

Tell the students the objectives of the lesson:
- to practise **making a positive impression**
- to revise the **present simple and continuous and the present perfect simple and continuous tenses**. You might need to remind students that although they may have studied these tenses before, you want to concentrate on using them correctly.
- to do some **pronunciation** work on **minimal pairs**. You might give students some examples of this so that they are clear about the aims of the lesson. You could write *seat* and *sit* on the board to demonstrate that students will be comparing the pronunciation of individual sounds. Reinforce this by writing the key words on the board or OHP.

Warm up

Ask the students the questions or get them to answer in pairs. Don't spend too long on this as it is just intended as a brief introduction to the topic of the unit.

Background briefing: Martinique

Martinique is a Caribbean island with a population of around 400,000, the majority of which are of African origin. It is an overseas 'department' of France which means that it has full representation in the French National Assembly. So, not surprisingly, it has a distinctively French feel to it and

refers to itself as 'a little bit of France in the Caribbean'. It has become known for a form of music called 'zouk'. For more information about Martinique, go to the *English365* website: www.cambridge.org/elt/english365.

Listen to this

Caribbean roots

- Look at the picture of Marc and read the caption. You could add that he works for a telecommunications company.
- Explain that students are going to listen to two different parts of an interview with Marc. Before you start, you might want to check the meaning of *unemployed*, *graduated* and *lack*. This will help students with their comprehension.
1 Ask students to read through the profile before you play track 1.1. They can compare their answers with a partner before you check the answers with the whole class.

Suggested answers

1 major telecom
2 1998
3 international environment
4 month, Italy
5 time
6 jazz / goes to jazz clubs / organises jazz events

Track 1.1 tapescript ▶▶

INTERVIEWER: So Marc, what do you do exactly?

MARC: So, I manage, lead a team of around 15 people and let's say that I work on sales and technical aspects for one, or my customer, a major telecom operator in France … I have to cover all aspects of doing business with the customer. So I'm the single person accountable for that customer. In fact, our chairman regularly repeats the motto: 'One company in front of the customer.'

INTERVIEWER: So how long have you worked for your company?

MARC: Since 1998.

INTERVIEWER: And why telecoms?

MARC: The main reason was to work in an international environment. And over the last five years I've visited many many countries … like Hong Kong, Israel, Ireland, Italy, Colombia, Chile, Singapore … I was also in Miami in the sun, as well, so around … 12 different countries over the world … across all continents. In fact, I've been working in the domestic market, at the headquarters, for one year now. But I travel every month to Italy.

INTERVIEWER: So, Marc, with all this travel, where do you say you're from: Paris, Europe, Martinique …?

MARC: I'd say that I'm from somewhere over the Atlantic, you know. I'd say that … I have a mixture of cultures, like everybody. I still have some West Indian feelings, hot temperatures are very important for me. On the other hand, I have moved or changed a lot, say, with the concept, my attitude ... to time. When I first came to France, it was very strange for me to notice a train left on time ... within one minute, or a few seconds. Caribbean people, like some southern countries, are more, let's say, relaxed about time. Time is really of less importance. But, on the other hand, people in the Caribbean have a very different approach to life, more positive, more taking time to actually enjoy life... more so than Europeans.

INTERVIEWER: So is your lifestyle very different?

MARC: Absolutely. In France I was surprised to see sunlight at 9 or 10 pm, it was very, very strange ... very, very, very ... because in tropical countries ... the sunset is around ... five-thirty ... six-thirty at the maximum. And the night comes very suddenly, you have only, maybe, half an hour's time ... but in France at night you can go out for a walk, see friends ... there are lots of things to do ... it's good for my social life.

INTERVIEWER: Do you still keep a contact with Martinique culture?

MARC: I love Creole jazz. In fact, in my spare time I work with an organisation that promotes Caribbean jazz in France. I try to because the job can be very stressful. So I love jazz, and I very often go to jazz clubs. We've got a lot of jazz clubs in Paris.

INTERVIEWER: And do you organise concerts and things like that?

MARC: Yes, exactly. We organise every year a Creole jazz festival in Paris in jazz clubs, yes. We've been doing that for ... for ... ten years, roughly.

2 • Doing this prediction exercise will help students to focus their listening and it might be useful to explain this before the activity.
  • Allow for variation in the wording of the answers but encourage correct grammar and use of vocabulary.

Track 1.2 tapescript ▶▶|

INTERVIEWER: And in the Caribbean now, what's life like there now?

MARC: Some things on Martinique, are improving. So the level of education is increasing with more and more people going to university. But there's also a big employment issue. Half of young people are unemployed, even students who have graduated – and there are a lot – can't find jobs. It's a small country with very few job opportunities, a small job market, in fact ... so this is an issue really.

INTERVIEWER: What about the tourism?

MARC: The opposite. It's decreased. It's partly, let's say, the relationship with France ... French territories like Martinique, we don't promote tourism enough ... we're not very focused on customer service. We don't have it enough in the culture, as with other countries in the Caribbean. Of course, it's mainly a lack of training in the tourism field.

INTERVIEWER: So what's the future for the people in Martinique?

MARC: It's interesting. People who live with these jewels in the West Indies, tropical island jewels, just see them as natural and tend not to see them as things to commercialise. Outsiders often have a different perspective. It's like Eskimos ... they'd never promote

skiing. But the local people are starting bit by bit to change their ways by developing a new sense of customer focus, maybe like in my job ... so I think there is a real opportunity for the future.

What do you think?

You could also ask students what the advantages and disadvantages are of working in an international environment. If there is time, you could do a quick classroom survey to find out who works in such an environment and who would like to.

Check your grammar

Present simple and continuous; present perfect simple and continuous

• It is likely that students will have studied these tenses at least once if not many times before. Stress that it is important to review such areas of English grammar and to concentrate on using them correctly. You could also get them to look through the tapescript for other examples of the tenses.
• Students could do these activities individually or in pairs.
• Depending on how well the students cope with this, you might want to refer them to the Grammar reference section in the Student's Book at this point.

Do it yourself

Students can do these activities alone or in pairs. Set time limits for each activity and then get students to compare their answers in pairs before you check the answers with the whole class. If students find these activities challenging, it would be a good idea to write the answers on the board so that they are clear for the whole group.

1 You could do the first question with the whole class to check that everyone is clear about the activity.

Answers

1 I usually travel to work by tram.
2 Martinique has had this problem for many years.
3 I have been living / have lived here for five months.
4 How long have you worked / have you been working for the company?
5 How long have you known each other?

2 Get them to read the whole text through quickly before completing it with the correct verbs.

Answers

1 has worked / has been working   2 has   3 exports
4 has grown   5 uses   6 is currently expanding
7 is building   8 has   9 believes   10 has received   11 sees

3 After you have checked the answers, as a brief extension, you could get students to ask and answer similar questions about each other in pairs. Pay close attention to the correct use of the tenses.

Answers

1 do you do   2 does the company do   3 Has it been
4 are you staying   5 Have you ever been
6 have you been coming   7 do you always eat
8 have you ordered

Sounds good

Minimal pairs

It is worth making a general point here that students should always try to identify areas of English that they have problems with. This will help them to become more efficient learners and so improve more rapidly. You may want to refer them to *Learner English* by Michael Swan and Bernard Smith, published by Cambridge University Press.

1 • Do the first word pair with the whole class so that the activity is clear. You could demonstrate it yourself before you play track 1.4.
  • In pairs, students could also create their own word sequences that their partner has to identify.

Answers

1 ABA   2 BBA   3 AAB   4 BAB   5 BBA   6 AAB

Track 1.3 tapescript ▶▶

1 sit – seat – sit
2 gate – gate – get
3 shop – shop – chop
4 yob – job – yob
5 worse – worse – worth
6 win – win – wing

2 • You will have to monitor this activity carefully as some students may not be aware of the words that they have difficulty with.
  • Once the sounds that students have difficulty pronouncing have been established, get them to write down five other words that contain the problem sounds.
  • Encourage students to make an effort to pronounce these sounds correctly in different contexts. It is often the case that students may have no problems with the sounds in class, but as soon as they go outside they revert to the incorrect pronunciation.

Track 1.4 tapescript ▶▶

See the Student's Book.

It's time to talk

• Explain that the *It's time to talk* sections in *English365* Book 3 are intended to improve students' social skills as well as language.
• Set the scene and ask students what they would do while the visitor is waiting. Elicit the fact that they would probably talk to the visitor and in this way introduce the concept of small talk.
• Give students a few minutes to look at their file cards, read the small talk guide and prepare what they are going to say.
• Depending on how confident the group is, you might want to allow students to practise in pairs before they perform for the rest of the class.
• Make sure the class is clear about what they should be doing while listening to the role-plays.
• Monitor and take notes yourself. Give both positive and critical feedback at the end. Focus on both language and social skills.

• You may want to use the Extra classroom activity here (see pages 92 and 99).

What did we do today?
Check the Remember section quickly and remind students of the aims of the lesson.

Follow up
Encourage students to:
• write down expressions for making small talk
• concentrate on using tenses correctly in different situations
• be aware of the problems they have with pronouncing particular sounds in English and focus on pronouncing them correctly.

2 The art of management

What did we do last time?

Although you may want to do some review work from the previous unit we recommend that you do the main review work before the next type 1 unit, i.e. Unit 4. This is more challenging for your students, as it involves longer recall, and should ultimately provide more continuity and improve learning effectiveness.

On the agenda: Why are we doing this?

Read about Type 2 units on page 9 and Teaching type 2 units on page 16.

Explain that this is the second of three types of unit. This type looks at vocabulary for work and communication skills. The main professional skills in business English are presenting, meetings, negotiating, telephoning, writing and socialising. In *English365* Book 3 we focus on writing, presenting, meetings and negotiating.

Tell students the objectives of this lesson (see On the agenda):

- to talk about **management**
- to build **vocabulary** in the area of **managing organisations**
- to practise **writing emails** and increasing awareness of **register and 'down-toning'**. You could explain at this point that *down-toning* means avoiding direct language.

Reinforce this by writing the key words on the board or OHP.

Warm up

Ask the students the questions or get them to ask and answer in pairs. You could also ask them to give real examples of the good management they have experienced.

Background briefing: PY Gerbeau

PY Gerbeau is the Chief Executive of X-Leisure and has worked in the leisure industry for over 18 years. Before this, he was Chief Executive of the Millennium Dome in London and Vice President of Park Operations at Disneyland, Paris. Before he became a management consultant he was a professional ice hockey player and qualified for the 1988 Winter Olympics. His initials stand for Pierre Yves. For more information about PY Gerbeau, go to the *English365* website: www.cambridge.org/elt/english365.

Listen to this

Good management

- Look at the picture of PY Gerbeau and read the caption. Check understanding of *runs* (a business) and the *art* of management.
- Ask students if they have heard of PY Gerbeau. What do they know about him?

1
- Get students to read the priorities and deal with any vocabulary problems. You might need to explain *vision* and *knowledge management*. Ask if they thought of any of these priorities in the Warm up.

- Play track 2.1 and ask students to identify which of the priorities PY mentions and in what order. Students could check their answers with a partner before you check the answers with the whole class.

Track 2.1 tapescript ▶▶

INTERVIEWER: What would you say are the most … most important things a manager has to focus on? What makes for success in managing a business or organisation?

PY GERBEAU: Well, briefly I think the product has to be right. You need a brand that consumers will connect to your business. So that's the first thing – the product – brand management. That has to be first.

INTERVIEWER: Yes.

PY: The second thing is obviously people management. Because if you hire the right employees, if you hire the right management culture, management attitude, you've also got a winner.

INTERVIEWER: OK.

PY: The third one is relationships. No matter what you do, you know you'll have relationships with your investors, relationships with your peers, relationships with your employees, relationships with your consumers.

INTERVIEWER: Yes.

PY: Relationship with your suppliers. It's all about this. And the last one which, which comes back to people, is knowledge management.

INTERVIEWER: Hmm.

PY: You have information, you have to get the right information and use it in the right way – we call that knowledge management. It means you learn from the past. You can take advantage of the past, know it and use the past. Use what you know – what you can find out.

2
- Get students to discuss their predictions in pairs. You could then talk briefly about how to take effective notes (see page 16 in the Introduction). Encourage students to write key words only rather than full sentences, and to use bullet points. Suggest that students use a separate piece of paper with clear headings for their notes. Then play track 2.2.
- Make it clear that the answers are suggestions only. You could ask students to write their answers on the board or OHP and get them to agree as a class on the best set of notes.

Track 2.2 tapescript ▶▶|

PY: I'll tell you something else. Managers can get more respect from people by being completely straight with people. You know, everybody makes mistakes. What's important is that you can learn from them. If nobody makes mistakes then nobody's taking any risks, which is no good. People have to be free to make mistakes.

INTERVIEWER: Yes, I get you.

PY: And we have to encourage employees to try things. To say, to encourage people to try out ideas. If you kind of encourage people to be autonomous, to take a risk and to be accountable for it then suddenly you create a culture which is very hard to manage. You want people to take risks. You cannot then, you cannot be the traditional boss – 'Do what I say, no questions.' So it's more difficult, but you let your employees be autonomous. You can't just say, 'I'm the boss', you shut up and you listen.

INTERVIEWER: OK.

PY: Which is very challenging. I accept that. Now what I said before about relationships, the people … you have to manage all that. You have to build relationships, look after people, know the people, talk to everyone, talk to your employees, your suppliers, all your colleagues, your consumers. You have to be there and not stay away locked up in your office looking at balance sheets. You have to talk to your shareholders too. Everyone.

INTERVIEWER: So tell us more about experience then. Where does that come in?

PY: Well, you can do a course, do an MA, read the books. You can read all the management gurus. You can read about all the management functions …

INTERVIEWER: Yes.

PY: Marketing function, finance functions, planning, leading, all that stuff. Ah, but if there's one thing you don't learn, it's management.

INTERVIEWER: Yes.

PY: You know and … you can learn HR, i.e. you know you need to have the kind of remuneration package to attract the right people …

INTERVIEWER: Yeah.

PY: … an incentive to keep them. But at the end of the day there's one thing in those books that you'll never learn, because it's taken from the field, that's management by experience. You can't learn experience from books.

INTERVIEWER: Of course not.

PY: Managers should manage by experience and lead by example. It's called 'Management by walking around', you learn from doing things, being there. So you don't learn management. I hate management gurus.

What do you think?

- Ask students to discuss the questions in small groups and give prompts. Check understanding of *management guru*.
- You could also ask students what aspects of management they would like to change or improve in their organisation and what experience they have of management training.

The words you need … to talk about managing organisations

1 Ask students to read the text quickly before getting them to complete it individually or in pairs. Check the answers.

2 Before getting students to do the matching exercise, you could ask them to look at the verbs and elicit possible prepositions or particles. Check the answers with the whole class. As you go through the answers, get students to define the words in context or ask checking questions. You could also mention the importance of not learning single words in isolation only. When students record new vocabulary they should make a note of common prepositions and collocations. This will help to improve their accuracy and range of vocabulary.

3 Explain that the underlined words have a similar meaning to the items in exercise 2. After doing this exercise, you could get students to test each other in pairs quickly and then make sentences about their own organisation.

It's time to talk

- Set the scene and deal with any possible vocabulary problems, for example, you might need to explain *working party*.
- Give students a few minutes to look at their file cards and plan what they are going to say. Set a time limit for the meeting and stress that they should attempt to reach an agreement. Monitor the conversations and record any mistakes to go over later with the whole class. When they have finished, get a spokesperson from each group to report back to the whole class on the decisions that have been made.
- Give feedback on their performance, both in terms of communication and linguistically. You could ask them how they feel they did. Was it a successful meeting? Is there anything that they would do differently?
- You may want to use the Extra classroom activity here (see pages 92 and 100).

COMMUNICATING AT WORK

Writing 1: Email, register and 'down-toning'

Before you begin, you could ask students how often they write emails in English and what sort of problems, if any, they have with them. You could mention that email use is increasing all the time and while this can improve communication, it does make it more important to get your message across clearly and effectively, with the right language.

1 Get students to look at the emails and to compare their ideas in pairs. Get them to say why one is effective and the other is not. In this way, you should be able to elicit the concept of down-toning.

The first email is very direct; the second is more effective because it is more indirect and softer in tone. The main differences are in the use of phrasing and the level of formality: a more informal register in the first email and a more formal register in the second. Quite often, a direct style can appear rude.

2 Get students to check their answers with a partner before checking with the whole class. Elicit the kind of language that is used to down-tone. For example, indirect language (*it seems*), moderating adverbs (*unfortunately*) and indirect style (*we need* rather than *I need*).

2 Dear Sam,
I'm sorry to say it seems there are some problems in the report you sent. Could you have another look at the data from the survey? We need to have a new version of the report next week – unfortunately, we don't have much time as the final project has to be completed within ten days. Do please call me if you need any further explanation or assistance.
Best wishes,

3 I think we should arrange a meeting soon. I suggest that we meet this Thursday at 3 in my office. Is that convenient for you? If not, could you suggest some other dates? It might be a good idea to send the agenda before we meet. It would also be useful to have the financial data before the meeting. Unfortunately, Kim may have to leave early on Thursday.

4 • Students could do this activity in class, if there is time, but set a clear time limit. Alternatively, you could set it for homework.
• If you do it in class, monitor while the students are writing and make a note of any good language used and any mistakes, and then go over them with the whole class after the activity. To finish, students could pass round their emails for others to read.
• If you set the activity as homework, check it and again make a note of any language that you would like to focus on with the whole class at the beginning of the next type 2 lesson.

Thank you for sending the market research report. I'm sorry to have to say it's not quite what I was hoping for, partly because it is only half the length I asked for. In addition, it is not very well organised and the conclusions are rather unclear.

I know that you've been under considerable pressure recently, but I would be grateful if you could find the time to do some further work on it. Please ensure it is the correct length, make some changes in the way it is organised, and clarify the conclusions.

I would appreciate it if you would send me the revised report by the end of next month. Do please call me if you would like to discuss anything.

What did we do today?

Check the Remember section quickly and remind students of the aims of the lesson.

Follow up

Encourage students to:
• write down useful language for talking about management
• write down the new words in their vocabulary books and record relevant information about the word grammar, collocation, pronunciation, etc.
• write down phrases they could use in an email
• bring in an email that they have written to show the rest of the class.

3 Hitting the headlines

What did we do last time?

Although you may wish to do some review of the work you did in the last lesson, we recommend that you do the main review work in relation to Unit 2 when you come to the next type 2 unit, i.e. Unit 5. This is more challenging for the students, as it requires longer recall, but should ultimately provide more continuity and improve learning effectiveness.

On the agenda: Why are we doing this?

Read about Type 3 units on page 10 and Teaching type 3 units on page 16.

Explain that this is an example of the third of three types of unit and that this type looks at speaking and social skills, and vocabulary which is useful to working adults in their lives outside work. In every type 3 lesson, students will learn and practise:
• social skills useful for everyday situations
• vocabulary for everyday subjects of discussion and conversation.

Type 3 units will help students manage better when they meet people socially.

Now tell students the objectives of the lesson (see On the agenda):
• to practise talking about **the news**
• to develop **social skills** for **starting conversations**
• to learn **vocabulary** to talk about **newspaper headlines**.
Reinforce this by writing the key words on the board or OHP.

Warm up

Get students to answer the questions in pairs. You could also ask them when they would make small talk. For example, when they first meet someone, at the beginning of a meeting, when they welcome a visitor, etc.

Getting started

What's the point?

1 Set the scene and get students to read the questions before playing track 3.1. You could also ask students how

they would feel in that situation. Get them to discuss their answers in pairs and encourage them to say what Marcus and Prisha do and don't do well. For example:

Marcus dominates the conversation.
He talks about himself too much.
He talks about his work too much.

You could write up advice on the board about how the speakers could improve. For example:

Marcus should introduce himself more effectively.
He should ask Prisha more questions.
He should show more interest in Prisha.

Answers

a He's an engineer
b At the local hospital
c Marcus dominates the conversation and doesn't seem interested in what Prisha has to say. He makes it difficult for her to break the ice and respond to what he says or tell him anything about herself.

Track 3.1 tapescript ▶▶|

MARCUS: Hello, I don't know anyone here and I saw you standing there so I thought I'd come over and introduce myself. My name's Marcus Todd. I'm an engineer with Ajax Construction. Maybe you've heard of us – we do a lot of work on new offices and factories, big projects mostly. How about you?

PRISHA: Hello, my name's Prisha. Prisha Joree. I work in the local hospital.

MARCUS: Really. We've just finished a big contract there, building the new wards and the staff restaurant. It was quite a challenge doing all the new building round the work of the hospital. I wasn't involved in it myself but …

2 Get students to read the questions before playing track 3.2. Check the answers and write what the speakers do better on the board.

Answers

a Delhi
b She's a nurse
c This is a two-way conversation, and Marcus is interested in what Prisha has to say. They both help to break the ice by asking questions, saying who they are and showing interest in what the other person has to say.

Track 3.2 tapescript ▶▶|

MARCUS: Hello, I don't know anyone here. Do you mind if I talk to you?

PRISHA: Not at all, I hardly know anyone here myself. My name's Prisha. Prisha Joree. I work in the local hospital.

MARCUS: Nice to meet you, Prisha. And I'm Marcus Todd. I'm an engineer. I work in construction.

PRISHA: Nice to meet you, Marcus.

MARCUS: Prisha, that's a Hindu name, isn't it?

PRISHA: That's right. My parents are from Delhi originally but I was born and brought up in the UK.

MARCUS: And what do you do at the hospital?

PRISHA: I'm a nurse. I've been there for over five years now, ever since I qualified, in fact.

MARCUS: I've got so much respect for nurses. I'd love to be able to do your job but I don't think I could. It must be very interesting helping different people with different problems.

PRISHA: Well, yes, and it's quite physically demanding as well …

3 Get students to complete the sentences from memory as far as possible first. You could write them on the board so that students can reach agreement on the answers before playing the track again to check. Play it once more, if necessary.

Answers

a mind if I talk to you
b an engineer. I work in
c do you do
d be very interesting helping different

4 You could ask different pairs to focus on different scenarios and get them to present their suggestions to the rest of the class. You could correct them yourself, if necessary, or write them on the board for everyone to look at. Check pronunciation, if appropriate.

Possible answers

Plane or train
Are you travelling on business?
Where are you travelling to?

On holiday
Have you been here before?
Where are you staying?

A visitor to your workplace
Let me show you round.
Did you find us OK?

Have a go

- Set the scene and give Students A and B a few minutes to prepare their roles and to think about what they are going to say.
- Ensure that the observer is clear about his/her role. They should concentrate on how effectively A and B communicate as well as their use of appropriate phrases and correct language. They could use the advice at the end of the unit as a checklist. You could demonstrate the kind of feedback that you are looking for. For example: *Student A asked a lot of questions and showed interest in what Student B was saying. I think Student B might need to get more involved in the conversation and give longer answers, but she did use some good phrases like 'I hardly know anyone here myself.'*
- Students should swap roles so that the observer can have an opportunity to practise making small talk.
- After the role-play, encourage students to reflect on their performance. Each group could feed back to the whole class.

Read on

The headlines

- This part of the unit aims to develop students' reading skills and to increase their awareness of the kind of language that is often used in newspaper headlines.
- Get students to discuss the opening questions in pairs. If they do read newspapers in English, ask them which ones and what the differences are between them. You could

elicit some of the differences between the popular and quality press and the kinds of stories they might run.

1
- Get students to compare their ideas about the headlines in pairs before getting suggestions from the whole class.
- At this stage it might be worth getting students to look at the headlines and asking them what some of the features of headlines are. For example, auxiliary verbs, prepositions and articles are frequently omitted and dramatic language is used. Tell students not to worry too much about the vocabulary, as this will be dealt with later in the lesson. The key thing here is to focus on the general meaning.
- Give a time limit for students to match the headlines to the stories. This will encourage students to get a general idea of each story before they read in more detail in the next exercise.

Answers

1 g   2 f   3 d   4 e   5 a   6 b   7 c

2
- Give students a longer time limit to read the stories in more detail and answer the questions.
- After doing the exercise, get students to discuss the questions in pairs. The stories are likely to appear in the popular press. You could ask students if they have the same kinds of newspapers in their country.

Answers

1 She says they look like famous people.
2 Alarm clocks – because some children didn't have them and were often late for school.
3 It sent a phone bill to a man who had been dead for 16 years.
4 It phoned a betting line. The call cost the owners £180.
5 They've been putting penguins into their fridges. This is not good for the penguins.
6 Aerobics classes because they are too fat.
7 She fell more than 30 metres down a cliff. Nineteen people came to her rescue. She was unhurt.

The words you need ... to read newspaper headlines

- Students can do these exercises in pairs. Check the answers and pronunciation, if appropriate.
- Make it clear that this kind of language is not normally used in everyday spoken English, but that it is helpful to have a passive knowledge of it so that they can understand newspaper headlines.

Answers

1 1 consists of   2 look like   3 look (closely) at
4 handing out   5 turn up   6 asking for   7 found out
8 turning up   9 set up   10 got away
2 1 prohibits   2 dismissed   3 supports   4 helped
5 dispute   6 unemployment   7 badly affected
8 agreement   9 promise   10 marries   11 resigns
12 stops

It's time to talk

- You could begin by telling the students a news story from your country. This will serve as a model.
- Give students a few minutes to think of their news stories and perhaps to make a few brief notes.
- Highlight the language for talking about the news in the Student's Book and encourage students to show interest and ask questions when listening to a story. Monitor and feed back on their language at the end of the activity.
- Depending on their level, some students might find writing headlines quite challenging, so monitor this carefully and help out where necessary. Students could write their headlines on the board or OHP so the whole class can see them easily. You might want to turn this activity into a game and award points for the pairs that get the most stories correct.
- You may want to use the Extra classroom activity here (see pages 92 and 101).

What did we do today?
Check the Remember section quickly and remind them of the objectives of the lesson.

Follow up
Encourage students to:
- write any new and useful vocabulary in their vocabulary books
- read English language newspapers as much as possible.

4 Orient Express

What did we do last time?
Do a review of the last type 1 lesson (see Teacher's notes for Unit 1) and do some quick revision as follows.

Present tenses
- Ask students what the differences are in the use of the present simple and continuous and the present perfect simple and continuous. At this level there shouldn't be a problem with the form, but it might be worth double-checking this.
- Put students in pairs or small groups and ask them to have brief 'small talk' type conversations using the different tenses.

Pronunciation: Minimal pairs
Ask students what individual sounds in English they have problems with; go over the pronunciation quickly.

On the agenda: Why are we doing this?
Tell students the objectives of the lesson:
- to practise talking about **selling**
- to revise **verb grammar**. You could write an example on the board so that students are clear about what they are going to study, e.g. *I love doing*, and *I need to do*

- to do some **pronunciation** work on **using pauses to add impact**.
Reinforce this by writing the key words on the board or OHP.

Warm up
Get students to discuss their answers to the questions in pairs. You could also ask them what kind of people they think might travel on this train.

Background briefing: Orient Express
In Europe, the Venice-Simplon-Orient-Express offers luxury train travel between the cities of London, Paris, Prague, Budapest and Istanbul, among others. In addition, it operates luxury train services in South America and South-East Asia. The company also owns a unique collection of hotels around the world. For more information about Orient Express, go to the *English365* website: www.cambridge.org/elt/english365.

Listen to this

Selling luxury
- Read the caption and look at the picture of Vicky. Tell students that they are going to listen to her talking about her magazine and her job. You could also ask them what kind of skills they think Vicky needs to do her job and what might be involved in it.
- Before students do the listening, elicit the following vocabulary that they will need for the listening tasks: *selling, persuade, brochure, promotion, existing client, fashion shoot*.

1 Get students to read through the arguments and techniques before you play track 4.1.

Answers
1, 3, 4, 6

Track 4.1 tapescript ▶▶
INTERVIEWER: So, Vicky, is it a tough job to persuade people to advertise in the magazine?

VICKY: Well, first of all I've got a most fantastic product so that anybody who I'm speaking to, marketing directors around Europe, if they've been to one of our hotels like Splendido in Porto Fino or Le Manoir in Oxford, or they've been on the Orient Express train, my job's done. They know the people who are staying there, the guests or travellers, are right for their products.

INTERVIEWER: Is there a problem with the magazine being free?

VICKY: Well, yes, a little. The advertising agencies are always looking at how much magazines cost and from an advertising point of view it's tough because we're giving away a magazine. But, you see, I say we're the most expensive and exclusive magazine in the world because you only get it free if you go for, well, as a minimum, lunch on the Orient Express, which is £500 for two.

INTERVIEWER: So, Vicky, what other selling techniques do you use?

VICKY: You need to meet people. If you're just cold calling on people and they hear it's a magazine on the phone they tend not to want to speak to you, because these marketing directors are getting an average of 30 or 40 telephone calls a day from someone selling something. So I don't try to sell the magazine on the telephone. You can't make people buy like that. I try to arrange a meeting because when you're actually there, it's easy, with the lovely brochures and magazine I've got, to make the whole story come alive.

INTERVIEWER: OK.

VICKY: And another thing, with someone I haven't spoken to, or don't know much about their company, I tend to look on their website. And then you say, 'Oh, I see you've just bought such and such', or 'I see you're expanding into this market' or 'that market', because people really, really appreciate it if you've actually done a little bit of research into their company. I would say it's probably the one ... the single most important thing about selling.

INTERVIEWER: And does it take time to persuade people?

VICKY: Oh, yes. I always tell myself to be patient. It might be ten years with some people. But we never give up with anybody.

Suggested answers
2 1 She telephones Europe.
2 About four hours each on telephoning and emailing.
3 About 50%.
4 A lot of fashion houses only advertise in fashion magazines.
5 The watch sector.
6 The proportion of corporate clients booking the Orient Express train.
7 The Orient Express to Istanbul for two people.
8 The current occupancy level for the Orient Express train.

Track 4.2 tapescript ▶▶
INTERVIEWER: So, what's a typical day for you?

VICKY: Well, I divide it up into sections. I'm usually at my desk just before 8 to speak to Hong Kong and Singapore ... their day is ending then. At around 11 o'clock I'll do Europe, which will be Italy, Germany, obviously France and Switzerland.

INTERVIEWER: How many minutes per day are you actually on the phone would you say? A couple of hours?

VICKY: Oh, I would think it's probably about four hours on the phone and four hours writing emails because, you know, emails are all very well and good, but things don't really come alive until you actually speak to people personally.

INTERVIEWER: OK. And in terms of how you divide your time between clients you're working with, is it like 80 per cent existing clients and 20 per cent new clients?

VICKY: Well, I should think it's about 50:50 actually. One area in the magazine we want to expand on is fashion. But a lot of the fashion houses won't advertise in anything that isn't a fashion magazine. So we've started doing live fashion shoots at one of our lovely hotels. And we're just beginning slowly to win clients like Missoni, Christian Dior, Dolce & Gabbana.

INTERVIEWER: OK.

VICKY: And one area we're very strong indeed on is watches, the Swiss watches. Now you know you've got watches for sport, watches for the evening, every year people like to have a new watch. So Cartier and Rolex, for example, are spending a lot of money on promotion around the world.

INTERVIEWER: And in terms then of who uses the Orient Express train, is it quite a diverse kind of client base?

VICKY: Yes. In England you get an awful lot of people celebrating Valentine's Day or Mother's Day. But about 40 per cent is corporate, the city boys taking clients for a day out. And then obviously you're talking about holidays, the Cipriani in Venice. And then we also do one to Istanbul; the price of that goes up to about £12,000 for two. But you stop off at Vienna, Budapest, Bucharest – that's a ten-day tour.

INTERVIEWER: Will it remain popular at that price?

VICKY: Yes, still very popular. And you know it's something – when I meet people, I love saying that I work for Orient Express, their faces light up, they say, 'That's something I really want to do one day.' And so, even though we've lost a lot of Americans as you can imagine over the last few years, we're still running the train at about 90, 95 per cent full. There's only one Orient Express and people will always plan to do it as a dream.

What do you think?

You could also ask students if they have received 'spam' telephone calls and text messages, and what they think should be done about it. This is when companies telephone people at home to say they have won a major prize. The recipients are then required to call a premium rate number in order to claim it. The prizes often turn out to be non-existent.

Check your grammar

Verb grammar

1 and **2**

- Tell students to work through these exercises individually or in pairs, as appropriate. Then check the answers with the whole class.
- You could also get students to look through the tapescript for other examples to match to the correct verb grammar type.

Answers

1 Type 1: b   Type 2: d   Type 3: a   Type 4: c
2 Type 1: ask, decide, forget, help, promise, want
Type 2: advise, allow, ask, encourage, help, want
Type 3: advise, finish, suggest
Type 4: help, let, make, promise

3 This may require some extra explanation so it may be worth having some examples prepared. For example:
I tried to scream. I tried screaming.
Students could then work in pairs to suggest possible contexts for each.

Answers

1 b   2 a   3 a   4 b   5 a   6 b   7 b   8 a

Do it yourself

1 Give students a few minutes to do this exercise on their own and then check the answers.

Answers

1 I wanted you to call me if there was a problem.
2 My boss didn't let me go to the sales conference.

3 Let's stop discussing this item and move to the next point on the agenda.
4 My company doesn't allow employees to smoke in their offices.
5 He told me that I should go immediately.
6 I really enjoy cooking at weekends.

2 Get students to read through the email quickly before they attempt the exercise. You could ask quick checking questions like: *What was delayed? Does Serge need a visa?* They can then do the exercise individually.

Answers

1 to redraft   2 making   3 to send   4 to include   5 to run
6 doing   7 to set up   8 know   9 to ask   10 to check

3 You could extend this activity by getting students to suggest qualities required in their jobs, using the verbs given.

Answers

1 remember/manage   2 learn/teach themselves
3 want/help   4 let   5 persuade/tell   6 hate
7 ask   8 explain

Sounds good

Using pauses to add impact

1
- Check understanding of *impact* before you begin.
- Play the track twice, if necessary. Alternatively, you could read it out yourself with clear pauses and stress on the connecting words.
- Get students to discuss their ideas in pairs before you talk it through with the whole group.
- When the students read the text, encourage them initially to exaggerate the stress and pauses so they are clear about what they should be doing.

Answers

The words in italics are pronounced with extra volume and stress, and are preceded and followed by a pause, which adds power to the argument being developed.

Track 4.3 tapescript ▶▶|
See the Student's Book.

2
- Play track 4.4 and get students to decide which speakers add impact effectively.
- Before students practise saying the sentences, you may want to play the track again, or model the sentences yourself.

Answers

1, 4

Track 4.4 tapescript ▶▶|

1 Firstly, the 2310 has good functionality. Secondly, the price is very attractive.
2 The 2310 is triband. As a result, it works in both Europe and the US.
3 You get 2,310 minutes of free talk time every month. In addition, you get 200 free text messages.
4 The 2310 is very popular. In fact, it's the best on the market at the moment.

3 You could extend this activity by getting students to persuade the whole class.

It's time to talk

- Tell students that they are now going to practise using the language that they have looked at in this lesson by performing a telephone call role-play.
- Make sure that they write the six words they choose on a piece of paper they can give to another pair.
- Students will need some time to plan their conversation and think about the benefits of the product they have chosen. Set a time limit for this.
- Give feedback on students' performance.
- You may want to use the Extra classroom activity here (see pages 93 and 102).

What did we do today?

Check the Remember section quickly and remind students of the objectives of the lesson.

Follow up

Encourage students to:
- write sentences about their organisation using the verbs in this unit
- record the grammar of new vocabulary items
- practise using stress and pauses to add emphasis to what they are saying.

5 Financial planning

What did we do last time?

Do a review of the last type 2 lesson (Unit 2). Remind students of what they worked on (see Teacher's notes for that unit) and do some quick revision as follows.

Talking about managing organisations
Ask students to give you the prepositions or particles that can collocate with the following words: *experiment, adapt, cut, take advantage, be accountable, sort* and *lead*. Then get them to make sentences about their own work situation.

Writing: Email, register and down-toning
Ask students how we down-tone in emails. Try to elicit that we use indirect language, moderating adverbs and an indirect style. Ask them to give you examples for each category.

On the agenda: Why are we doing this?

Tell students the objectives of the lesson:
- to talk about **financial matters**
- to develop **vocabulary** to talk about **financial planning and control**
- to develop skills for **presenting progress reports**.

Reinforce this by writing the key words on the board or OHP. Some students may not be very interested in finance so it could be a good idea to emphasise how centrally important it is to business, and of course in our personal lives as well.

Warm up

Get students to give you short answers to these questions and don't worry if they don't know too much about financial planning as these are intended to introduce the topic.

Look at the picture of Rachid and ask some checking questions about him. Students may want to know what an actuary is, but don't explain at this stage as the definition appears in the listening section.

Listen to this

Actuaries and finance managers

Proceed as suggested in the teaching hints for type 2 units in the Introduction (page 16).

> **Answers**
>
> **1** investments   financial planning   risk management
> **2** 1 b   2 a   3 c   4 a

Track 5.1 tapescript ▶▶

INTERVIEWER: Rachid, can you start by telling us about Norwich Union and what you do?

RACHID: Well, I work for Norwich Union Life, which is a subsidiary of Aviva PLC, one of the largest European insurance and investment providers. We are a provider of investment products, in other words products based on long-term savings.

INTERVIEWER: Yes.

RACHID: So, for example it could be pensions or life protection products or health care insurance, that kind of thing. And me, I'm an actuary.

INTERVIEWER: And what's your role as an actuary?

RACHID: It's risk management. It involves a lot of financial modelling.

INTERVIEWER: What's that?

RACHID: Well, the actuary's job is to model the future, so we assess the performance of investments over future time – this is called modelling. We have to take account of financial economics, the financial environment – an important area for us. So one of the things we do is cash flow projection.

INTERVIEWER: So the role of the actuary is much more to do with financial planning in relation to products? Is it a form of financial forecasting? You forecast what will happen?

RACHID: Well, yes. For example, we have to design products and we have to price them and we have to take account of everything that's going to happen in the future. This is cash flow projection.

INTERVIEWER: Yes. I see.

RACHID: We have to make projections about how different financial indicators are going to behave, how the policy is going to behave, how the markets, the risks and the investment markets are going to behave.

INTERVIEWER: Yeah.

RACHID: So it's all about making these projections.

INTERVIEWER: So in effect there is a big difference between the actuary, who is involved in financial planning, and the finance manager, who is involved in financial reporting?

RACHID: Yes, there's a big difference because we tend to take decisions about the future ...

INTERVIEWER: You're projecting ahead and ...

RACHID: Yes, and making decisions, whereas the finance department look just, you know, they look at the expenses, they look at ...

INTERVIEWER: Performance. So budgets, looking at overspending, for example? Maybe they work mostly with checking if a project is over budget?

RACHID: Exactly, but the past, past performance or what's happening now. And of course, the control function – classically a lot of financial management is monitoring and control. We're not really involved with that, except our colleagues in finance give us important documents to work from, like profit and loss accounts and income statements. They prepare all the classic tools of financial reporting.

INTERVIEWER: I understand.

RACHID: But we really focus on the future, on projecting forward.

What do you think?

You could do a quick classroom survey to find out how many people have financial responsibility and if they would like to have more.

The words you need ... to talk about financial planning and control

1 and 2

Get students to complete these exercises on their own or in pairs. There is potentially a lot of new vocabulary here, so it is important to stress to students that they should be selective when they choose which items they would like to learn.

Answers
1 1 management   2 environment   3 projections
4 planning/modelling   5 indicators
6 management/reporting   7 profit and loss   8 statements
2 1 budget   2 income   3 expenditure   4 invest
5 breaks even / has broken even   6 assess   7 forecast
8 interest payments   9 overrun   10 borrow

3 It is worth spending some time going over some of the wrong answers and explaining the difference between *investment* and *expenditure*, for example. You could also get students to make sentences with some of the new items of vocabulary as a means of consolidation.

Answers
1 budget   2 loans   3 overran   4 environment
5 forecast   6 borrow   7 income   8 expenditure
9 interest   10 investment

For further work or revision on finance, you could refer students back to Unit 11 in *English365* Book 2. Unit 27 in this book is also finance related.

It's time to talk

- For this activity you may wish to move the class around and put students with new partners.
- Set the scene and give Student A time to look at their file card and assimilate the information and for Student B to look at their card and to write questions to ask.
- Encourage students to focus on the vocabulary that is new for them and try to use it during the role-play. When you give feedback on their performance, ask how many new words they used.

- You may want to use the Extra classroom activity here (see pages 93 and 103).

COMMUNICATING AT WORK

Presenting 1: Progress reports

1 • You might want to begin with the students' books closed. Explain what is meant by a *presentation* or *briefing* and a *progress report*. Ask about the possible structure of a progress report, eliciting ideas like background, what has been done and what still needs to be done.
- Alternatively, play track 5.2 and ask students what the structure of the presentation is.
- Then get students to look at the explanation of the structure of a progress report in the book.

Answers
Background; what has been done; what still has to be done or will happen

Track 5.2 tapescript ▶▶

PRESENTER: So, a short briefing on what's going on. First, the background. As you know, we introduced a new system last year but it has never worked very well. We think the main problem concerns administration procedures. And research has shown that we can improve the quality of information – the information flow – for example, what we tell customers about supply and delivery dates.

So far, we've already made a lot of changes to our warehousing. We are in the middle of upgrading our software and we have much better technical support than we had last year. The most important benefit is that our internal information handling is better.

What's next? Well, we need to continue the improvements. A key step is to have more administrative help, so we need to recruit and train more staff. We also want to introduce more specialist functions and more staff training. In the coming weeks we will plan a lot more training events.

2 Before students hear the recording a second time, ask them to suggest suitable language to fill in the spaces. Otherwise, get them to fill in the spaces as they listen to the recording a second time. You could also ask them to suggest alternatives. Elicit suggestions and perhaps write up some of the good ones on the board.

Answers
1 a short briefing   2 the background   3 we introduced
4 the main problem concerns   5 we can improve
6 made a lot of changes   7 are in the middle of
8 most important benefit   9 What's next?
10 we need to continue   11 we will plan

3 Give students a few minutes to plan their presentation. Stress that the presentation should retain the basic three-part structure. To finish, you could ask volunteers to present their progress reports to the whole group. Monitor and give feedback on the students' performance.

What did we do today?

Check the Remember section quickly and remind students of the objectives of this lesson.

Follow up

Encourage students to:
- write down useful words related to financial planning in their vocabulary books
- write down useful phrases for giving progress reports.

6 Top cities

What did we do last time?

Do a review of the last type 3 lesson (Unit 3). Remind students of what they worked on (see Teacher's notes for that unit) and do some quick revision as follows.

Social skills: Getting started

Ask students to give you some strategies for making effective small talk. For example:
- break the ice
- ask questions
- show interest.

Then ask for examples for each of them. They could then have a brief conversation in pairs using the language and strategies.

Talking about the news

Ask students to give you verbs plus prepositions that mean the same as: *resemble, discover, appear, escape, arrive* and *comprise*. Ask them to make sentences using the words.

You could also get students to tell a partner about a recent news story from their country. Remind them of the language suggested in that lesson, for example: *Did you see that article in the paper about ...? Have you heard the news about ....?* etc.

On the agenda: Why are we doing this?

Tell students the objectives of this lesson:
- to talk about **current affairs**
- to develop **social skills** for **building rapport**
- to learn **vocabulary** to talk about **economic issues**.

Reinforce this by writing the key words on the board or OHP.

You could point out that *rapport* is a French word.

Warm up

Look at the questions and get students to discuss their answers briefly in pairs. Get students to feed back ideas about how to build rapport to the whole class.

Building rapport

What's the point?

See the Introduction (page 16): Type 3 units – social skills.

Answers

1 a A big new office block in the city centre
  b At least six months
  c Marcus dominates the conversation and only talks about himself and his work. He doesn't ask Prisha any questions – she has to do all the work.

Track 6.1 tapescript ▶▶|

MARCUS: ... It was quite a challenge doing all the new building work round the work of the hospital. We had to do some very careful planning – of course, it would have been so much easier just to close down different parts of the hospital at different times.

PRISHA: Yes ... but it's much better now that it's all finished ... So what are you working on at the moment?

MARCUS: Oh, we're building that big new office block in the city centre, the one right next to the station. It's one of the biggest contracts we've ever had – and we've got a lot of our people working on it. It's very important to us.

PRISHA: Oh, yes, I think I know the one you mean ... Will it take long to finish?

MARCUS: Oh, it'll be another six months at least. Hard work. We normally do ten-hour days because we can't afford to miss the deadline. There'll be a massive penalty to pay if we're late. So it's six, sometimes seven, days a week down there on site at the moment.

PRISHA: Really.

Answers

2 a Australia
  b He's a journalist.
  c This is a two-way conversation with a much better balance. Both Marcus and Prisha help by asking questions, looking for common areas of interest and keeping the conversation going.
3 a Do you like your job?
  b Do you like sport?
  c I was there as well.
  d Who does your brother work for?

Track 6.2 tapescript ▶▶|

MARCUS: ... I've got so much respect for nurses. I'd love to be able to do your job but I don't think I could. It must be very interesting helping different people with different problems. Do you like your job?

PRISHA: Well, yes, I love the job, although it's quite physically demanding. You have to do a lot of lifting.

MARCUS: Yes, I can imagine. And where did you train?

PRISHA: I did my training in Leeds but I was really lucky and did a year's work experience in Australia as well.

MARCUS: Really! Whereabouts in Australia were you?

PRISHA: Sydney. Have you been to Australia?

MARCUS: Yes, I have. When were you there?

PRISHA: For the whole of the millennium year – 2000.

MARCUS: So you were there for the Olympics. Do you like sport?

PRISHA: Yes, I absolutely love it – and I got to see quite a lot of the events, especially the athletics.

MARCUS: How incredible! I was there as well.

PRISHA: Really? Are you a sports fan too?

MARCUS: Well, my brother's a journalist. He covered a lot of the athletics for his paper and he found a cheap deal for both of us, so I went too and had a great time.

PRISHA: My sister's husband is a journalist too. Who does your brother work for?

MARCUS: Well, actually he's gone freelance recently, but at that time he was working for …

Possible answers

4 With someone who says he/she doesn't like parties very much

I don't like them very much either.

What do you prefer?

With someone who asks you what sport you're most interested in

I'm quite keen on football. How about you?

I like playing badminton. Have you ever played?

With someone who says you look like their brother/sister

Really? Do I?

How incredible! What does your brother/sister do?

Have a go

See the Introduction (page 17): Type 3 units. After the activity, you could get selected pairs to perform for the rest of the class and perhaps write some of the best ways of building rapport on the board.

Read on

The news

Get students to close their books and explain that they are going to read a text about cities. Ask them the question, which they can discuss in pairs.

1
- Write the title of the text on the board and explain that they are going to predict the content of the article. Before they do this it might be a good idea to ask why they think they are going to do this. Try to elicit that prediction can help to understand a text more easily. In this way, the rationale behind the activity should become clear.
- You could ask the questions and get students to discuss them in pairs or they could read them in the Student's Book.

2
- Stick to the time limit – you can always give students more time to read the text later, if necessary. It is important for students to realise that they do not need to read every word to answer the questions.
- When you go through the answers, it might be beneficial to ask students where in the text they found the answer and what made them look there.

Answers

1 Mercer Human Resource Consulting
2 Switzerland and Germany   3 New York   4 215
5 Calgary   6 Athens   7 air pollution   8 39

The words you need ... to talk about economic issues

1 You could ask students to say what kinds of things might appear in each category before they do the matching exercise individually or in pairs.

Answers

1 a 7   b 8   c 6   d 10   e 2   f 3   g 5   h 1   i 9   j 4
2 a 4   b 5   c 1   d 10   e 8   f 2   g 7   h 9   i 6   j 3

3 Before doing the activity, you could see if students can predict what term each quotation might refer to. They can then look at the article to check. It is a good idea to get them to read the article quickly so they have a general idea of what it is about.

Answers

1 f   2 d   3 i   4 j   5 e   6 a   7 b   8 g   9 c   10 h

It's time to talk

- You could suggest five determinants for students to choose. If they live in the same city, you could ask them to choose three different determinants per pair. Alternatively, they could comment on a city that they know well.
- Get students to expand on each determinant and tell them not to worry if they do not know a great deal about it – tell them to use their imagination.
- Encourage them to use the vocabulary from the previous section.
- After they have presented their results to the rest of the class, you could ask them to choose the top city from the ones presented.
- You may want to use the Extra classroom activity here (see pages 93 and 104).

What did we do today?

Check the Remember section and remind students of the objectives of the lesson.

Follow up

Encourage students to:
- start a new section in their vocabulary book on economic issues
- write down useful phrases for building rapport.

7 Motivating careers

What did we do last time?
Do a review of the last type 1 lesson (Unit 4). Remind students of what they worked on (see Teacher's notes for that unit) and do some quick revision as follows.

Verb grammar
Ask selected students to make sentences with the following words: *advise, allow, ask, encourage, finish, forget, help, let, make, promise, want, suggest.*

Pronunciation: Using pauses to add impact
Get students to choose a product or service and explain its benefits to a partner. Tell them to use emphatic stress and pauses. Before they do this, you might like to remind them of the types of connecting words that can be stressed. For example: *firstly, as a result, in addition, in fact,* etc.

On the agenda: Why are we doing this?
Tell students the objectives of the lesson:
- to practise **talking about the past**
- to revise the **past simple**, **past continuous** and **past perfect simple** tenses
- to do some **pronunciation** work on **emphasising important words.**

Reinforce this by writing the key words on the board or OHP.

Warm up
Point out that the unit characters have followed very different career paths – trade unionist and capitalist entrepreneur. Ask students what they think might motivate people to do such different things.

Background briefing: Norwegian Confederation of Trade Unions (Landsorganisasjonen) and Rotecna
Norwegian Confederation of Trade Unions
The Norwegian Confederation of Trade Unions (Landsorganisasjonen or LO) is the largest and most influential workers' organisation in Norway. Established in 1899, its affiliated unions represent some 800,000 workers across the country. LO currently plays a central role in collective bargaining settlements both nationally and locally to improve workers' pay, working hours, holidays and other employment rights. LO also works internationally to support and strengthen the trade union movement in countries where trade unionism struggles to assert itself. Its longer-term objective is to contribute to the evolution of democratic government.

Rotecna
Founded in 1991 by its President, Gener Romeu, Rotecna S.A. specialises in the manufacturing of pig farm equipment – plastic and cast iron slatted flooring, wet and dry feeders, drinking bowls, etc. – and has gained a leading position in national and international markets. Its products are made to a high quality standard and designed to increase the profitability of modern pig farms.

For more information about the Norwegian Confederation of Trade Unions and Rotecna, go to the *English365* website: www.cambridge.org/elt/english365.

Listen to this

Work choices

1
- Give students time to read the statements and help them with any vocabulary problems. Then play track 7.1. You could choose to play track 7.2 immediately or go through the answers for Terje's profile first.
- Alternatively, you could do this as a jigsaw listening. If you decide to do this, you will need two CD players as half the students will listen to Terje and half will listen to Gener. After listening to each person, the students can then pair up with someone from the other group and exchange answers with them.

Answers

1 a carpenter   2 transport company
3 President of the Transport Workers' Union   4 Oslo
5 1996   6 2,000   7 1991   8 owned bars and restaurants
9 60%   10 specialisation   11 a little luck

Track 7.1 tapescript ▶▶|

INTERVIEWER: So how did you move into the world of trade unions?
TERJE: Well, I trained as a carpenter actually, building houses.
INTERVIEWER: And after that?
TERJE: Then, in 1976, I started with a transport company and, during this time, I was elected as president of the Transport Workers' Union.
INTERVIEWER: When was that?
TERJE: I became president in 1982.
INTERVIEWER: And did you enjoy your work with the transport company?
TERJE: Yes. We were always looking to find ways to run the company more effectively. Most important for us was not to kick people out, maybe move people from the bus to the tram, to the metro and so on. But not kick them out.
INTERVIEWER: Then after ten years you decided to do something different, to go into the public sector?
TERJE: Yes, I became commissioner for urban planning and cultural affairs for Oslo city council. I was elected for the Socialist Left Party which had taken power, together with the Labour Party. That was in January 1992.
INTERVIEWER: A big challenge?
TERJE: Yes, we didn't have so much money. Oslo city had very big economic problems.
INTERVIEWER: And then you decided to move back to the union movement, to LO?
TERJE: Yes, I joined Landsorganisasjonen, LO, in 1996.
INTERVIEWER: The international department means a lot of travel?
TERJE: Yes, and I put together a magazine about all our work abroad. We printed 2,000 last year and sent them to the various trade unions. It's all about sharing experiences and, in the end, giving support to trade unions abroad in developing countries which are working to build democracy.

Track 7.2 tapescript ▶▶

INTERVIEWER: So, Gener, how did Rotecna start?

GENER: OK. I set up the company in January of '91.

INTERVIEWER: Did you know anything about running a company?

GENER: Yes, I knew a bit about business because I'd been a partner in another company and also had bars and restaurants near Barcelona. So I'd been in business for over 20 years before I set up Rotecna.

INTERVIEWER: Was it risky to start Rotecna?

GENER: Of course, when you take a decision like this, it's risky. But when you decide, it's because you have confidence in your project.

INTERVIEWER: With Rotecna, was it a strategy to get into the export market quickly?

GENER: Yes. We started exporting, I think, in the second year, in '92. And now 60 per cent of our sales go to export markets, to the rest of Europe, all of America – North and South, some Asian countries and Australia. So, we're present in over 50 countries.

INTERVIEWER: How do you explain your success?

GENER: Well, specialisation was important. It was a good decision to concentrate on one specific activity, pig farm equipment. Also, investment strategy. I've always reinvested my profits in the company for new products, always.

INTERVIEWER: You make it sound like business is easy.

GENER: Yeah. I'm a hundred per cent sure about this. If you're honest, clever, practical and you take risks … and, of course, you need a little luck.

2 • Before you begin, check understanding of *tough* and *apartheid*.

• There may be quite a lot of new vocabulary in the tapescripts, so it may be worthwhile, after doing the exercises, giving students some time to go through them and choose, say, six words that are new to them. Encourage them to work out the meaning of the words in context, if possible, at first and then explain them, if necessary.

Answers

1 Colombia
2 €1.5m is the amount invested by LO in South Africa from 1985 to 1996.
3 Meeting people
4 To help the local economy
5 Strong but not strong enough sometimes
6 He now takes every Wednesday afternoon off.

Track 7.3 tapescript ▶▶

INTERVIEWER: Terje, you've travelled a lot … to some tough places?

TERJE: Yes, Colombia was difficult. I only went there once and, you know, it'd had a long history of civil war, many people – politicians and trade unionists – had died, people never given their human rights. Things were improving when we visited but Colombia was a tough place, yes.

INTERVIEWER: Did it motivate you that you made a difference, you helped to improve things?

TERJE: Absolutely. Like in South Africa. We started to consult with trade unions in 1985 and we were right in the fight against apartheid. I think we invested around €1.5 million from 1985 until 1996. So, yes, it was good to make a difference.

INTERVIEWER: I guess money isn't really a motivator for you?

TERJE: I don't think about money. I think the main motivation is just meeting people. You have to talk to people, to share experiences, not to think about yourself, but get on the road and meet people, and then maybe you can help.

Track 7.4 tapescript ▶▶

INTERVIEWER: Gener, just a few questions on what motivates you now. I know you've developed your business with local people. Is that a motivator for you?

GENER: Yeah, it's part of my philosophy or motivation. I've always tried to employ local people to help the local economy. But because we are in a province in Spain with little unemployment, I have to use people from outside the community too.

INTERVIEWER: What about management style – are you a hard manager, Gener?

GENER: I don't think so. I've got a strong character, and as a manager I'm strong, but sometimes I'm not strong enough. When I need to fire some people, I give them five … ten more opportunities.

INTERVIEWER: And what's the future for you? What will keep you motivated?

GENER: For business, well, a new vice-president joined the company two weeks ago so I can dedicate more time to customers and new products. And privately, I decided on new objectives to increase my quality of life, to reduce the pressure of work.

INTERVIEWER: OK. Did you work too hard in the past?

GENER: Yeah. I used to work very long hours when I was young … all, all of my life. So I decided to take every Wednesday afternoon off. This means I can do some training courses, more leisure activities … this is my big, big objective.

What do you think?

You could do a quick classroom survey to find out if the motivation for students' careers is similar.

Check your grammar

Past simple, past continuous and past perfect simple

1, 2 and **3**

• Explain to students that they are now going to look at the grammar Terje and Gener use to talk about their pasts.

• Students can do the exercises in pairs and then check the answers. Afterwards you could get students to look through the tapescripts and get them to find other examples of the tenses.

Answers

1 1 Past continuous
  2 Past simple
  3 Past perfect simple

2 1 We were looking (past continuous)
  2 Did you enjoy (past simple)
  3 I knew (past simple), I'd been (past perfect simple)
  4 We started (past simple)
  5 I went (past simple), it'd had (past perfect simple)
  6 Things were improving (past continuous), we visited (past simple)

3 1 a The 'situation getting worse' was in progress when the person left the country.
  b The situation got worse after the person left the country. In other words, the two events are a sequence: event A (the person left the country) followed by event B (the situation got worse).

2 a The improvement of the local economy happened before the setting up of the company.

b The improvement happened after the person set up the company. In other words, the two events are a sequence: event A (the person set up the company) followed by event B (the local economy improved).

Do it yourself

1, 2 and 3

Ask students to do the exercises alone or in pairs, and then check the answers.

Answers

1 1 When I started to read English newspapers, I learned a lot about the UK.

2 I had just written an important report when my computer crashed. I think I've lost all the data.

3 When I finally found the meeting room, the meeting had already started.

4 I joined Techno Ltd in 1996. At that time the company was doing well.

5 When I got to the office I realised I hadn't brought my keys.

2 1 left 2 selected 3 had finished 4 shaped 5 was studying 6 did 7 worked 8 left 9 had reached 10 was carrying 11 wrote 12 had had 13 honoured 14 continued 15 made

3 1 arrived 2 had set up 3 had increased 4 asked 5 had 6 had not gone 7 told 8 had stayed up 9 discovered 10 had forgotten 11 was 12 had used

Sounds good

Emphasising important words

Remind students of the importance of sentence and word stress in English pronunciation and how different stress can change the meaning or implication of what we say.

1 Play track 7.5. You might need to do this more than once, or model it yourself.

Get students to say how the different stress patterns change the meaning. For example:

In sentence 1, *off* is stressed. The speaker is emphasising that he will be *off*, i.e. not at work. In sentence 2, he is emphasising that he *wants* to be off work, i.e. it is not definite. In 3, he is emphasising that he wants to take the *afternoon* off, i.e. not the morning.

Answers

The following words are emphasised:
1 off 2 want 3 afternoon

Speaker B changes the emphasis according to the context of each sentence. In 1, the word *off* is emphasised to answer the idea of relaxation in the original question. In 2, *want* is emphasised to contrast with *you'll definitely* in the question, to highlight the fact that although the speaker may want to take time off, it may not be possible. In 3, *afternoon* is emphasised to highlight the fact that the speaker will still work on Wednesday mornings and so won't put the business under pressure, as indicated in the question.

Track 7.5 tapescript ▶▶

See the Student's Book.

2 Give students plenty of time to read the different situations and absorb what is being said. You could get them to predict which word will be emphasised.

Answers

1 a2 b1
2 a1 b2
3 a2 b1
4 a1 b2
5 a2 b1

Track 7.6 tapescript ▶▶

1 1 Did you say <u>you</u> would post the report to me?
  2 Did you say you would <u>post</u> the report to me?

2 1 I'm not free on Monday <u>morning</u>.
  2 I'm not free on <u>Monday</u> morning.

3 1 I <u>think</u> it's my suitcase.
  2 I think it's <u>my</u> suitcase.

4 1 Could I <u>observe</u> the team-building seminar?
  2 Could <u>I</u> observe the team-building seminar?

5 1 <u>I</u> didn't delete all of this data.
  2 I didn't delete <u>all</u> of this data.

3 You might need to suggest some sentences and situations here. For example:

Sentence: *Could you ask Anna to write up the minutes of yesterday's meeting?*

Situations:

The speaker wants Anna to write up the minutes and not something else. (emphasise *minutes*)

The speaker wants Anna and not somebody else to write up the minutes. (emphasise *Anna*)

The speaker wants Anna to write up the minutes of yesterday's meeting and not an earlier one. (emphasise *yesterday's*)

Monitor this activity carefully. After the pairwork, you may want to get selected students to say their sentence with different words emphasised in front of the whole class. The class should say what each situation is.

It's time to talk

- This is a good opportunity to move the class around and get students to work with students they haven't worked with before.

- Read the instructions and make sure that students understand what they should do. You may want to suggest students use these ideas for their stories.

Professional past	Personal past
• career: previous jobs	• a happy childhood memory
• training courses	• a bad travel experience
• a business trip	• a famous person you met or saw
• a tough meeting	• a wonderful dinner
• interesting colleagues	• a great party

- Give them a few minutes to prepare their stories, but encourage them to make brief notes rather than write sentences.
- Remind students of the tenses they should use and perhaps write some examples on the board.
- Monitor the questions and answers and give feedback on the students' linguistic performance.
- You may want to use the Extra classroom activity here (see pages 93 and 105).

What did we do today?
Check the Remember section quickly and remind students of the objectives of the lesson.

Follow up
Encourage students to:
- write sentences about their past experiences
- write down their short story from *It's time to talk* and hand it in to you.

8 Twin towns

What did we do last time?
Do a review of the last type 2 lesson (Unit 5). Remind students of what they worked on (see Teacher's notes for that unit) and do some quick revision as follows.

Talking about financial planning and control
Get students to make sentences with the following words:
borrow, break even, invest, forecast, expenditure, income.
Get them to talk in pairs about their own finances or those of their organisation. If you feel that this might be a sensitive subject, tell them what they say does not have to be true.

Presenting: Progress reports
Ask students what the three parts of a progress report often are. Elicit:
1 Background
2 What has been done
3 What still has to be done or what will happen.
Ask students to give you appropriate language for each stage. For example:
The background is ...
We've already completed ...
The next stage is ...
You could get students to talk about their progress through this book, using the model and language above.

On the agenda: Why are we doing this?
Tell students the objectives of this lesson:
- to talk about **the role of government**
- to develop **vocabulary** to talk about **politics**
- to improve **presentation skills – structuring**.
Reinforce this by writing the key words on the board or OHP.

Explain that this unit is a basic introduction to some political vocabulary and also the opportunity to reflect on some typical political subjects. Some students may think they are not very interested in politics, but the focus here is on local government and its support for local communities, young people and business. All this is very political.

Warm up
Brainstorm local government activities and ask what students think of them. You could also ask if they know anything about twinning in Europe or elsewhere. If they do, ask why councils organise such relationships. If they don't, say that they will find out in the listening.

Background briefing: Leeds and Hangzhou
Leeds
Situated in the north of England, Leeds is one of the fastest growing cities in the country, with a population of around half a million people. It is regarded as vibrant culturally and is a key financial and commercial centre. It is also home to one of the most famous football teams in Europe, Leeds United.

Hangzhou

Hangzhou is a large city in south-east China, on the Yangtze delta, and is home to over six million people. Well known for its historical and cultural heritage, it is the political, cultural and economic centre of the Zhejiang province.
For more information about Leeds and Hangzhou, go to the *English365* website: www.cambridge.org/elt/english365.

Listen to this

Local goes global
Before you listen, read the caption and look at the photo of Adrian and ask students if they think local government has any international role.

1 Get students to look at the areas of work. You might need to check understanding of *Chamber of Commerce* and *citizenship* before you play track 8.1.

Answers
He mentions: businesses   schools, colleges and universities Chamber of Commerce   international relations strategy citizenship

2 Look at the Introduction on page 16 for guidelines on taking notes.

Answers
1 colleges   2 universities   3 communities 4 departments   5 Leader   6 Chamber of Commerce 7 health   8 trade   9 investment   10 global 11 citizenship   12 confidence / self-esteem / standards

Track 8.1 tapescript ▶▶
INTERVIEWER: Adrian, you're the Head of International Relations for Leeds City Council. What does that involve?

ADRIAN: Well, it involves coordinating the local authority international role with all the other key stakeholders' international relations, so in particular with … that means … the stakeholders are businesses, business support services, schools, colleges and universities, community groups, faith communities, and obviously council departments, everything that's international, basically.

INTERVIEWER: Yes, that's a wide brief. I'm interested in, for example, the connection with business. How does that work in practice?

ADRIAN: Yeah, OK, we have local strategic partnerships. So local authorities are now required to do this, to create local strategic partnerships. We launched the Local Strategic Initiative, which had the Leader of the City Council as its chair, and the President of the Leeds Chamber of Commerce as its vice chair, and along with the universities, the local media, the health authority.

INTERVIEWER: That's all local.

ADRIAN: Yes, but our international work fell neatly into place. We would create … we would agree an aspiration to compete more effectively in the global economy. Now I work primarily with schools, universities, colleges, Chambers of Commerce, and other organisations that promote business links. All these organisations help us fulfil our two broad aims for international relations strategy, which are firstly to support businesses in trade and investment, and secondly in supporting citizens of Leeds, particularly young people, as we help them to become global citizens, to become internationalist in their perspectives. This is what we call citizenship.

INTERVIEWER: So that's important, helping young people.

ADRIAN: Yes, developing an understanding of citizenship makes them more confident, their self-esteem grows, they do better in school – an international dimension to the curriculum helps in raising standards and in so doing improves their employability …

Answers

3 1 T   2 T   3 F (it is about education and citizenship)   4 T
4 A twinning arrangement with Durban in South Africa; a conference with partners in the Czech Republic on education and citizenship, rights and responsibilities

Track 8.2 tapescript ▶▶|

INTERVIEWER: Yes. And how do you get people, and young people in particular, how do you get them interested in politics and citizenship? I mean a lot of people think, 'Oh, politics, I'm not interested.'

ADRIAN: Well, I'll give you two examples. We've got a twinning arrangement with Durban in South Africa. One of our schools works with a township school to sponsor the children and one of them, one of the township children, got a place at university. And some of our teachers have visited Durban and come back with ideas about international education, about global citizenship. They can use these ideas. The link to Durban is something real, the children learn from it, they become more internationally interested.

INTERVIEWER: That sounds good.

ADRIAN: Yes, and another example, yesterday I was in a meeting where … in which we were planning a conference with our partners in the Czech Republic. The central theme is actually education and citizenship, about rights and responsibilities. We believe that the international dimension is central to citizenship.

INTERVIEWER: Right.

ADRIAN: So the connection for young people, why it's important is in order to understand their role in society, how society works and how the local can become global, and all the interconnectivity.

INTERVIEWER: Yes, I'm sure you're right.

Answers

5 1 An economic cooperation agreement
2 To establish direct links, linking company to company, creating new business projects, and more trade and investment
3 Young people, education and assistance to the new democracy
4 Benefits for people and for businesses through trade and investment

Track 8.3 tapescript ▶▶|

INTERVIEWER: And how does it all impact on businesses then?

ADRIAN: Well, our international work is part of what we're trying to achieve as a city. We've just returned from a three-day visit to Dortmund, in Germany, our partner city, twinned for 35 years. We've just renewed our economic cooperation agreement through which we work to create direct links between companies. So we match company with company in creating new business projects, and more trade and investment. These are direct benefits to businesses here in Leeds.

INTERVIEWER: I see, so what are your other twin towns or cities, beyond Dortmund?

ADRIAN: Lille, in northern France, Brno in the Czech Republic, we've moved further afield to Hangzhou in China, our twin city – probably the ninth most successful city in China, with a population of six or seven million people. We have university offices there, a business link office, a regional development office has opened there …

INTERVIEWER: And you talked before about Durban, in South Africa.

ADRIAN: Yes … Durban, which at this stage is very much focused around young people and education, and assistance to that new democracy, but which we confidently predict will have benefits for people and for businesses through trade and investment later. So these are all long-term partnerships with long-term objectives.

What do you think?

- Ask students what their experiences are. You can prompt responses here by asking further questions such as: *Have you, or do you know anyone who has, ever been on a school or college exchange? What do you remember about it? Does your town or city have any twinning links in other countries? Does the local Chamber of Commerce organise links with other countries? If so, where?*
- You could also ask them about young people and politics: *Are young people interested? What might help to get them interested?* Students can discuss their answers in small groups before sharing opinions with the whole class.
- Give prompts to help students express their opinions: *I think …, In my opinion …*

The words you need ... to talk about politics

To begin, relate this section to the work context by asking: *Do you ever talk about politics at work or with foreign visitors?* If they answer no, it may be that they think politics is something that 'people don't talk about'. Ask general questions about what the main political issues in their countries are, and whether the government is good for business, helps their particular sector, or has little impact, etc.

1 After students have done the exercise, ask them in what ways the collocated terms affect their organisation. Can they think of any examples?

2 When you check the answers, make sure that students are clear about the meaning of the collocations. For example, check that they understand the difference between *Prime Minister* and *Head of State*. You could quickly get students to say who the political leaders in their countries are, what their titles are and the roles they have.

3 Get students to read through the texts quickly before they fill the gaps.

It's time to talk

- This discussion activity is designed to connect the political issues and the political vocabulary of the unit to the students' own experience. Avoid sensitive political issues if you judge there may be some in your class.
- You could do this as a pyramid discussion. Get individuals to choose five important issues and then compare them with a partner, saying why they feel they are important. They then have to agree on five with their partner. They then compare with another pair, and so on.
- You may want to use the Extra classroom activity here (see pages 94 and 106).

COMMUNICATING AT WORK

Presenting 2: Structuring

Background briefing: Guggenheim Museum, Bilbao
Designed by architect Frank Gehry and opened in 1997, the Guggenheim Museum in Bilbao, Spain, is seen as an architectural masterpiece and the city's main tourist attraction. The outside is covered in titanium, and inside the building's most notable feature is the 50 metre high atrium which is connected to the 19 galleries by a series of metal walkways and glass elevators. It is central to the regeneration of this industrial city and is now home to some of the most important art of the twentieth century, including works by Picasso, Robert Motherwell, Robert Rauschenberg, Clyfford Still, Antoni Tàpies and Andy Warhol. For more information about the Guggenheim Museum, go to the *English365* website: www.cambridge.org/elt/english365.

- Ask students what key elements make a presentation effective. Emphasise that clarity in the structure helps the speaker, as well as the audience, and that the introduction is a key part of a presentation.
- Typically presentations have three parts: introduction, main part, conclusion. The main part is often in different sections. A key function of an introduction is to make this structure clear.
- Emphasise that the target language illustrated in the recording is important: it applies to any presentation, whether formal or informal, to a large audience or a small one, and whether on a major topic or a small internal matter.

1 The content of the recorded introduction is less important than the language it illustrates for structuring a presentation. But in any case, ask students if they know about or have visited the Guggenheim. There is a political connection here too: the museum was built in Bilbao to aid the economic regeneration of the city, which was suffering from industrial decline.

Track 8.4 tapescript ▶▶│

PRESENTER: OK, ladies and gentlemen. My intention is to give a short presentation – basically an introduction to one of Europe's great modern buildings, the Guggenheim Museum in Bilbao, in the north of Spain. My talk will last about 15 minutes.
I'm going to divide the talk into three parts and I'll begin with an overview, looking at the background.
In the second part of my talk I'll talk about the architecture of the building and say a few words about Frank Gehry, the architect.
Finally, I want to describe the impact of the museum on the city and the region.
I'm going to talk for about 15 minutes and later there'll be time for questions and a discussion.
First then, a few words on the background and on the place where the museum was built.

3 • All the suggested topics listed here are work-related. If your students are pre-service, they could talk about an aspect of their studies. Some learners may prefer to choose a non-work related topic. Students should regard the Guggenheim presentation as a model introduction.
• They will need a short period of preparation – give them a time limit. Stress that the topic is not what matters, but they should concentrate on the language of structuring in their presentation.

What did we do today?
Check the Remember section quickly and remind students of the objectives of the lesson.

Follow up
Encourage students to:
• write sentences about politics in their country
• record phrases for structuring a presentation in their vocabulary books.

9 How's the weather?

What did we do last time?
Do a review of the last type 3 lesson (Unit 6). Remind students of what they worked on (see Teacher's notes for that unit) and do some quick revision as follows.

Social skills: Building rapport
Ask students for ways in which they can build rapport. Elicit the following:
• find things in common
• get the balance right
• keep the conversation going.
Get students to do short role-plays in pairs in order to revise and practise the techniques.

Economic issues
Get students to give you words to describe the following situations:
• rising prices

• many people do not have work
• exchange rates do not change
and also the following:
• part of the economy that includes insurance and tourism
• part of the economy that includes the production of goods.

On the agenda: Why are we doing this?
Tell students the objectives of the lesson:
• to talk about **the weather**
• to develop **social skills** for effective **listening**
• to learn **vocabulary** connected to **the weather**.
Reinforce this by writing the key words on the board or OHP.

Warm up
After discussing the questions, you could also ask what makes someone a bad listener. Tell the students that this unit will focus on active listening skills; stress how important this is in effective communication. Highlight that effective communication is a two-way process involving speaker and listener equally.

Listening

What's the point?
See the Introduction (page 16): Type 3 units – social skills.

Answers

1 a With her sister in LA (Los Angeles)
 b The facilities had been double booked
 c Debbie isn't really listening to Ann. She doesn't pay attention and sounds bored.

Track 9.1 tapescript ▶▶│

ANN: Yeah, we had a fantastic time.
DEBBIE: Uh-huh.
ANN: We stayed with my sister in LA for a few days and then we went to Jed and Judy's wedding.
DEBBIE: Right.
ANN: But there was a problem with the hotel in LA – the facilities for the wedding and the reception had been double booked so it was almost a disaster, but one of their friends offered them her house in Palm Springs. It was huge … great view, pool … and everyone was really friendly.
DEBBIE: I thought they were having the wedding in LA.
ANN: I just told you! There was a problem with the hotel they originally booked, so this friend of theirs offered them the use of her house for the whole weekend, and the house was in Palm Springs.
DEBBIE: Oh. OK. Would you like to go for lunch now or do you want to wait for a while?

Answers

2 a Fantastic the whole time (warm with clear skies)
 b At a friend's house in Palm Springs
 c Debbie shows that she's listening and that she's interested by responding to what Ann says, asking questions to check she's understood, and interacting with Ann.
3 a great. I'm glad to hear it
 b you! How was it?
 c I thought that
 d sounds as if you had a great time

Track 9.2 tapescript ▶▶

Possible answers

4 Holiday
How did you get there?
Would you go again?

Where somebody lives
Oh yes, I know that street.
That's a nice part of town.

Planning a surprise
Does she like surprises?
What's the occasion?

Have a go

- See the Introduction (page 17): Type 3 units. Tell students not to worry too much about the story or how interesting it is. The most important thing is to practise the active listening skills.
- To finish, you could get selected pairs to perform for the rest of the class.

Read on

The weather

Get students to discuss the questions quickly in pairs. You could also ask what the weather is like during the different seasons in their countries and what kind of weather they prefer.

1
- Exploit the pictures by getting students to tell each other in pairs what they can see in them.
- Check the meaning of *swell* before you start.
- Once again set a time limit for the reading. When you go through the answers ask students to tell you the key

words that helped them decide which story matched which headline.

Answers

1 1 d, ii 2 c, iv 3 a, i 4 b, iii
2 1 tornado 2 tidal waves 3 floods 4 blizzard

3
- Get students to read the questions and answer them as fast as they can. Alternatively, get the students to cover the questions and read them out yourself. You could give points for the first person to answer correctly. This will energise the lesson and change the focus slightly.
- Brainstorm other kinds of extreme weather on the board. You could elicit words such as *thunderstorm*, *hurricane*, *flood*, etc. You could ask if any of the students have experienced any of these kinds of weather and what happened.

Answers

1 A broken leg
2 The police (the cops) found them in a field
3 Six to eight metres high
4 At least a minute and a half
5 Because of the risk of contamination (of the water being polluted)
6 Four weeks
7 First thing in the morning
8 Because they were dangerous and icy

The words you need … to talk about the weather

Look at the quote and ask students if they knew English people were famous for this. You could ask them if they think it is true!

1 Get students to do this individually and then check their answers in pairs. Once they have done this, they can use their dictionaries, if necessary.

Answers

Rain: drizzle   light showers   heavy showers   thunderstorm
Winter weather: hail   snow   ice   frost   sleet
Temperature: warm   hot   freezing   cool   mild   boiling   chilly
Light: sunny   clear   dull   hazy   cloudy   bright

2 When you have checked the answers, it is worth mentioning how this affects the sentence construction. For example:
It + adjective – *It is chilly.*
There + noun or noun phrase – *There was a thunderstorm.*

Answers

Rain: all nouns or noun phrases
Winter weather: all nouns
Temperature: all adjectives
Light: all adjectives

Answers

3 Temperature (from hottest to coldest):
boiling → hot → warm → mild → cool → chilly → freezing

4 When you have checked the answers, check any problems with meaning. For example, *gale force* might be new for students.

5 You could also get students to make their own sentences using the word combinations. They could revisit the first part of the *Read on* section by talking about today's weather, but this time by incorporating the new vocabulary.

It's time to talk

- Give students a few minutes to prepare their briefing. They could also think about different activities people might be able to do in their country at different times of the year, for example, skiing.
- Encourage students to give a structure to their briefing – this will link with Unit 8 – and to use new vocabulary from this lesson.
- Give feedback on their performance.
- You may want to use the Extra classroom activity here (see pages 94 and 107).

What did we do today?
Check the Remember section quickly and remind students of the objectives of the lesson.

Follow up
Encourage students to:
- practise using active listening techniques in real situations
- record useful phrases for active listening
- record new vocabulary in their vocabulary books
- read the weather forecast in English.

10 Emotional computers

What did we do last time?
Do a review of the last type 1 lesson (Unit 7). Remind students of what they worked on and do some quick revision as follows.

Past simple, past continuous and past perfect simple
Ask students for examples of the three tenses and then get them to interview each other about their careers and lives.

Pronunciation: Emphasising important words
Write the following sentence on the board: *I drove to the cinema last night.*
In pairs, get students to emphasise different words in the sentence to change the meaning. Their partner should say

what the meaning and difference in emphasis is. For example, if *I* is stressed, it means *I was the driver, not somebody else.*

On the agenda: Why are we doing this?
Tell the students the objectives of the lesson:
- to **describe** objectives
- to revise the use of **multi-word verbs** – write an example on the board to make this clear, e.g. *look at*
- to improve **pronunciation: polite disagreement in short answers**.
Reinforce this by writing the key words on the board or OHP.

Warm up
- Begin by asking students what the title of this unit might mean. Don't worry if they don't come up with the correct answer at this stage as you just want to stimulate interest.
- Before students look at the possible commercial applications, it might help to engage them further by asking if they can think of any possible uses of an 'affective computer'. Students can brainstorm in groups. It is worth spending time on this so that students are clear about the concept before looking at the applications.

Background briefing: MIT Media Laboratory
Founded in the 1980s, the MIT Media Laboratory has been at the forefront of research into, and invention of, digital technology to enhance the way people express and communicate ideas. It helped to develop now familiar areas such as digital video and multimedia. Today the Media Lab is exploring new frontiers such as wireless, 'viral' communications, wearable computing, machines capable of commonsense reasoning, new forms of artistic expression, and how children learn. These themes outline a future where the bits of the digital realm interact seamlessly with the atoms of our physical world, and where machines not only respond to our commands, but also understand our emotions. For more information about the MIT Media Laboratory, go to the *English365* website: www.cambridge.org/elt/english365.

Listen to this

Affective computing
1 There is potentially a great deal of new vocabulary in this listening. Depending on the level of the group, you could either pre-teach it, or get students to look through the tapescript once they have done the listening activities. Perhaps highlight: *emotion (stress, frustration), to smile, skin, facial movement, to sweat, frustration, to monitor, immune system, to lecture (to give a serious talk), to measure, to interpret, to get the wrong impression, controversial, to enhance, to miss (a flight).*

2 This could be quite challenging, so put students into small groups to see which group can predict the most. This will add a competitive element.

Track 10.1 tapescript ▶▶|

INTERVIEWER: On the website your group's research sounds wonderful. I liked the idea, for example, of computers recognising emotions in users like stress and frustration.

ROSALIND: We should be careful what we're monitoring here. Computers can't really read your internal feelings, only what's on the outside, if you're smiling, moving in a certain way, temperature of your skin, etc. You really have to distinguish between what the technology is doing and what people do, and the computer only knows that certain facial and body movements and sweat reactions are typical of frustration or stress.

INTERVIEWER: What are the commercial applications of all this?

ROSALIND: We've been looking at many things, for example, how to monitor stress in different ways. Stress has direct effects on the heart and the immune system.

INTERVIEWER: Is that from the corporate world, looking to monitor stress levels among staff?

ROSALIND: Yes, but I had one chief technology officer who asked me if they could monitor stress in their employees without their employees knowing … , so I gave him a long lecture about why I thought that was a bad idea. He eventually backed down.

INTERVIEWER: Good.

ROSALIND: I really think it's better to give these tools to people to learn about their own bodies, not to feel monitored. And I think it would be dangerous if your boss knew something you didn't know. And there's the problem that there is air in these measurements. The big challenge with using computers to measure emotion is to interpret the data accurately. So your boss could easily get the wrong impression.

INTERVIEWER: So it's using technology to help people?

ROSALIND: Yes, it is. I want to develop tools so people can build up emotional intelligence. I really think it's better to give these tools to people to learn about their own bodies and, hopefully, better manage emotional states and feelings in the service of their goals – maybe with something you wear at work, clothes, or so-called intelligent earrings, to monitor stress. But to impose this on people is actually, well, is definitely controversial and I'm not following up that line of research.

INTERVIEWER: Do you see these technologies creating a more personal contact across the virtual internet world?

ROSALIND: Yes. For example, in online chats, etc. If someone in a chatroom cracks a joke and somebody laughs, there are changes on the skin which computers can read and then express as an icon turning red or looking a little more excited, or laughing.

INTERVIEWER: OK, so you can know that they're laughing for real?

ROSALIND: Yes. Or when there's a video-conference brainstorming session online, when you're really in a room with somebody and you throw out an idea, you can sort of see by their response immediately, you know, they sit back in their chair and their eyes look big.

INTERVIEWER: So you would use visual representation to show people are unsure or support the idea?

ROSALIND: Oh, yeah. On the icon, I could just see the mouth smile or you know one eyebrow raised, the head at an angle, eyes open, for eye contact … looking at you.

INTERVIEWER: I can imagine working in the way you've done with emotion and communication at such a deep level, has it enhanced the way you interact with people and machines?

ROSALIND: Hmm, I really don't know! I think it certainly makes you appreciate more the importance, for example, of empathy, recognising people's feelings, of human interaction. And maybe not just trying to solve somebody's problems but truly trying to understand their feelings.

INTERVIEWER: Interesting. I have to ask one last question, although I'm sure the answer is yes. Has the military been interested in this kind of research?

ROSALIND: Increasingly since nine eleven.

INTERVIEWER: They'd be looking to be aware of highly stressed individuals in an environment like an airport, for example?

ROSALIND: Yeah. Although, frankly, I'm sceptical about this. You quickly come up against problems. So identifying stressed people in airports, for example, maybe they're late for their flight, it might be cancelled, they're going to miss it. They're extremely stressed but they're certainly not trying to commit crimes. It's impossible to know the cause of traveller stress.

What do you think?

Having listened to Rosalind, ask if students can think of any more possible uses of this technology. Is there anything else that they would like computers to be able to do?

Check your grammar

Multi-word verbs

Please note that in our look at multi-word verbs we have used the word *particle* to refer to both prepositions and adverbial particles. Our definition of multi-word verbs includes verbs which sometimes take dependent prepositions, or adverbial particles (such as *learn about*) as well as phrasal verbs.

- Before doing the exercises, tell students that multi-word verbs are an important part of English. Explain that they tend to be more informal and so are used more often in spoken than in written English. Ask if they have any problems with them and elicit that one of the key difficulties is that the meaning is not always clear, even if the individual words are known. This part of the unit will introduce some new multi-word verbs and revise their grammar and use.

- Encourage students to refer to the Grammar reference section in the Student's Book, either in class or for homework. You could also get students to look through Tapescript 10.1 to see if they can find other examples of multi-word verbs and to see if they can work out the meaning from the context and what kind of verb it is. For example: *build up*, *follow up*, *throw out*.

Do it yourself

1, 2 and 3

- Students can work through all three exercises in pairs, or you could check the answers after each one.
- Potentially, there are a lot of new vocabulary items here, so encourage students to record and learn the ones that they feel will be useful to them. Suggest that they use their dictionaries while doing the exercises.

Answers

1 1 I'm sorry about cancelling the meeting but I had to call it off.
2 You don't have to write the report. I will look after it.
3 I'm not sure about the answer to your question. I will have a look at it later.
4 My son grew up in England.
5 OK. Shall we meet up at seven o'clock in reception?
6 I look forward to seeing you next month.

2 1 3   2 3   3 2   4 2   5 3   6 2   7 2   8 2   9 2   10 3

3 1
A: I can't *live with* this old computer any more. It's so unreliable.
B: OK. I wanted to *put off* buying a replacement / *put* buying a replacement *off* but let's get a new one next week.

2
A: I think we need to *focus on* the network problems in detail today.
B: Don't worry. I'm sure we can *work out* a solution / *work* a solution *out* soon.

3
A: We have to *build up* more in-house IT competence / *build* more in-house IT competence *up*. Consultants are too expensive
B: I totally agree. Perhaps we should *talk about* this at our next meeting.

4
A: You'll be pleased to hear that the project is almost ready. I think we can *finish off* everything / *finish* everything *off* by 10 June.
B: I'll *note down* that date / *note* that date *down* in my diary. It's the best news I've had all day!

Sounds good

Polite disagreement in short answers

Ask students what makes someone sound polite in English. Elicit that it involves use of vocabulary, but also, and perhaps more importantly, polite pronunciation. Tell them that this part of the unit will help them to sound more polite when disagreeing with someone.

Answers

1 1 A   2 D   3 A   4 D   5 D
In dialogues 2, 4 and 5 the second speaker communicates polite disagreement by speaking with a little hesitation, elongating the initial word *Yes*, stressing key words such as *could*, *may* and *possible* and speaking with a higher and/or slightly weaker tone of voice.

Track 10.2 tapescript ▶▶|

1 A: I think this technology will be great in the fight against crime.
  B: Yes, you could be right.
2 A: Computers will never be able to think in the same way as human beings.
  B: Yes, you could be right.
3 A: I think we need to invest in more computer research.
  B: Yes, I think so. That may be the case.
4 A: Intelligent computers will make our lives easier in the future.
  B: Yes, I think that may happen.
5 A: Emotional computers will create a new world.
  B: It's possible, yes.

Answers

2 1 D   2 A   3 D   4 D   5 A

Track 10.3 tapescript ▶▶|

1 A: I think that increasing computer memory will solve the software problem.
  B: Yes, it seems so.
2 A: I think the answer is to reinstall the software.
  B: Yes, I think so.
3 A: I think this new IT system could save us a lot of money.
  B: It's possible, yes.
4 A: I think outsourcing is cheaper.
  B: You might be right.
5 A: It looks as if we're going to finish the project on time.
  B: Yes, you could be right.

It's time to talk

- Set the scene by explaining that students are going to talk about objectives. Start by asking them what objectives they have in different work situations or what the objectives of any current projects are.
- Give students a few minutes to choose a situation, think about what they are going to talk about and how to use the multi-word verbs.
- If they need help with the use of the multi-word verbs, refer students to the Grammar reference section in the Student's Book.
- Write the following prompts on the board to help them:
  The aim (of ...) is to ...
  The (main) objective (of ...) is to ...
  I've arranged this meeting to ...
- It is important that students perform in front of another pair so they can check if the multi-word verbs have been used correctly.
- You could get selected pairs to perform their role-plays in front of the whole class.

- You may want to use the Extra classroom activity here (see pages 94 and 108).

What did we do today?

Check the Remember section quickly and remind students of the objectives of this lesson.

Follow up

Encourage students to:
- record the grammar of multi-word verbs when they write them in their vocabulary books
- write sentences using new multi-word verbs.

11 Quality control

What did we do last time?

Do a review of the last type 2 lesson (Unit 8). Remind students of what they worked on (see Teacher's notes for that unit) and do some quick revision as follows.

Talking about politics and the role of government

Ask students to give you words that collocate with the following: *Prime, general, economic, Member of, political, Head of.* Get them to talk about the political situation in their countries using the words. For example: *The Head of State is …*

Presenting: Structuring

Ask students how to do the following in English:
- state the subject of a presentation
- say how long you will talk for
- signal the different parts of a presentation
- say if the audience can ask questions.

On the agenda: Why are we doing this?

Tell students the objectives of this lesson:
- to talk about **quality**
- to build **vocabulary** to talk about **quality assurance**
- to develop skills for **meetings: listening and helping understanding**.

Reinforce this by writing the key words on the board or OHP.

Warm up

- Quality is a key management and organisational concept. It is widely accepted that the success of any business or organisation depends on the quality of its work, relative to price.
- Get students to discuss their answers in pairs or small groups. You could also ask what kind of quality control measures their organisation has. You might need to explain that TQM stands for *Total Quality Management.*

Background briefing: Montex

Montex is based in Paris. It is a leading high fashion embroidery company that works for some of the major fashion houses in Paris. Montex employs around 25 full-time staff, but this can increase to around 40 depending on client needs.

Listen to this

What could be more important than quality?

Look at the picture of Maria and read the caption. Check understanding of embroidery.

1 Note that you need to play both parts of the recording (11.1 and 11.2) for this exercise. Get students to read through the statements and check understanding of *continual* and *visual.*

2 Before you play track 11.1 again, ask students if they can remember what the numbers refer to.

Track 11.1 tapescript ▶▶|

INTERVIEWER: Maria, what does Montex do?

MARIA: We do high fashion embroidery for top fashion houses.

INTERVIEWER: How many people work for Montex?

MARIA: Well, we have a core staff of 25 and then at peak periods, leading up to a show, we have maybe 40. So, that's between 25 and 40.

INTERVIEWER: I imagine the work is very labour intensive, handmade?

MARIA: Yes, it is. Some of the garments we make take about … the work could be up to 900 hours.

INTERVIEWER: That's a long time … so the prices …?

MARIA: Are very high, yes, very expensive.

INTERVIEWER: How do you ensure the quality you need?

MARIA: First of all, the first thing is I would say – the quality of the people that we have here. We employ highly skilled and experienced people.

INTERVIEWER: They're all highly trained?

MARIA: Yes, they are. They're professionally trained specialists, they have done a minimum of three years' education at a specialist school. At least three years. And then there's experience. Some of the women who work here, they are nearly all women, about 98 per cent of the people in this work are women, some of them have been here at Montex for 20 years – and they're the best ones.

INTERVIEWER: Right. What other quality monitoring do you have?

MARIA: Well, there's the process of working, there's a continual checking process – a lot of visual checks – we check quality at every stage of the work, at every level. And we have the overall supervisor of the work, maybe she doesn't do any of the work herself. Her job is standing up and walking around, monitoring, checking, controlling. So she makes visual checks at every stage, all part of the quality process. She's walking and looking at the work all the time.

Track 11.2 tapescript ▶▶|

INTERVIEWER: Maria, if you were talking to people in another industry about quality, what would you advise them is the most important thing?

MARIA: I'd say every company has to find its own ways because it really depends on the company and the work they do. For example, our main concern is creativity, design. The workers here are not 100 per cent production-focused.

INTERVIEWER: I see.

MARIA: In a production-oriented business you want speed and efficiency. I can't ask my staff to be the fastest people. They look, they think. They need to think about how beautiful the result will be, and that takes time.

INTERVIEWER: Yeah.

MARIA: And it's the same for quality. Every business has to set its own rules. So if you make simple products, they have to be produced in large quantities, at low cost. So you have maximum efficiency. We can't work like that.

INTERVIEWER: Yes, I see.

MARIA: The work is very labour intensive.

INTERVIEWER: So it's quite traditional?

MARIA: Yes, everything is made by hand. It's very traditional. And it's slow.

INTERVIEWER: Right.

MARIA: It's really exactly like a hundred years ago, except we're using modern materials.

INTERVIEWER: So, one last question. What are the rewards, what are the positive outcomes of working with Montex?

MARIA: Well, seeing the results, seeing our beautiful work at the top Paris fashion shows. It really is very beautiful. And also, we work for such famous names, we do an excellent job. These are important rewards. We can be proud of what we do.

What do you think?

This could be developed by getting students to write down a list of things that bring them satisfaction. They could rank them in order of importance and then compare with another student or pair of students.

The words you need ... to talk about quality assurance

1 An alternative to looking at the tapescripts would be to play the tracks again.

> **Answers**
>
> **1** 1 handmade   2 intensive   3 skilled   4 experienced
>   5 professionally / highly   6 specialist   7 monitoring
>   8 visual
> **2** 1 production-oriented   2 efficient   3 cost savings
>   4 Automated   5 quality monitoring   6 visual
>   7 customer needs   8 feedback   9 market research
> **3** 1 use highly skilled, professionally trained and experienced
>   people
>   2 automated systems, visual checks, customer feedback
>   3 handmade products, labour-intensive production
>   4 market research, customer feedback

It's time to talk

- The option for students to talk about their own organisation or another organisation they know should avoid them all talking about the same thing. They could refer to an amenity in their town, a sports club, a supermarket, or any organisation they have worked with.

- Tell them to consider issues like customer support and after-sales, communication with customers, quality control systems, staff training, staff experience and good management. Also, encourage them to use vocabulary from the previous section.

- You may want to use the Extra classroom activity here (see pages 94 and 109).

COMMUNICATING AT WORK

Meetings 1: Listening and helping understanding

Refer to the social skills section in Unit 9, which focuses on active listening and checking understanding. There is some overlap: here the emphasis is on helping others to understand in meetings, while in Unit 9 the focus is on social language, but the principle of active listening is the same.

1 Check understanding of *chunks* and *minutes* before students read through the tips. Get them to do this individually and then compare their answers with a partner before playing track 11.3.

> **Answers**
>
> Alan recommends:
> Try to understand chunks of language, not listen for every word.
> Keep good eye contact with the other participants.
> Show you follow and understand.
> Paraphrase what people say to check your understanding.
> Ask for repetition.
> Write notes.
> Ask for the minutes of the meeting.

2 You may need to play the recording more than once and stop the track after each phrase in order to allow students time to write. You could get suggestions from students and write them on the board. Then build them up as a class, playing the track again where necessary.

> **Answers**
>
> KONSTANTIN: OK; Right, I think I understand that; Right, that's clear; OK; I see; Of course; Thanks, Alan, that's all very useful.
> ALAN: I see, yes; I understand; Right; OK; Sure.

Track 11.3 tapescript ▶▶|

KONSTANTIN: Alan, I know you're a communications consultant. As you know, I often have meetings where everyone is speaking in English. What advice can you give to help people like me, you know, not native speakers, to understand better in meetings?

ALAN: Well, it's true that people listening can try to listen in particular ways.

KONSTANTIN: OK.

ALAN: The first thing is to try to listen to chunks of language, not individual words. This is very important.

KONSTANTIN: Right, I think I understand that.

ALAN: And related to that, I think, is don't try to translate things in your head – it just doesn't work. You are not a simultaneous translator. In fact, translation doesn't help at all – it takes much too long.

KONSTANTIN: Right, that's clear. What about using electronic translators?

ALAN: Some people think electronic dictionaries help them – I don't think they do – the whole business just takes too long and you lose your concentration, so no translation.

KONSTANTIN: OK.

ALAN: The next point I think is an obvious one, but keep good eye contact, look at people as they speak and show you follow and understand by your expressions. Look interested, and say things like: 'I see, yes', 'I understand', 'Right', 'OK', 'Sure'. All this is sometimes called 'active listening'.

KONSTANTIN: I see.

ALAN: Another thing is it's good – it's useful to paraphrase what people say to check your understanding. Also, if you're not sure, ask them to repeat what they've said.

KONSTANTIN: Of course. I do that.

ALAN: And then there's writing. You can't ask other people to write everything down, but you can take notes yourself – in English, of course. And you can ask for the minutes of the meeting. Most formal meetings have someone taking the minutes, and these are distributed later.

KONSTANTIN: Thanks, Alan, that's all very useful.

3 Again, stop after each phrase to allow students time to write. Check the meaning of *maintain* before you start.

Track 11.4 tapescript ▶▶

KONSTANTIN: Alan, what about the other way … how to be clear, how to help other people to understand me in a meeting?

ALAN: Well, I usually recommend ten simple steps to help people understand what you're saying in meetings. The first is obvious: be well prepared. It's easier for you to be clear if you're well prepared. Secondly, and just as obvious: speak slowly and clearly. In other words, don't speak too fast. Third: always maintain good eye contact. Look at people, don't look at the table or out of the window! Fourth, it's a good idea, if possible, to use visual supports.

KONSTANTIN: So that's a bit like in a presentation, using visual supports can underline your message.

ALAN: Exactly. The next point, five, is possibly the most important: keep to the point. Say exactly what you need to say and make sure it's relevant to the discussion. Then number six: it's always best to use short and simple sentences. That way, you'll be easier to understand.

KONSTANTIN: Keep it short and simple.

ALAN: Yes, K-I-S-S. Kiss.

KONSTANTIN: Right. So what comes next?

ALAN: Well, point seven: summarise your main point, or points – so you briefly sum up your main ideas. Point number eight is: try to use listing and sequencing language, things like: 'first, second, third' or 'then, next, finally'. Next, number nine: be aware of other people and check that they understand you. You want to make sure people understand you. Finally, point ten: if you think it's appropriate, give out handouts with your main points. So people take away a paper with your main ideas. So obviously that connects to the first one, which was to be well prepared.

KONSTANTIN: Thanks, Alan. You make it sound very easy!

4 • Set the scene and mention that *lilac* is a kind of light purple colour.
• Give students time to read through their file cards and prepare what they are going to say. Stress the importance of paraphrasing and clarifying and encourage them to use the techniques from the previous exercises.
• Monitor the activity and give feedback on performance. Remember to give positive feedback on good language and techniques used.

What did we do today?

Check the Remember section quickly and remind students of the objectives of this lesson.

Follow up

Encourage students to:
• record new vocabulary in their vocabulary books
• write a paragraph about quality control in their organisations.

12 I was a couch potato

What did we do last time?

Do a review of the last type 3 lesson (Unit 9). Remind students of what they worked on (see Teacher's notes for that unit) and do some quick revision as follows.

Social skills: Listening

Ask students for three ways they can listen actively. Try to elicit the following:
• show that you are listening
• check understanding
• manage the conversation by summarising and asking questions.

Then elicit phrases that perform these functions. For example: *That's great. Where exactly did you go? So you had a good time?*

Talking about the weather

Ask students what the weather is like today. Then ask them to describe the weather in the different seasons in their countries. Try to elicit as much vocabulary from Unit 9 as possible.

On the agenda: Why are we doing this?

Tell students the objectives of this lesson:
- to practise talking about **television**
- to develop **social skills** for **dealing with 'no'**
- to learn **vocabulary** connected to **TV and TV programmes**.

Reinforce this by writing key words on the board or OHP.

Before you begin, explain the meaning of the unit title, *I was a couch potato*. Draw a picture on the board of a potato watching television and try to elicit that it means a lazy person who watches too much TV.

Warm up

You could also ask if students have said 'no' to someone recently. What was the situation? What happened? Additionally, to link into the next section of the unit, ask if students have ever had their flight cancelled or delayed. What happened? What did they do? Did they ask for compensation?

Dealing with 'no'

What's the point?

See the Introduction (page 16): Type 3 units – social skills.

> ### Answers
>
> **1** a Manchester
> b Because the first plane was late
> c André is angry and aggressive and is not prepared to listen to the airline assistant.

Track 12.1 tapescript ▶▶

ASSISTANT: Good morning, can I help you?

ANDRÉ: Yes, I'm supposed to be flying from Manchester to Lyon via London with your airline but I've missed my connection here, basically because the first flight was late. I've also lost a very important bag. I've already talked to two different Jetair people and still haven't got a clear idea about what you're going to do, so I'd like to talk to your manager and get some action on my problem.

ASSISTANT: I'm sorry, but the Jetair customer service manager is not available at the moment. Perhaps I can …

ANDRÉ: What do you mean? He's not available. It's his job to be available, isn't it?

ASSISTANT: I'm sorry, sir, she's in a meeting with …

ANDRÉ: Look, you have an increasingly angry customer standing here who is not going to go away until he gets some satisfaction on this so I suggest you call your manager and …

> ### Answers
>
> **2** a She's in a meeting on airport security
> b At least an hour
> c André's tone is more positive and he is less aggressive. He tries to find another way to approach the problem by asking questions, and is more constructive.
> **3** a tell me when she will be
> b that you're trying to help
> c anyone else I can talk to
> d the name and number of someone I can call

Track 12.2 tapescript ▶▶

ASSISTANT: Good morning, can I help you?

ANDRÉ: Yes, I'm supposed to be flying from Manchester to Lyon via London with your airline but I've missed my connection here, basically because the first flight was late. I've also lost a very important bag. I've already talked to two different Jetair people and still haven't got a clear idea about what you're going to do, so I'd like to talk to your manager and get some action on my problem, please.

ASSISTANT: I'm sorry, but the Jetair customer service manager is not available at the moment. But perhaps …

ANDRÉ: Can you tell me why not?

ASSISTANT: She's in a meeting on airport security at the moment.

ANDRÉ: Well, can you tell me when she will be available?

ASSISTANT: I think it's likely to go on for at least an hour. But perhaps I can help you if you could give me the details?

ANDRÉ: I understand that you're trying to help but I'd really prefer to talk to someone more senior this time, if you don't mind. Is there anyone else I can talk to?

ASSISTANT: I'm sorry, not at the moment. Her deputy is off duty and I'm the only one here apart from the check-in staff. I could take the details and phone through to head office if you like.

ANDRÉ: I'd rather do it myself this time. Do you have the name and number of someone I can call?

ASSISTANT: Well, yes, you could call the customer service manager for the London area. Look, here's the number. His name is Gerry Atwood. You can use this phone if you like. Tell Mr Atwood that you're with Fiona and that I can …

> ### Possible answers
>
> **4** Afternoon off
> *I know it's a busy time, but this is very special.*
> *Can I make up the hours another time?*
>
> Cake refund
> *Could I have another cake then?*
> *Can I see the supervisor?*
>
> Retirement party
> *He's been with us for a long time.*
> *I understand you are busy, but she'd be very pleased if you were there.*

Have a go

See the Introduction (page 17): Type 3 units. Get students to prepare for this carefully and to think through various strategies for dealing with 'no'. For example, they could be encouraged to think of reasons for doing the charity work and why it might benefit the organisation.

Read on

Television

- Tell students that in this part of the unit they are going to develop their reading skills by focusing on improving their reading speed and ability to read for gist. They will also focus on differentiating between facts and opinions in written texts.
- Discuss the initial questions about reality TV and ask students for their views on it.

- If you have a weaker group, you may wish to do the first vocabulary exercise in *The words you need* before the reading. There is quite a lot of new vocabulary in the texts and you may feel that it is too much for your students without more initial help.

1 Give students a time limit and tell them not to worry about vocabulary at this point as it will be dealt with later in the unit. Initially they should concentrate on getting the gist of the TV programmes.

2 Explain that *shattered* means extremely tired. You might also want to point out that 'Big Brother' comes from George Orwell's novel *1984*. In it, citizens are ruled and constantly watched by the mysterious 'big brother'.

Answers

1 Stay awake for a week
2 By using a panel of ethics advisers and employing medical staff
3 The ethics panel vetoed (stopped) the use of door handles which gave electric shocks
4 They both changed the world of the British
5 Because it started the reality TV craze (it was the first reality TV show)
6 Virtually 24 hours per day
7 A member of the public pretends to have won a vast sum of money on the lottery
8 After five days
9 A luxury holiday for all those successfully hoaxed

3 Mention that distinguishing between facts and opinions can often cause difficulties, as opinions can often be presented as facts.

Answers

1 F   2 O

4 Elicit that facts and opinions may be presented in the same way linguistically and grammatically, but there is no way to quantify, test or measure the opinions. Sentence 2 is a good example of this.

Answers

1 F   2 O   3 O   4 F   5 O   6 F   7 F   8 O

The words you need ... to talk about TV and TV programmes

1 • Students can do this individually or in pairs. You could get students to try and work out the meaning of the words from the context before they do the matching activity.
  • There is a lot of vocabulary in the texts so once again, encourage students to be selective about the vocabulary they would like to record and learn.

Answers

1 g   2 e   3 d   4 i   5 f   6 j   7 b   8 h   9 c   10 a

2 • Start by brainstorming kinds of TV programmes and writing them on the board. Students can then look in their books to see how many they thought of.
  • If you have a weaker group, you might explain some of the kinds of TV programmes first. Make it clear that in a *quiz show*, contestants have to answer questions and in a *game show* they might have to do some other kinds of task or game, hoping to win a prize. A *soap*, or *soap opera*, is a long-running drama following the lives of a group of people in a particular place. You could mention that the most popular soap in the UK, *Coronation Street*, has been running since the 1960s. It is set in a working class suburb of Manchester.
  • Encourage discussion about the different types of programme. You could ask students to think of programmes in their own countries which fit into these categories.
  • You could also ask students what kinds of programme are popular in their countries and which ones they like. You could ask questions like: *Which is your favourite TV programme?* and get them to describe it to a partner.

Answers

A Question of Sport: quiz show
Ground Force goes to Hollywood: makeover
Question Time: studio debate
Friday Night with Jonathan Ross: chat show
The Simpsons: cartoon
The Good Life: sitcom
In Search of Genius: documentary
Rick Stein's Food Heroes: cookery
Coronation Street: soap
Who Wants to be a Millionaire?: game show
Midsomer Murders: police drama
I'm a Celebrity ... Get me out of here: reality show
UEFA Cup: live sport

It's time to talk

- If possible, bring in an authentic TV listings page.
- You could get students to mark the programmes they would like to watch individually first, then compare with a partner and try to agree on what to watch. You could then proceed with a pyramid discussion and get them to compare with another pair and try to agree on what to watch.
- Encourage students to say why they want to watch a particular programme and write the following phrases on the board to help them:
  I think we should watch ...
  I prefer ... to ...
  Why don't we ...?
  What about ...?
- You may want to use the Extra classroom activity here (see pages 94 and 110).

What did we do today?

Check the Remember section quickly and remind students of the objectives of this lesson.

Follow up

Encourage students to:

- record new vocabulary for talking about TV
- be selective with the vocabulary they want to learn
- record expressions they can use for dealing with 'no'
- watch TV in English, if possible.

13 Developing people

What did we do last time?

Do a review of the last type 1 lesson (Unit 10). Remind students of what they worked on and do some quick revision as follows.

Multi-word verbs
Write the following multi-word verbs on the board or OHP:
back down, follow up, look at, come up against.
Get students to write sentences using the verbs and then say what the grammatical features are. Ask them to think of other verbs of the four main types. They could then talk about their current work or study situation using as many of the verbs as possible.

Pronunciation: Polite disagreement in short answers
Get students to work in pairs and take it in turn to make suggestions. Their partner should either agree or disagree and take care to use the correct pronunciation.
You could use the following as a model to start them off:
I think we should improve staff training.
Yes, I think so.

On the agenda: Why are we doing this?

Tell students the objectives of this lesson:

- to improve speaking skills: **analysing possibilities in the past and present**
- to look at the **grammar** of **modal verbs to express certainty**
- to improve **pronunciation: stress in word families.**

Reinforce this by writing the key words on the board or OHP.

Background briefing: TMSDI

Based in York, England, TMSDI was founded in 1989 as a management consultancy company with the aim of supporting human resource managers. It offers customised leadership, communication and individual and team development programmes. For more information about TMSDI, go to the *English365* website: www.cambridge.org/elt/english365.

Warm up

- Ask students what they think a management consultant does. Don't worry if they can't give you much at this stage as this should become clearer later. Explain there are some

complex concepts so you are going to look at some of the vocabulary first.

- Some students may not have had experiences of coaching – it is more likely that appraisal and performance review are more familiar concepts. Ask if they have appraisals and how successful they are. What is the process? Who carries out the appraisals? How often do they take place? If you have pre-service students, ask if there is anything like an appraisal or performance review where they are studying. If not, should there be? Are the principles the same for students and for employees? Would they like to have their performance reviewed?

Answers

1 d	2 c	3 e	4 a	5 b

Listen to this

Coaching success

Explain that students are going to listen to Sue talking about her job as a management consultant. Before listening, get students to read through the sentences and deal with any vocabulary problems.

Answers

1 1 kick-off meetings   2 works well   3 difficult
   4 was aggressive to   5 help people find their own solutions

Track 13.1 tapescript ▶▶|

INTERVIEWER: Sue, can you say something about what you do?

SUE: Well, I have a multi-functional role, so I do a lot of one-day team-building events, I do a lot of one-to-one coaching with managers, some 360 degree feedback and I occasionally deliver the workshops which accredit trainers and human resource managers to use the team profiling systems that we have.

INTERVIEWER: You do a lot of work with team building, I think, with new teams especially?

SUE: Yes, a central part of our work at TMSDI now is team kick-off meetings for client teams who don't want anything to go wrong from the beginning of projects. And so we give them a framework in which they can discuss what they think they should be doing and how they think they should be doing it.

INTERVIEWER: You also mentioned that you do one-to-one coaching.

SUE: Yeah, I do actually. I was very unsure about doing it in the beginning, especially the telephone work, because I'd always done it face-to-face, but it works very well actually and I think people, particularly with the telephone coaching, feel they can be very honest about things and have a very private and honest conversation with someone like myself.

INTERVIEWER: But what is coaching? Is it about telling people what to do, or suggesting the reasons for problems ... like 'The problem may have been a personality clash' or 'It could be you need to improve your communication skills' – that kind of thing? It must be a difficult role!

SUE: Coaching I do very flexibly at the moment and any specific issues that people have we talk through, you know – what's happening, why they think it's happening and what to do about it.

INTERVIEWER: OK.

SUE: For example, we have one system or process, which is 360 degree and that is the most challenging and difficult for managers to receive the feedback from and it can be quite disappointing for people sometimes. I had a case recently where one guy was rated very low by his team. I knew he'd be very disappointed and we sat down and looked at the specific feedback. In fact, it was all down to one case of quite aggressive bullying. Even though it had happened in the past, it was still an issue for people working for this man. So the coaching was to set up some positive things he had to go and do to change.

INTERVIEWER: And did he change?

SUE: He might have changed after our session. I hope so. I see him next week. Good coaching should help people to find and explore their own solutions to problems. But you never know.

Suggested answers

2 1 personal and work–life or work–home balance
2 how to motivate people
3 how to manage virtual teams
4 change; a lot of problems
5 try something differently

Track 13.2 tapescript ▶▶

INTERVIEWER: Do you see any trends in leadership skills for modern organisations?

SUE: I spend a lot of time talking to leaders about managing their personal and work–life, work–home balance.

INTERVIEWER: That's because people work too much.

SUE: You may be right. But for leaders, it's also often about how they manage other people's work–life or work–home balances. That is quite an issue.

INTERVIEWER: OK.

SUE: I'd say the second big issue is about how they continue to motivate people when business is changing at such a rapid rate. Quite often staff can't finish things that they've started, before they have to change and do something different. It's frustrating. So I think, through constant change, a lot of managers also want advice on how to actually motivate others.

INTERVIEWER: You must have heard the buzz term 'change management' a lot.

SUE: Yeah, it's been around for a long time now, since the eighties. But I think that the nature of change is different. It's very technology-driven. And a third thing, something managers request more and more, is how to manage virtual teams.

INTERVIEWER: Virtual teams?

SUE: Yes, you know, linking with other people is a big issue really. Plenty of people are happy to work in their own virtual bubbles but it doesn't suit a lot of others. I think that technology-driven change at the moment is causing a lot of problems.

INTERVIEWER: OK. And just one final question, as you're dealing with people facing change and challenge, you'll have had some pretty tough experiences in your time. It can't be easy at all. So, what's the most enjoyable part of the job for you?

SUE: *(silence)*

INTERVIEWER: That was a strong silence there.

SUE: Yeah, there's loads actually. But I would just say that it's when that light bulb goes on for people. Whether it's in a team situation or whether you're one to one with them. If I don't have that at the end, I actually feel as if I've failed. In a way, there's no job satisfaction. But you feel you've done something if people leave wanting to and excited to try something differently, that's really, really nice.

What do you think?

Ask students how they feel their work–life balance could be improved. Is this something they find practical? What does it actually mean in practice? Generate discussion by mentioning that employees in an institution in the UK have been advised to delete all emails in their in-boxes on return from holiday. The intention is that employees will not have double the work to do when they come back to work and that people who have sent emails will write again if they have no reply and it is important. Ask students what they think of this. Would it work in their organisation? What are the possible advantages and disadvantages?

Check your grammar

Modal verbs to express certainty

- Explain that you will now look at some of the grammar that Sue uses to express herself in the interview. Note that you are only focusing on one function of modal verbs in this lesson. The passive voice form of modals is looked at in Unit 19.
- Students can work through these exercises individually or in pairs.
- Refer students to the Grammar reference section.

Answers

1 1 present A   2 past C   3 past A   4 present C
5 present B   6 present A   7 past C   8 past A
2 1 must / will   2 should   3 may / could / might
4 can't / won't
The answers are for both present and past.
3 1 c   2 d   3 b   4 a
4 2
5 Present: modal verb + infinitive without *to*
Past: modal verb + *have* + past participle

Do it yourself

Students can do these exercises individually or in pairs.

Answers

1 1 I'm not sure where Marie-Louise is. She *could / may / might* be in the canteen.
2 You must *have* been tired when you arrived last night.
3 Xavier's flight was due to arrive at 8 o'clock. It's half past eight now so he will *have* arrived.
4 It's just before nine o'clock and the post normally arrives at nine. I'm sure it *will* be here soon.
5 I sent you the report three weeks ago so you *must / should have* received it by now.
2 1 could   2 must   3 may be   4 will   5 may know
6 must   7 should   8 can't
3 1 will be   2 won't have seen   3 may / might / could get
4 can't have received   5 must be / must have been
6 may / might / could be / have been
7 must / might / may have been
8 must be / must have been   9 should have received
10 could / might / may be

Sounds good

Stress in word families

Explain how learning word families can help students to improve their range of vocabulary and ability to express ideas in different ways. They should be careful when using different forms of words as the syllable that is stressed can change. This part of the lesson will help them with this.

1 Remind students of how word stress is commonly marked in dictionaries. Get them to check if they are not sure.

Answers and Track 13.3 tapescript ▶▶|

'politics   poli'tician   po'litical   po'liticise

2 After students have done this exercise, you could get them to see if they can match words with the same stress pattern. For example: *organiser* Oooo and *innovator* Oooo.

Answers and Track 13.4 tapescript ▶▶|

1 compe'tition	com'petitive	com'petitor	com'pete
2 a'nalysis	ana'lytical	'analyst	'analyse
3 negoti'ation	ne'gotiable	ne'gotiator	ne'gotiate
4 organis'ation	'organised	'organiser	'organise
5 'management	mana'gerial	'manager	'manage
6 inno'vation	'innovative	'innovator	'innovate

3 As students do this exercise, get them to identify what part of speech each word is.

Answers and Track 13.5 tapescript ▶▶|

1 re'sign	resign'ation
2 au'thority	'authorise
3 e'lectrical	elec'tricity
4 'document	docu'mentary
5 re'sponsible	responsi'bility
6 cre'ate	crea'tivity
7 en'thusiasm	enthusi'astic
8 de'mocracy	demo'cratic
9 'pharmacy	pharma'ceutical
10 'technical	tech'nique

It's time to talk

- Give students time to prepare their role-plays.
- Encourage them to make their conversations as natural as possible and not simply to say the sentences. Get them to expand on the theme as much as possible.
- You may want to use the Extra classroom activity here (see pages 95 and 111).

What did we do today?

Check the Remember section quickly and remind students of the objectives of this lesson.

Follow up

Encourage students to:
- record modal verbs and their different uses in a special place
- mark the word stress when they write new words in their vocabulary books
- record different members of word families.

14 Project management

What did we do last time?

Do a review of the last type 2 lesson (Unit 11). Remind students of what they worked on (see Teacher's notes for that unit) and do some quick revision as follows.

Talking about quality and quality assurance
Ask students about:
- ways of ensuring staff are of good quality
- ways to monitor quality
- ways businesses can find out what a customer wants.

Meetings: Listening and helping understanding
Ask students what techniques they can use to listen in meetings. Try to elicit:
- try to understand chunks of language
- avoid translating in your head
- use active listening techniques
- ask for repetition and summarise what you understand.

On the agenda: Why are we doing this?

Tell students the objectives of this lesson:
- to talk about **projects and product development**
- to build **vocabulary** to talk about **project management**
- to develop skills for **negotiating: stating positive expectations and preferences, suggesting alternatives.**

Reinforce this by writing the key words on the board or OHP.

Warm up

Ask students what they think project management involves. Brainstorm ideas and vocabulary, for example, *setting deadlines*, *budgeting*. This will link to the listening.

Background briefing: Melly Still

Melly has worked extensively in theatre and as well as directing and co-directing productions she has taken on the roles of designer, movement director, choreographer and adaptor. Among other productions, she has worked on *Grimm Tales*, a reworking of the fairy stories at the Young Vic Theatre in London, and adaptations of some of Salman Rushdie's novels for the Royal National Theatre and Royal Shakespeare Company. She has worked on productions around the UK and toured in Hong Kong, Australia and New Zealand. For more information about Melly Still, go to the *English365* website: www.cambridge.org/elt/english365.

Listen to this

Project management in the theatre

- Before you start, ask students what they think is involved in putting on a play. Mention that theatre production is often used as a classic model of project management.
- Look at the picture of Melly and read the caption.

1 Get students to read through the activities and check the meaning of *recruitment* and *sponsorship*.

2 Check the meaning of *rehearsal* and *stakeholders*.

Track 14.1 tapescript ▶▶

INTERVIEWER: Melly, I'd like to ask you about project management as a theatre director. First, tell us about teamwork or team management in the theatre.

MELLY: Well, a production has to be the work of a whole team. First of all there's what's called a creative team, which is the director and the designer, and then there's the composer, and the lighting designer, and a sound designer.

INTERVIEWER: So that's like a core team?

MELLY: Yeah, the creative team. But also you have many different departments, different teams in fact, with specific responsibilities – metalwork, carpentry, sound, electrics, painting, you know – every department, so yes, teamwork is really important.

INTERVIEWER: I see. Then what about working out schedules? I mean obviously you have a start date for a performance but you have to plan over a long period.

MELLY: Yes, planning begins a long time in advance. For example, at the moment I'm working with a writer, it takes months, years even. Then you get the go-ahead for a production, and you start planning talks with the designer, the composer, lighting designer, sound design. And then you need to plan lots of deadlines … up to the performance, design, costumes – meetings with every department. Meetings happen over several weeks.

INTERVIEWER: And this is before you've approached any actors.

MELLY: Absolutely, way, way months in advance. Much later you get the cast, the actors.

INTERVIEWER: And another tight schedule?

MELLY: Yes, a very short rehearsal period, usually four or five weeks …

INTERVIEWER: Only?

MELLY: Yes. After months of planning you have this short period of intensive work in rehearsals.

INTERVIEWER: So are you involved in recruiting all these experts, and the actors? There's a lot of recruitment?

MELLY: Yes, there are a lot of jobs, so yes, recruitment, auditions of course, you have to get the right actors.

INTERVIEWER: And are you also responsible for costs, budgets and budgetary planning?

MELLY: Well, no, I'm not. There's a production manager who oversees all the costs – he's in control of the budget.

INTERVIEWER: Right.

MELLY: … but there is a set budget, absolutely fixed. You can't overrun the budget.

INTERVIEWER: Right. The next area is communication. Obviously the whole project management depends on good communication. How much are you involved with stakeholders? You know, all the people affected by the production?

MELLY: Well, it's true I have to communicate with everyone, including the artistic director of the theatre, the publicity, local schools, maybe groups in the community. And then every department, the set building, the costumes, lighting, and all the actors, musicians, but not with, for example, sponsors. I don't have to deal with the executive board either.

INTERVIEWER: That's the theatre's business?

MELLY: Right, they manage that, and the producer. Oh, and of course there's the media, I have to get in touch with local media, national newspapers, television, radio. It's a key part of communication, the publicity.

INTERVIEWER: Sure. What about regular or formal monitoring and controlling systems?

MELLY: Yeah, we have what's called a production meeting, or a progress meeting, once a week. There every department reports on progress, and if there are any problems to solve. That's a time to discuss any changes of minds or … problems.

INTERVIEWER: That's quite a big meeting then, it's important.

MELLY: Yes, and it can be very tense, sometimes it's difficult, but it should be positive, because we're all after the same …

INTERVIEWER: Result.

MELLY: … the same result, and so it's absolutely vital that we just sort out any difficulties together.

What do you think?

You could also ask students what kind of job they would like to do in a theatre. Again stress the similarity with project management and get them to think of ways that their jobs are similar. You could prompt with questions like: *Do you set deadlines? Do you recruit new staff?* etc.

The words you need ... to talk about project management

1 See if students can put the words in the gaps before you check the meaning of new vocabulary.

2 • There is a Gantt chart in *It's time to talk*. It is a common tool for displaying planning and progress in project management. It is named after its inventor, Henry Laurence Gantt, an American engineer and management consultant (1861–1919).
   • Check the meaning of the collocations when students have done the matching.

It's time to talk

- Set the scene and give time for students to absorb the information and look at the chart.
- Set a time limit for preparation and encourage students to give details and say what they are going to do and when. Write the following on the board to help them:
  We're going to ...
  We plan to ...
  The deadline for ... is ...
  Then, ...
  After that, ...
  At the same time, ...
- When they present their plan, get them to use a flip chart if you have one. Alternatively they could use the board or OHP. At the end of the presentation, encourage other students to ask questions and to clarify what they have been told. This would be a good opportunity to remind students of the techniques they looked at in Unit 11.
- Give feedback on the presentations. Some students may appreciate written feedback.
- You may want to use the Extra classroom activity here (see pages 95 and 112).

COMMUNICATING AT WORK

Negotiating 1: Stating positive expectations and preferences, suggesting alternatives

- Explain that negotiating is an important part of business and work and is not only connected with high-level finance. It is often something we have to do every day. You could ask students to give you situations in which they have had to negotiate. This could be as mundane as booking time off for holidays.
- The aim here is to facilitate students' use of useful language for negotiating. Before playing the recording, it may be helpful to elicit examples of the three areas of language: phrases that emphasise positive expectations in a negotiation; phrases to state preference; phrases to suggest alternatives.
- After playing the recording and identifying the phrases actually used, you could elicit further alternatives.

1 Explain that a *local authority officer* works for the council or local government. Get students to say why they chose their answers. What helped them to choose?

Answers

1 at an early stage   2 friendly and cooperative

2 Give students time to read through the text and predict the missing phrases before playing the track again, if necessary.

Answers

1 we're confident that we can work together
2 we share the same aims
3 we're looking forward to a positive outcome
4 our main concern is

5 we'd like to see
6 we'd like to suggest
7 There are a number of possibilities
8 Alternatively, we can
9 A third possibility is

Track 14.2 tapescript ▶▶|

LOCAL AUTHORITY OFFICER (LA): In general terms, we're confident that we can work together constructively. We think that we share the same aims.

PROPERTY DEVELOPER (PD): Yes, of course, I'm sure that's true. For our part, we plan to bring many improvements to the area and we're looking forward to a positive outcome. At the beginning, we'd like to emphasise that our main concern is that the development offers benefits to the local community.

LA: Yes, of course, that's essential. Also, we'd like to see a design which is sympathetic to the natural environment. So, we'd like to suggest a central area for the community with plenty of open spaces – we'd like trees, walkways, water features and so on, to enhance the appearance of the development. We could have the retail outlets and leisure facilities such as bars and restaurants around the outside …

PD: Excellent. We can discuss that kind of idea. Can we begin with some of the alternatives that we've been thinking about?

LA: Yes, of course.

PD: There are a number of possibilities. First, we can create a central retail area with a range of community assets on the outside. Alternatively, we can create an integrated design with both retail and leisure facilities side by side throughout the development. A third possibility is a combination, with some residential development, some housing, we think at the cheaper end of the market.

LA: Well, we can talk about all of those, but the idea of open space is very important to us.

PD: And I'm sure you're right, we can do something like that …

3
- Stress that the objective is to use the language presented in the previous exercise, so make sure that students prepare suitable language to use as well as think about the content in the preparation stage.
- You could get selected pairs to perform for the rest of the class.

What did we do today?
Check the Remember section quickly and remind students of the objectives of this lesson.

Follow up
Encourage students to:
- write sentences about project management in their organisations
- write down useful phrases for negotiating.

15 Are customers always right?

What did we do last time?

Do a review of the last type 3 lesson (Unit 12). Remind students of what they worked on (see Teacher's notes for that unit) and do some quick revision as follows.

Social skills: Dealing with 'no'

Ask students how they would deal with 'no' in the following situations:

- you ask your boss for overtime payments for the extra work you've been doing recently
- you ask a colleague to lend you his/her car
- you ask a friend to play badminton with you
- you ask a colleague for some help with some photocopying.

Talking about TV and TV programmes

Ask students for words for the following definitions:

- people who watch TV
- a group of programmes that deal with the same subject, often shown weekly
- a programme about real people or situations
- someone who takes part in a competition
- a famous person
- a person or an organisation which sends out TV or radio programmes.

On the agenda: Why are we doing this?

Tell students the objectives of the lesson:

- to practise talking about **customer service**
- to develop **social skills** for **complaining**
- to learn **vocabulary** connected to **consumer issues**.

Reinforce this by writing the key words on the board or OHP.

Warm up

Ask questions to prompt students: *What was the problem? What did you do? What did you say?*

Complaining

What's the point?

See the Introduction (page 16): Type 3 units – social skills.

> **Answers**
>
> 1 a The shower and the window
>   b Once before – this is the second time
>   c Sylvia does not make it clear what the problems are. She should get to the point more quickly, and be more direct and less apologetic.

Track 15.1 tapescript ▶▶

RECEPTIONIST: Good morning. What can I do for you?

SYLVIA: Yes, sorry, but I have a slight problem …

RECEPTIONIST: Oh, I'm sorry to hear that? Can we help in any way?

SYLVIA: I was just wondering if there was a problem with the plumbing …

RECEPTIONIST: Well, I think everything is OK. Is there a problem with the water in your room?

SYLVIA: Well, the water is certainly hot enough but it's just that … I'm not sure if I understand how to make the shower work properly. I don't seem to be able to get it to …

RECEPTIONIST: Would you like me to send someone up to show you how it works?

SYLVIA: Oh, that shouldn't be necessary. But actually, I wonder if it might not be a bit damaged – you know, when I turn it on, quite a lot of water seems to go on the floor. So actually … there is rather a lot of water on the floor now. I'm very sorry about this. I did actually mention it to your colleague yesterday. He said someone would look at it but I'm not sure that anyone has.

RECEPTIONIST: I think I'd better send someone up to have a look at it now. We'll have someone up in the next hour.

SYLVIA: Oh, thank you. I'm sorry to put you to trouble when you must be very busy … but, in fact, if someone is going to come up …

RECEPTIONIST: Is there anything else you'd like him to look at?

SYLVIA: Well, I do find it rather stuffy at the moment. And a little bit too hot.

RECEPTIONIST: Have you tried opening a window?

SYLVIA: Well, yes, actually, I have, but it seems quite difficult to open. In fact I can't get it to open at all. It must be sticking. Either that or I'm just not very strong – it's probably that!

RECEPTIONIST: Don't worry, madam, I'll get someone to look at that as well.

SYLVIA: Thank you, I'm really most grateful …

> **Answers**
>
> 2 a The water in the shower goes on the floor
>   b She can't open the window
>   c Sylvia explains the problems clearly in a more assertive tone. She makes it clear that it's the hotel's responsibility and expresses her disappointment. But she also shows her appreciation of the way the receptionist deals with her complaints. The outcome is positive.
> 3 a to make a complaint
>   b I'd like you to do something about it
>   c very disappointed with
>   d appreciate the way you've responded

Track 15.2 tapescript ▶▶

RECEPTIONIST: Good morning. How can I help you?

SYLVIA: Hello. I want to make a complaint. Yesterday evening I told your colleague that there was a problem with the shower in my room – the water goes all over the floor – and today it's still not working properly.

RECEPTIONIST: I'm sorry about this, madam. I thought that someone had looked at it.

SYLVIA: Well, it's still not working and I'd like you to do something about it.

RECEPTIONIST: I apologise for this. Could you give me your room number?

SYLVIA: Yes, it's room 16.

RECEPTIONIST: … I'm very sorry, madam, I'll get someone to look at it in the next hour. Is that all right?

SYLVIA: Well, I'd like to take a proper shower but I suppose I can wait. But there's another problem as well – I can't open the window – it's stuck. So the room's really stuffy and I couldn't sleep properly last night.

RECEPTIONIST: I'm very sorry. I think this may be because the windows have been repainted recently and they may be a bit stiff. I'll get the window looked at at the same time.

SYLVIA: It's not a very good start to my stay. I'm very disappointed with the general standard so far.

RECEPTIONIST: Yes, I can understand your disappointment. Can I suggest that you change your room? I think we can offer you a slightly bigger one with a better view. And perhaps we could offer you a half bottle of champagne with your evening meal tonight by way of apology?

SYLVIA: Thank you. Yes, I'd be happy with that. I appreciate the way you've responded.

Possible answers

4 In a restaurant
Sorry, but this food is cold. Could you heat it up?
Can I have another one which is hot, please?

In a shoe shop
I bought these very recently.
You can see the problem.

In a travel agency
I wasn't happy with the hotel.
We were told that the beach was five minutes away.

Have a go

See the Introduction (page 17): Type 3 units.
As a simple model for complaining, write the following on the board:

1 *Explain the problem.*
2 *Say what you want.*
3 *Say what you will do if you don't get it.*

Encourage students to remain polite and not to get angry.

Read on

Consumer report

Explain that *horror story* means that something went very wrong and that students are going to read about the experiences of two dissatisfied consumers. You could tell your own story, if you have one, before students discuss their experiences in pairs.

1 • You may want to tell students that these articles were taken from *Which?*, the magazine of the Consumers' Association in the UK. With more than 700,000 members, it is the largest consumers' organisation in Europe. The texts come from the *Which?* lawyers' files.
   • Explain that being able to identify the main points in a text is an important reading skill that can save them time and so improve their reading speed.
   • Check the meaning of *conservatory* and *taken for a ride*.
   • As an alternative, you could do this as a jigsaw reading. Half the class reads *Delayed action* and half *Taken for a ride*. They could then pair up and compare their answers.

Answers

Delayed action:
1 A new conservatory
2 The company did not do the work properly.
3 The company finally did the work and gave Mr Dowlah some vouchers by way of compensation.

Taken for a ride:
1 A new car
2 The company did not deliver the car on time.
3 Mr Planner sold his old car and then had to pay for a hire car while he waited for the new one. The company paid him for the cost of the car hire.

2 Explain that students are now going to read the text in more detail. You could add an element of competition here by getting students to complete the sentences in groups and see which group can do it the fastest.

Answers

1 conservatory/extension   2 £9,088   3 nine   4 £908
5 four   6 inspection   7 replastered and redecorated
8 £8,180

3 • Alternatively, you could get half the class to read the first half of the text and the rest the second half. They could then write questions for a partner to answer as quickly as possible.
   • For the discussion, write some phrases on the board to help students:
   I'd have … Check the pronunciation of this also.
   You could ask further questions like:
   Is it common to complain in your country? How do people generally complain?
   • A possible extension: in small groups, get students to describe a situation in which they have complained. The others should try to guess what the outcome was.

Suggested answers

1 Neil wanted to buy a new car (a Volkswagen Golf 1.6 Auto).
2 He decided to buy it from Showroom4cars.com.
3 He placed his order in June.
4 The company said they would tell him two or three weeks before it was delivered.
5 He tried to phone the company in August.
6 The company told him it would arrive in September.
7 He sold his own car but the new car didn't finally arrive until November.
8 The company finally paid him all the money he had spent on car hire.

The words you need … to talk about consumer issues

1 Encourage students to look at the whole sentence in the text when they try to work out the meaning of the words.

Answers

1 1 adverb   2 verb   3 noun   4 noun   5 verb   6 noun
   7 noun   8 noun   9 verb   10 multi-word verb
   11 noun + verb   12 noun
2 1 g   2 k   3 i   4 c   5 j   6 d   7 e   8 a   9 l   10 b
   11 f   12 h
3 1 small print   2 best buy   3 deposit   4 recall   5 refund
   6 fine   7 warranty   8 claim   9 expiry   10 entitled

It's time to talk

- Set the scene and check the meaning of *mail order*. Give students time to prepare for the role-play and remind them to use the vocabulary from this unit and to plan a structured approach to their complaint.
- After the role-plays, students can summarise to the rest of the class what the outcome was. Ask how successful they were and what they would do differently next time, and in a real situation.
- You may want to use the Extra classroom activity here (see pages 95 and 113).

What did we do today?
Check the Remember section quickly and remind students of the objectives of the lesson.

Follow up
Encourage students to:
- record new vocabulary from this unit
- write a letter of complaint.

16 Thomas Cook in India

What did we do last time?
Do a review of the last type 1 lesson (Unit 13). Remind students of what they worked on (see Teacher's notes for that unit) and do some quick revision as follows.

Modal verbs to express certainty
Ask students how we can express the following degrees of certainty in both the past and the present:
- 99%
- 80%
- 50%
- 1%

Get students to make sentences about their work situation using the modal verbs. For example: *The intranet was very slow today. There must be a problem with the server.*

Pronunciation: Stress in word families
Write the following on the board:

Noun	Verb
competition	
	analyse
negotiation	
	organise
management	
innovation	
	create

Get students to tell you the missing words and then ask them to mark the stress and pronounce the words correctly.

On the agenda: Why are we doing this?
Tell students the objective of this lesson:
- to improve speaking skills: **making what we say interesting**

- to revise using **adverbs**
- to improve **pronunciation: adding impact and interest.**
Reinforce this by writing the key words on the board or OHP.

Warm up
- You may want to bring in a map of India so students can discuss tourist sites, etc. while looking at it.
- After looking at the photo of Ameeta, ask if students have heard of Thomas Cook. If not, explain that it is a travel company. See the Background briefing below.

Listen to this

The golden triangle
It would be better to discuss the information in the Background briefing after students have done the listening exercises, to avoid giving away details covered in the listening.

1 • Explain that *in-house* means that the newsletter is only available to the employees of the company.
 • Give students a few moments to read through the fact sheet and to check any vocabulary problems.

Track 16.1 tapescript ▶▶

INTERVIEWER: Can you just tell me a little about the history of Thomas Cook in India?

AMEETA: Yes, Thomas Cook in India was set up in 1881. When it was set up, it basically catered for the British administration based in India and the Indian royal families, these were the first customers. There's a great story of Thomas Cook making arrangements for a prince to travel to Queen Victoria's coronation with an enormous retinue of 200 staff, 50 family attendants, 10 elephants, 33 tigers and 1,000 packing cases … all by sea, of course. These were gifts for the queen.

INTERVIEWER: Nice. And how many people work for Thomas Cook in India now?

AMEETA: Ah, around 900. As of today, we have 45 branches across 16 cities in India, plus operations in Sri Lanka, in Mauritius, and we've also got a licence to operate in Bangladesh.

INTERVIEWER: So, tell me a little bit about how Indians like to travel on holiday, as distinct from Europeans.

AMEETA: Well, one big difference is that group travel, families, is very popular in India.

INTERVIEWER: Is Europe a big market?

AMEETA: Yes, and the UK is a must – London is a must. To an Indian, London is Europe. And another spot that you have to have is

Switzerland. Indians love snow because we never have snow here. So, European tours will start from London or end in London. Most families plan their itineraries in such a way, the reason being because most Indians have some family or friends staying in the UK.

INTERVIEWER: The corporate market is also important for you. Do you have the same problem as in Europe with competition from the budget airlines using websites only?

AMEETA: Yes, and we do foresee a squeeze on margins. But e-ticketing in India hasn't really taken off here yet like in Europe. You know, not everybody has a computer … and people still like to have a physical ticket in their hand. And in India, companies, especially, don't have the time to stop work and say, 'I'll get on the net and find out how much it is on Emirates and Lufthansa.' That's why they depend on a travel agent. So we aim to give a quality service in four main areas. First of all, we offer very up-to-date information. We can tell you on the spot, 'This is the best deal you can get right now.' Secondly, we have more extensive travel insurance and foreign exchange services, so we try to position Thomas Cook as a one-stop travel shop.

INTERVIEWER: So service is your added value?

AMEETA: Absolutely. We also have a call centre in India which operates 365 days from eight am to eight pm. And finally, the fourth point, another very important part of our service, and we're really proud of it, is our website – we're constantly innovating and offering new features with it. This new technology is going to help us expand the market. So, yes, service is very important in a growing market, that we look out and maintain contact with all our customers.

INTERVIEWER: Just to look at things the other way a little, which nationalities come as tourists to India and what are the major destinations for these foreign travellers?

AMEETA: Basically, there are four big countries for tourists coming to India. It's the UK, France and Germany, and Russia is again another big market. The popular destinations – remember we have a very big coast line – are Goa and Kerala. Another popular circuit is Delhi, the capital city of India, along with Agra, because of the Taj Mahal, and then Rajasthan. These three are very close to each other and so are known as the 'golden triangle'. And travellers often do it within five days. The French, in particular, love to come to Rajasthan.

INTERVIEWER: Why's that?

AMEETA: They just love it and Rajasthan is great. It's a desert landscape but it still has a lot of colour and festivities. There's a festival which is known as the Jaisalmer festival, which is a camel fair. The Indian Tourist department sends very good, five-star quality tents over there, and these fairs take place out in the desert. They set up these tents, and these are almost booked up, as I say, by the French, by almost two to three years in advance.

INTERVIEWER: I suppose many people also organise more spiritual, religious type trips?

AMEETA: Yes, and there's something now happening which is in the last two to three years, which has again become very popular, called Kumbh Mela. It's basically something that is connected with mythology – it depends on how the moon and the sun are travelling. There are four cities which are considered to be the holiest places, and they have what is known as the biggest congregation of holy people, you know, and thousands and thousands of people go. You also get celebrities, stars like Demi Moore, she was here last year, and Goldie Hawn, you know? They all visited Kumbh Mela. And this visiting of stars, because of this, again this is becoming really, really popular with other foreign travellers now.

Background briefing: Thomas Cook, the golden triangle, Jaisalmer and Kumbh Mela

Thomas Cook

Thomas Cook is one of the world's leading travel services groups with operations in more than 100 countries, employing over 30,000 people. Thomas Cook in India was set up in 1881 with the intention of providing guided tours of India for the first-time visitor. Besides holidays, Thomas Cook India also provides foreign exchange services, travel insurance, corporate travel management and other customised travel related services.

The golden triangle

The golden triangle is the most popular tourist route in India and links the cities of Delhi, the capital of India, Agra, home of Taj Mahal, and Jaipur.

Jaisalmer

This desert fortress close to Rajasthan's border with Pakistan is straight out of an Arabian fairy tale, glowing with the luminescence of a mirage at sunset. Jaisalmer is a golden sandstone city with crenellated city walls, a magnificent fortress and exquisitely carved stone and wooden havelis. Jaisalmer's impressive fort crowns an 80 m (260 ft) high hill, and about a quarter of the city's 40,000 inhabitants reside within its walls. Little has changed here for centuries; houses, temples and palaces are packed in like sardines, it's honeycombed with winding lanes, and has formidable gateways.

Kumbh Mela

The Kumbh Mela is held every three years in each of four different locations, returning to each of the four places every 12 years. It is a sacred Hindu Pilgrimage and bathing festival. The festival lasts just over a month and many of the pilgrims stay in a large tented city. The Kumbh in 2001 was probably the largest human gathering in history, with over 30 million people attending; the authorities spent millions of dollars on security and other arrangements.

For more information about Thomas Cook and Jaisalmer, go to the *English365* website: www.cambridge.org/elt/english365.

What do you think?

If there is time, get students to work in pairs and present their town or a part of their country to other students. If they come from the same place, they could present a town or area that they know well.

Check your grammar

Adverbs

- Explain that you are now going to look at the use of adverbs. Perhaps write some examples on the board so that students know exactly what they are.

- Before you continue with the Student's Book, you could get students to look through Tapescript 16.1 to find examples and then try to explain what function they have. Tell students that using adverbs effectively can help them to sound more expressive when they speak in English.
- You could get students to cover the examples of each adverb and ask them to find an example in the tapescript.

2
- Highlight the fact that many adverbs can be used in different positions in a sentence.
- Refer students to the Grammar reference section.

Do it yourself

1 Students can do this individually or in pairs.

2 Make it clear that you are not asking students to tell you the effect of each adverb in each sentence – you just want to know the overall effect in the text.

3 When you go through the answers, check the meaning of the wrong answers. For example, *massively*.

Sounds good

Adding impact and interest

1 Play track 16.2 and try to elicit the differences between the two versions of the conversation. You could also demonstrate the good model yourself. Stress that both appropriate use of language and pronunciation can make a speaker sound interesting.

2 There may be some resistance from some students when it comes to practising the use of intonation, volume and pauses. Try to keep things light-hearted and emphasise the importance of being able to vary these features in English.

Track 16.3 tapescript ▸▸|
See the Student's Book.

3 Give students some prompts to help them with this activity. For example, they could think about historical attractions, restaurants, parks, etc.

It's time to talk

- Handle this in the normal way for file cards (see Introduction page 13).
- Remind Students B and C that they are trying to persuade Student A to include their hotel in the magazine, so they should practise using language from this unit to add impact.
- You may want to use the Extra classroom activity here (see pages 95 and 114).

What did we do today?

Check the Remember section quickly and remind students of the objectives of the lesson.

Follow up

Encourage students to:
- write sentences about their organisation with a range of different adverbs
- look at the Thomas Cook website
- practise their pronunciation – students should try varying their intonation, stress, volume and pausing outside the classroom

17 The marketing mix

What did we do last time?

Do a review of the last type 2 lesson (Unit 14). Remind students of what they worked on (see Teacher's notes for that unit) and do a quick review as follows.

Talking about projects, product development and project management
Brainstorm useful vocabulary for talking about *projects*, *product development* and *project management*. In pairs, get students to talk about a project they are currently involved in.

Negotiating: Stating positive expectations and preferences, suggesting alternatives
Ask students for ways of doing the following in English:
- stating positive expectations
- stating preferences
- suggesting alternatives.

On the agenda: Why are we doing this?

Tell students the objectives of the lesson:
- to talk about the **marketing mix**
- to build **vocabulary** to talk about **marketing**
- to develop skills for **presenting: using visual supports**.
Reinforce this by writing the key words on the board or OHP.

Warm up

Ask students what they think the pros and cons of working in marketing might be. Do they have a marketing

department in their organisation? What do they know about it? If they know about the Four Ps, can they expand and give examples? Don't give too much away at this point as students will learn more about it in the listening which follows.

Background briefing: University of York

The University of York is one of the top universities in England. It was founded in 1963 with 200 students. Since then it has expanded to 10,000 students and has over 30 academic departments and research centres. The main campus, with the colleges and academic buildings, is set in a large landscaped park near the city of York. For more information about the University of York, go to the *English365* website: www.cambridge.org/elt/english365.

Listen to this

The marketing mix – still useful?

- Ask students if they think the marketing mix is still useful.
- This listening is in five short parts. You will need to judge whether students need to hear each part more than once.
1 The first task is predictive, or checks what students know already. They can try to correct the statements, compare with a partner and then listen to the recording to check whether they are right.

Answers
1 Correct
2 No – it is simple
3 No – it works for products and services
4 No – it works for both
5 Correct
6 No – place, not people

Track 17.1 tapescript ▶▶|

INTERVIEWER: Nicky, what is the marketing mix? What are the Four Ps? And do you think the concept is relevant to modern organisations and businesses?

NICKY: Well, the marketing mix is basically an idea that uses the Four Ps as a framework for thinking about, and answering questions about, how you're going to position your product with your consumers. And the idea is very simple, which is why it can be used in different ways for different situations. It works for services as well as products, and also for public and for private organisations. It fits all kinds of situations. It's been around for years, maybe 50, I don't know how long, but yes, it's still useful.

INTERVIEWER: Right. So the Four Ps, what are they?

NICKY: OK, well, I think the Four Ps really … it's just a useful checklist to look at what you do under four clear headings: product, price, promotion, and place.

Answers
2 1 compare   2 customer   3 in competition / competing
4 target   5 benefits / strengths   6 weaknesses

Track 17.2 tapescript ▶▶|

INTERVIEWER: Yes. So explain about product, then.

NICKY: Product means what exactly it is that you're offering. Is it a hairbrush or is it a garden maintenance service? What product is it and how does it compare with those other products that a customer might choose instead?

INTERVIEWER: Yes.

NICKY: You're not in competition with everyone and anyone. You're able to target exactly who you're competing against and what your differences and benefits or strengths are compared to them, what your weaknesses are compared to them and why your consumers might choose you or might not choose you.

Track 17.3 tapescript ▶▶

INTERVIEWER: OK, and what about price? I suppose you're looking at the competition and how much other businesses or organisations charge …?

NICKY: … for that service or that price … and how you're positioned. Are you positioned as a premium product, highly priced in the market, or are you economy, at a low price in the market, or are you positioning yourself as good value …?

Track 17.4 tapescript ▶▶

INTERVIEWER: OK. And promotion?

NICKY: Well, promotion is a good one I think to answer your question really about whether the mix – the Four Ps – is still relevant because promotion means, to me, any way of making your product or service known to your potential buyer. So that might be leaflets through the door, it might be posters in the village for a very small local business. It might be television or radio advertising for a national product, or it might be the internet – if you're looking to market your product worldwide, that would be a good solution. But it's still the same idea, it's still how you make your product or service known about to your consumer …

5 After the listening, ask students if they were right about the marketing mix still being useful or not. They should be able to tell you that it is.

Track 17.5 tapescript ▶▶

INTERVIEWER: So place is the market in fact, where you're selling the product?

NICKY: Yes, place is in terms of the geographical area, the location, that you're looking to enter to market your product, so you can see yourself within a more sensible competitive set … So, if you've got a service, unless you franchise it out, you know – sell a kind of licence to use your name, like McDonald's do, and Gap and Benetton – it's probably more difficult I think to broaden the geographical scope. Whereas if you're selling a very standard product in a factory and you can make millions of them and ship them around the world because they're quite light and they're quite easy to carry and they're not fragile …

INTERVIEWER: Yes.

NICKY: Then your place and your opportunity for broadening the place is easier.

INTERVIEWER: Right. So in summary, the Four Ps is a management tool, it helps decision making?

NICKY: Yes, I think that's right. It's still useful, and it's still simple.

What do you think?

Students can answer these questions about any organisation which they are familiar with.

The words you need … to talk about marketing 1

Students can do these exercises individually or in pairs. In some cases you will be able to check understanding further by asking for examples or alternatives with a similar meaning.

It's time to talk

- In pairs, students could give short presentations to other students. To link in to the next part of the lesson, ask students if visual aids would help them make their points.
- You may want to use the Extra classroom activity here (see pages 95 and 115).

COMMUNICATING AT WORK

Presenting 3: Using visual supports

You may want to start with a short brainstorming exercise on general principles.

- Pictures should support what the speaker says, not be the dominant feature; they should be clear and easy to read; they should be introduced slowly, giving the audience time to look at them and understand the main points; the speaker should highlight main points from the pictures.
- Common errors: too much information; standing in front of the image; turning one's back on the audience; going into too much detail; going too fast; using too many pictures (or too few).
- PowerPoint can be an excellent tool for presenting, but it is important to avoid the following: having too much information on the slides; allowing the slides to become more important than the speaker; overdoing the special effects available from computer technology; using inappropriate colours.

1 This exercise is a basic vocabulary check. Remind students that in a presentation more or less any kind of visual support can be called *a picture*, and that a range of other terms can be used, for example, the *flowchart* could be described as a *diagram*.

2 The recording provides a model for how to describe the visual supports in exercise 1. Get students to read through the extracts and then listen and write down the missing words. You may need to play the recording again.

Track 17.6 tapescript ▶▶|

A: Look at the pie chart here. It shows that P&G has a market share of 20% whereas Caplo has 30%.

B: This picture shows a graph that compares sales over five years from 2000 to 2004. It also shows both turnover and costs.

C: The map represents the volume of exports to different international markets – the USA is clearly our main export market.

D: The table compares imports and exports between three regions in 2003. The figures are in billions of dollars, so for example, Western European exports to North America are almost 300 billion.

E: The flowchart shows the distribution channel for our products in the domestic market. It begins with suppliers and ends with the consumers.

F: This graph shows the trends in foreign direct investment in four economies. The solid line shows the US, the broken line represents the UK, and the dotted line is for Germany. The thin line here is for France.

3 Students should take it in turns to describe each picture to their partner, and add more information about it. Give feedback, particularly on examples of good language produced by students.

4 Here students can practise describing pictures of their own choosing and can produce a picture themselves, if they wish. You may want to bring in some magazines or books into class, or tell students to bring some for the lesson.

What did we do today?

Check the Remember section quickly and remind students of the objectives of this lesson.

Follow up

Encourage students to:
- write sentences about the marketing mix in their organisation
- write up their presentation in *It's time to talk* as a homework task
- write up their description of pictures in *Communicating at work*.

18 Wish you were here

What did we do last time?

Do a review of the last type 3 lesson (Unit 15). Remind students of what they worked on (see Teacher's notes for that unit) and do some quick revision as follows.

Social skills: Complaining

Ask students how they would complain about the following:
- a DVD player that has poor sound quality – in an electrical shop
- the cancellation of a plane – in an airport
- a hair in some soup – in a restaurant
- food that is past its sell-by date – in a supermarket.

If you have time, you could get students to role-play the situations.

Talking about customer service and consumer issues

Ask students for words for the following definitions:
- a written promise from a company to replace or repair a product that becomes faulty within a certain time period
- an amount of money that is given back to you
- an amount of money that is paid in advance for a product
- text in a formal agreement that is smaller than the rest of the document, often because it contains information that may not be good for the person signing the agreement
- a formal agreement that finishes an argument
- faults or problems
- money you are paid as a repayment for damage or loss.

Tell students that the title of this unit is what people commonly write on postcards when they are on holiday.

On the agenda: Why are we doing this?

Tell the students the objectives of the lesson:
- to practise talking about **holidays**
- to develop **social skills** for **persuading** – check the meaning of this, if necessary
- to learn **vocabulary** related to **holidays and holiday problems**.

Reinforce this by writing the key words on the board or OHP.

Warm up

To develop interest and discussion, you could also ask questions like: *In what kinds of situations do people persuade other people to do things?* Mention that persuading is something we have to do in everyday situations – at work, at home and socially – and is, therefore, an important skill.

Persuading

What's the point?

See the Introduction (page 16): Type 3 units – social skills.

Track 18.1 tapescript ▶▶|

MIKE: So Dieter, where are you going on holiday this year?

DIETER: Oh, I don't know, I guess I'll go on a beach holiday somewhere as usual.

MIKE: But you do that every year. It's very boring. Be more adventurous. Go scuba diving. You'll enjoy it.

DIETER: Oh no, I don't think so, that kind of thing's not really for me.

MIKE: You must. I'm going scuba diving soon. One of our friends can't come. You can take his place. You must come.

DIETER: Oh, I don't know, I've never done it before … I just like to relax … I couldn't do anything like that …

MIKE: But you must come. You'll enjoy it.

DIETER: No … no, thanks … Thanks all the same, but that kind of thing isn't for me.

Answers

2 a Four

b The brochure

c Mike's tone is persuasive and friendly. He listens to Dieter's points this time, but he makes scuba diving sound attractive, explaining why Dieter would enjoy it, and making his message clear by repeating it in different ways.

3 a It's absolutely brilliant.

b I'm sure you'd love it.

c believe that you'd enjoy it.

d I'd love you to come.

Track 18.2 tapescript ▶▶|

MIKE: So Dieter, where are you going on holiday this year?

DIETER: Oh, I don't know, I guess I'll go on a beach holiday somewhere as usual.

MIKE: Didn't you do that last year? And the year before? Why don't you think about doing something a bit different this time? Listen – I've got a good idea. Four of us had a scuba diving holiday booked but now one of the others can't go. Why don't you come along? It's absolutely brilliant. You're a good swimmer. I'm sure you'd love it.

DIETER: Oh, I don't think so, that kind of thing's not really for me.

MIKE: But tell me why not? It's not that difficult. It doesn't take long to learn the basics. And we've all booked to do a course anyway. What's the problem?

DIETER: But isn't it scary? What about sharks?

MIKE: Well, driving a car is probably more dangerous! Really, when you go diving, it's just fantastic seeing all those fish all round you, and there are wonderful plants too. It's a whole new world. It really is an incredible way to spend a holiday.

DIETER: But it's expensive!

MIKE: It's no more expensive than the holidays you take at the moment. I honestly believe that you'd enjoy it – more than just going to the beach every day. I wouldn't talk about it if I didn't think so. Let me show you the brochure. And the other guys are great. You'd really get on with them.

DIETER: Well, I don't know …

MIKE: It's up to you, but I'd love you to come.

DIETER: Well, maybe I'll take a look at the brochure …

Possible answers

4 A film

It's a great film. A real classic.

I know you'll love it.

A report

You know more about it than me.

It's up to you, but I'd really appreciate it.

Help with a household job

It won't take long with two of us doing it.

It must be your turn by now.

Have a go

- See the Introduction (page 17): Type 3 units.
- It will help if each group thinks of a town they would like to talk about. Encourage them to brainstorm types of things that visitors could do there and to think about why they would be interesting. Get Student B to list the plus points and try to relate them to Student A.

Read on

Travel

- After discussing the initial questions, also ask students if there is anything they think they could have done to avoid those problems.
- Introduce the concept of predicting and stress that when we read a text in our own language, we always have some idea of what the text is going to be about. It is important that students learn to do the same in English.

1 Get students to read through the titles and headlines and try to guess what they think the subject of each one will be before they do the matching exercise. Tell students not to worry too much about the vocabulary at this stage. They should use what they already know to make calculated guesses.

Answers

1d 2e 3f 4a 5c 6b Photo: Rainbow's end

2
- Explain that being able to understand the main points in a paragraph will help students to understand a text more quickly. It is, therefore, an important reading skill.
- Look at the title first and get students to say what they expect will be in the text. Tell them not to worry about the vocabulary, as this will be dealt with later.

Suggested answers

1 Pickpockets   2 Thieves   3 Short-changing   4 Pollution

5 Harassment   6 Mugging

3 After answering the questions, ask if students would recommend anything else.

Answers

1 Under your clothes

2 Radio or CD player

3 Get to know the local currency

4 Because you will be away from the traffic and the pollution

5 Close to other people

6 Into streets which are not well lit

The words you need ... to talk about holidays and holiday problems

Did you know?

The top ten tourist destinations were in this order:

1 France 2 Spain 3 USA 4 Italy 5 China 6 UK
7 Austria 8 Mexico 9 Germany 10 Canada

1 After students have done the exercise, check the meaning of any words they are not clear about, or get them to use their dictionaries.

Answers

1 snatched 2 keep your eyes open 3 remove 4 smashed
5 check 6 get to know 7 book 8 look 9 choose
10 keep away from

2 Before doing this, ask students what they think good travellers should do.

Answers

1 Minimise 2 leave 3 lock 4 Hide 5 bother 6 Avoid
7 report 8 distract 9 Make 10 Deter

3 Mention that there may be more than one right answer.

Answers

1 g 2 e 3 j 4 a 5 i 6 c 7 h 8 b 9 d 10 f

Reading tip

Tell students also to look out for other features of vocabulary when they are reading. This is a good way to improve their range.

It's time to talk

- Set the scene and go through the possible areas to deal with.
- After the activity, students could choose which is the best or safest destination from what they have heard.
- You may want to use the Extra classroom activity here (see pages 96 and 116).

What did we do today?

Check the Remember section quickly and remind students of the objectives of this lesson.

Follow up

Encourage students to:
- record new vocabulary
- write down useful phrases for persuading people to do things.

19 Media world

What did we do last time?

Do a review of the last type 1 lesson (Unit 16). Remind students of what they worked on (see Teacher's notes for that unit) and do some quick revision as follows.

Adverbs
Get students to give you different examples of the following adverb types:
- manner
- frequency
- time / place
- degree
- attitude marker.

Ask them to make sentences using the different adverbs. For example: *She wrote the report very badly.*

Pronunciation: Adding impact and interest
Write the following dialogue on the board:
A: *How is the new software?*
B: *Not bad at all. I was able to get the work done much more quickly.*
A: *Is it easy to use?*
B: *It was quite complicated at first, obviously, but I soon got the hang of it.*

Get students to practise saying the dialogue in pairs, using appropriate pauses and stress to add impact and interest.

On the agenda: Why are we doing this?

Tell students the objectives of this lesson:
- to improve **speaking skills: updating**
- to revise the **passive: present simple and continuous, past simple, present perfect, modals**
- to improve **pronunciation: linking.**

Reinforce this by writing the key words on the board or OHP.

Warm up

Before you look at this section, you could ask students what kinds of newspaper they read and about the different parts of a newspaper, for example, national news, international news, sport, financial, features, etc.

Background briefing: Göteborgs-Posten

Based in Göteborg, Sweden, *Göteborgs-Posten* has become one of the leading newspaper titles in Sweden since it was founded in 1813. Politically, it is liberal in its orientation and has a circulation of around 250,000. For more information about *Göteborgs-Posten*, go to the *English365* website: www.cambridge.org/elt/english365.

Listen to this

My most interesting interview

1
- Before you start this, ask students what skills they think a good interviewer requires.
- Get students to read the list of skills to see if they had thought of any of them.

She mentions:
2 3 4 6
The most important is 6.

Track 19.1 tapescript ▶▶

INTERVIEWER: So, are you out there on the road quite a lot interviewing people or do you do a lot of work which is office based on the phone?

YLVA: Both, I would say. It depends on how lazy I am on the day! But I try to be out of the office as much as possible.

INTERVIEWER: So, what makes a good interviewer?

YLVA: Well, it depends on who it is and the kind of interview. The most important thing is to make people comfortable, make them feel that they are not being interviewed by a journalist, just talking. It's interesting, 'cause sometimes, afterwards, having a cigarette break, people can be really relaxed and that's when I get some of the best quotes, interviewing with a cigarette.

INTERVIEWER: OK.

YLVA: Generally, I work to make people talk, which means asking the right questions. I'm not the star, the person being interviewed is. And, yes, I need to be a good listener so I can get back and ask … 'Well, yes, ten minutes ago you said this and now you say that. How does this work together and what do you mean by that?' But perhaps the most important thing for a journalist always in most situations and in all countries, I think, is the confidence that people around you have in you, both the people that you are interviewing and the readers. I mean, they have to trust you. You need to have a reputation in the business for being trustworthy.

2 1 a woman from Nepal
  2 a conference in Beijing on women's issues
  3 real impact on the lives of women around the world
  4 never heard / no knowledge
  5 earned anything / a single penny
  6 always smiling and positive

Track 19.2 tapescript ▶▶

INTERVIEWER: So who's the most famous or interesting person you've met?

YLVA: Well, I wouldn't say that the most interesting thing as a reporter is to meet the most famous people. The most interesting – I've got a picture of her here on my desk – was a woman from Nepal. I covered the world conference on women's issues in Beijing in 1995 and I was sitting here in my office a year later and I thought, 'Are these conferences having any impact at all on the daily life of women around the world in Africa, in Asia, Chechnya, Russia, whatever?' So we decided to go and see.

INTERVIEWER: OK.

YLVA: So reporters were sent to five different places in the world, and I got Asia and decided to go to Nepal. We went out, three hours by a very small plane from Kathmandu, then five hours by car, to a small village close to the Indian border and I eventually got to interview a woman called Jamuna.

INTERVIEWER: And had the UN conference made any difference?

YLVA: She'd never heard of the conference. And you know, in Nepal, the value of a woman was, and maybe still is, quite low. So in the article we tried to cover different issues about women: the fact that she'd never in her life earned a single penny, her husband had gone to India and never come back and she had four kids. But seeing her daily life, despite working 18 hours a day, she was always smiling and positive. So this kind of story, this is the thing that you really remember and value as a journalist … not so much the government ministers.

3 1 CNN is very fast to give us pictures of what is happening
  2 Support for the military / the war in Iraq
  3 The variety of news is decreasing

Track 19.3 tapescript ▶▶

INTERVIEWER: What do you think of news media such as CNN?

YLVA: Well, everything in CNN is done very fast, they're always where something is happening, in Kabul or in Africa. On the one hand it's good, as they can give us the pictures about what's happening. But it's also a negative thing that they are the first ones to tell the story. You know, the first ones that we listen to are the ones that we believe the most. And … CNN is an American channel with its own agenda. I wouldn't say that it's a threat but you really need to be aware of this.

INTERVIEWER: You wouldn't go as far as saying something like CNN is propaganda though?

YLVA: No, not yet. I think there are other channels in the United States that are more like 'propaganda', if you can say that. When I visited the United States, quite early on in the war, and with the situation in Iraq, these channels really said, 'We are supporting the military.' And as a viewer you can either like it or you can dislike it.

INTERVIEWER: Are you positive or negative about global trends in media?

YLVA: Well, things are changing very fast and dramatically, I would say. Now you have a few very big companies like AOL Time Warner, and the big bosses like Murdoch … these are very important and very powerful players. And I think that, as a result, the variety of news, the variety of how to cover a story has decreased and is still decreasing. And that's worrying.

What do you think?

You could also ask students the following questions: *Do you watch international news channels? Are they different from your national ones? Which do you prefer? Why? Are news channels always objective? What is the role of a journalist? Should they just report what they see, or should they intervene if, for example, a crime is being committed?*

Check your grammar

Passive: present simple and continuous, past simple, present perfect, modals

1 You could mention that in all cases, the passive is used to distance the speaker or writer from the action. It makes it more impersonal.

1 1 b   2 e   3 a   4 c   5 d
2 1 and 3 are active; 2 and 4 are passive.
  The passive is used in both examples because the real agents of the verbs in the passive are not known or are not necessary to specify. It is not important to describe specifically the people doing the work at CNN (it is obvious that Ylva means CNN staff). It is not necessary to state who exactly sent the reporters round the world: it may not be known exactly or the decision may have involved a lot of people.

3 When you have done this, highlight the different forms used in each tense and check students know how each passive tense is formed. Tell students to look at the Grammar reference section either in class or for homework.

Do it yourself

2 Mention that while these sentences may not sound very natural, they are good practice for using the passive form.

Sounds good

Linking

1 • Read the first sentence yourself and ask students what they notice. Students can then do the others in pairs. It will be useful to have these sentences written on the board or OHP when you go through the answers.
  • Highlight the importance of linking in English and how an awareness of it will help both listening and speaking. Tell students that it is not necessary to use linking when they are speaking – people will still

understand them – but it will help them to sound much more fluent.
  • Read the example sentences out to highlight the features of linking.

2 After students have done the exercise, you could point out a dialogue that they could use, for example in Unit 14 on page 50 in the Student's Book.

It's time to talk

• Set the scene and give students time to read through the information and their file cards. Help them with any unfamiliar vocabulary. You could write the following prompts on the board:
  Has ... been done yet?
  ... hasn't been done yet because ...
  The reason for this is ...
• After students have practised their role-plays in pairs, get volunteers to perform for the rest of the class. Students are usually more willing to do this once they have had a chance to practise with their partner first.
• You may want to use the Extra classroom activity here (see pages 96 and 117).

What did we do today?
Check the Remember section quickly and remind students of the objectives of this lesson.

What did we do today?
Encourage students to:
• write sentences about processes in their organisation using the passive
• find other dialogues in the Student's Book and mark the word linking, and to practise saying them.

20 Everybody's business

What did we do last time?
Do a review of the last type 2 lesson (Unit 17). Remind students of what they worked on (see Teacher's notes for that unit) and do some quick revision as follows.

Talking about marketing and the marketing mix
Brainstorm vocabulary connected to *marketing* and the *marketing mix*. Then ask students to talk about marketing in their organisation, using as many of the words as possible.

Presenting: Using visual supports
Brainstorm different types of visual support: *table*, *map*, *graph*, *pie chart*, *flowchart*.
Get students to draw two or three of these, inventing the information or statistics that they illustrate, and describe them to a partner.

On the agenda: Why are we doing this?
Tell students the objectives of this lesson:
- to talk about **marketing** and **market research**
- to build **vocabulary** related to **marketing**
- to develop skills for **meetings: teleconferencing** – check the meaning of this.

Reinforce this by writing the key words on the board or OHP.

- This is the second marketing unit. Unit 17 was mainly concerned with general principles of consumer marketing (marketing goods and services to the public), whereas this unit has a focus on a different category of marketing, as becomes clear in the first interview. The second interview is more general, covering marketing from all perspectives.
- You may want to reflect on the title of the unit. Just about anyone involved in any business or organisation is interested in or affected by marketing, either as a seller or as a consumer – hence marketing is 'everybody's business'.

Warm up
Also ask students what kinds of marketing they know. Which are the most effective? Don't worry if students don't offer a great deal here, as this will be covered in the listening.

Background briefing: Lafarge Zement and QA Research

Lafarge Zement
Lafarge Zement is the German subsidary of the company Lafarge, the world leader in building materials. Lafarge holds top-ranking positions in each of four different divisions: Cement, Roofing, Aggregates and Concrete and Gypsum. The head office of Lafarge Zement in Germany is based in Oberursel near Frankfurt.

QA Research
QA Research is a research and marketing company based in York, UK, established in 1989. Its managing director is Peter Harrington. QA is involved with market research, creative communication and sales consultancy. QA works mainly in the business-to-business context, but also in the marketing of consumer goods and services, and has particular expertise in promotion and sales strategies and in matching these to specific market needs.

For more information about Lafarge Zement and QA Research, go to the *English365* website: www.cambridge.org/elt/english365.

Listen to this

What's important in marketing?
1 Get students to read the information first, and choose the answers they think are correct. They then listen to check their choices.

Answers								
1 a	2 c	3 a	4 a	5 c	6 b	7 a	8 b	9 a

Track 20.1 tapescript ▶▶

INTERVIEWER: Right. What do you think are the most important issues in marketing for Lafarge Zement?

KRISTINA: Well, we work on a b-to-b scale, it's not a c business.

INTERVIEWER: So, business to business.

KRISTINA: Yes, business to business. And we market both standard and specialised products as well as specialist services, so it's completely based on technical characteristics of the products.

INTERVIEWER: Right. And how do you communicate with your customers? Is it direct marketing or through trade journals, magazines?

KRISTINA: It depends. The direct marketing approach is very important for us. Sure, our sales staff go out and talk to the customers themselves. But we also use a lot of internet marketing. We've got two websites.

INTERVIEWER: Right.

KRISTINA: And we use product brochures and magazines, but mainly our sales staff talk to our customers.

INTERVIEWER: So mostly it's direct marketing.

KRISTINA: Yes, mostly it's direct marketing with a focus on technical characteristics. But we also use brand image. Brand image is important, so we use the Lafarge image – as a large international company. The brand name is important to us. So we promote the brand on our websites, through magazines and brochures, we display our logo where we can. And we use sponsorship. We try to sponsor events where we use our logo. For example, we work on sponsorship with universities, so we offer our cement to the students for student projects and we get our logo on their brochures.

INTERVIEWER: Right. On another track, how important is relationship marketing?

KRISTINA: Yeah, that's very important to us because we have relationships over several years, over a long time. A dam project for example, it may take ten years. One other thing to mention is something we also take very seriously, which is market research. We're working on customer segmentation, and we carry out detailed customer satisfaction surveys. All that is, you know, really important these days.

2 You may need to play both parts of the recording more than once.

Track 20.2 tapescript ▶▶|

INTERVIEWER: What do many businesses do wrong in terms of marketing?

PETER: One thing businesses rely heavily on in terms of sales and marketing … is they don't take the trouble to find out about you, so you end up getting lots of rubbish in the post. So people still … you know, have this attitude of mass marketing. It's just not personal enough. And then the second side of it is they phone you up and everything is too rushed … they'll phone you up and they'll try and sell there and then, or it's 'Someone's in the area …' It's all too fast, too pushy.

INTERVIEWER: So what do you think has changed for the better over the years?

PETER: Well, obviously the IT side of marketing. You can buy computers now which are ten times as powerful for a fifth of the price now … compared with not so long ago …

INTERVIEWER: Yes.

PETER: … which has had a natural sort of impact on quality and also now that, you know, digital printers are around. You can sort of get your material to press without it going through any long drawn out process. So there are speed benefits too, everything is easier and quicker to produce and to receive.

Track 20.3 tapescript ▶▶|

INTERVIEWER: You've mentioned mass marketing. Do you think that with consumer marketing the secret is to avoid mass marketing, even where one is talking about consumer products?

PETER: Yeah, I would say it's all about careful market segmentation. And you have to develop database tools to do that.

INTERVIEWER: So, good research.

PETER: Yes, good market research, making sure you've segmented the data so that when … whilst you can't absolutely personalise it, you can at least send something to somebody who's expressed an interest, so you know you need good use of sales promotions. And I'll tell you one thing about the real big things that's important, it's all to do with after-sales service and customer satisfaction. It's to do proper customer satisfaction surveys.

INTERVIEWER: Right.

PETER: I would say to anybody, 'Look one thing if you're going to do anything, everybody, every business, if you sell to customers, whether they're consumers or businesses, run customer satisfaction surveys which are robust and, you know, just do it.'

What do you think?

How could the students' organisations improve their marketing? What could they do better? Is there anything else they should do?

The words you need ... to talk about marketing 2

1 Students may be able to complete the collocations without referring to the tapescripts. Also, rather than looking at the tapescripts they may prefer to listen to the recordings again to check their answers or fill in any gaps.

3 Make it clear to students that they should use the vocabulary in the previous exercises to answer the questions.

It's time to talk

- Guide individual students towards choosing an organisation they know well, so that they will be able to answer the questions.
- After doing the activity in pairs, selected students could present a brief summary of their chosen organisation, answering the file card questions, to the rest of the class who have to try to guess the identity of the organisation. They can ask other questions and the student 'in the chair' could draw its products, or its logo or offer other clues.

- You may want to use the Extra classroom activity here (see pages 96 and 118).

COMMUNICATING AT WORK

Meetings 2: Teleconferencing

- Ask students if they have ever taken part in a teleconference. You could also ask them to brainstorm the pros and cons. For example:
  Pros: participants don't have to travel, saves time
  Cons: no visual help, difficult to know when to speak, not clear who is talking to whom, people can start talking at the same time, problems with time zones.
- If your students never use teleconferencing, emphasise that the work included here revises a lot of general telephoning language as well as language for meetings.

1 • Introduce the scene and tell students that Rotaronga is fictional.
   • Get students to read the questions before you play all four extracts and elicit the answers. You may need to play the recording one part at a time.

1 Osaka
2 São Paulo
3 Oslo
4 She asks if she can record the meeting
5 Kyoji – it is impossible to continue there; the situation is unstable
6 They need more information; reports on the economic and political situations
7 There is an echo and there's a delay on the line
8 Kjell loses the connection / he gets cut off
9 She summarises the discussion
10 She will try to get the reports

2 Check the answers after each part. You may need to play the tracks more than once.

1 Dominique asks about the weather in Osaka.
2 Can you hear me all right?
3 Right, if everyone agrees, I'd like to record the meeting. Is that OK?
4 Give us your opinion about Rotaronga.
5 Kjell, you haven't said what you think.
6 Does everyone agree with that?
7 Kyoji: There's a strong echo on the line.
8 Maria Luisa: There's a delay on the line. I can hear you, Kyoji, but there's a delay of a few seconds.
9 Maria Luisa, can you repeat what you were saying about ...?
10 OK, I think we can finish here. Thanks, everyone.
11 Does anyone have anything else to add?
12 Dominique says: 'I'll summarise the discussion.'
    Alternatives: *Let's sum up. In summary ... In conclusion then, three points ...*

Track 20.4 tapescript ▶▶|

DOMINIQUE: Hello? Is that Kyoji? How's the weather in Osaka? Can you hear me OK?

KYOJI: Yes, everything's fine here, including the weather.

DOMINIQUE: Good. Now, hello Maria Luisa? How's the connection to São Paulo? Can you hear me all right?

MARIA LUISA: Yes, it's perfect.

DOMINIQUE: Kyoji, can you test your connection to Maria Luisa? Can you hear each other?

KYOJI: Yes, it works.

MARIA LUISA: It's OK.

DOMINIQUE: Finally, Kjell, how's everything in Oslo? Can you hear us?

KYOJI: Yes, it's very clear, no problem.

DOMINIQUE: Excellent. Right, if everyone agrees, I'd like to record the meeting. Is that OK?

ALL: Yes, OK. Fine, no problem.

Track 20.5 tapescript ▶▶|

DOMINIQUE: Kyoji, give us your opinion about the situation in Rotaronga.

KYOJI: On my last visit I thought it was impossible to continue in Rotaronga. The situation is too unstable.

DOMINIQUE: Who wants to respond to that? Does anyone have anything to say? Kjell, you haven't said what you think.

KJELL: I think we need more detailed information – a study of the economic situation in Rotaronga and also the political situation.

DOMINIQUE: Does everyone agree with that?

KYOJI: Yes, certainly, we need more information.

MARIA LUISA: We need a meeting.

DOMINIQUE: OK, but first we need more information. I'll get some reports organised and then we can discuss these by teleconference. It's too soon for a meeting.

Track 20.6 tapescript ▶▶|

DOMINIQUE: Please speak slowly and clearly. Don't talk over people. If you lose the connection, please redial. And please address everyone by name if you have a specific question.

KYOJI: Dominique, there's a strong echo on the line. But I can hear OK.

MARIA LUISA: Kyoji, there's a delay on the line. I can hear you, Kyoji, but there's a delay of a few seconds. Dominique, I wanted to tell you about the situation in Brazil ...

DOMINIQUE: OK, please. When anybody speaks, please leave a short space before you respond. If you can't hear anyone, please say so. Kjell? I think we've lost the connection to Kjell. Kjell, can you hear me? I don't think we can hear Kjell any more ... Maria Luisa, can you repeat what you were saying about the situation in Brazil?

MARIA LUISA: Yes, things are going OK – we are very optimistic, though it has not been easy.

KJELL: Hello. I'm back. I got cut off for a moment.

DOMINIQUE: OK, hello again. Welcome back.

Track 20.7 tapescript ▶▶|

DOMINIQUE: OK, I think we can finish here. Thanks, everyone. I'll summarise the discussion. We need detailed reports on the economic and political situation in Rotaronga and then we should have another teleconference. After that we will probably need a meeting in Paris, maybe in about a month. I think that's all. Does anyone have anything else to add?

ALL: No, OK, that's agreed.

DOMINIQUE: I'll send a summary of this teleconference by email. I hope we can have another discussion in two weeks. I will try to get the reports this week. Does everyone agree to that?

ALL: OK, thanks. Good.

DOMINIQUE: Bye for now.

ALL: Bye. Goodbye.

3 • Check that students understand the context. It may be worth eliciting what the rules of teleconferencing are, and remind them to follow the rules in their role-play. The key objective is to practise the language in the unit rather than focus on the content of the discussion. Ensure that each group appoints a chair, and elicit what the role of the chair is, i.e. he/she gives everyone the chance to speak, keeps an eye on the time, etc.
   • Before they begin, you could remind students of the work done on active listening and checking in Units 9 and 11.
   • As you listen to different groups, provide supportive feedback and constructive suggestions.

What did we do today?

Check the Remember section quickly and remind students of the objectives of this lesson.

Follow up

Encourage students to:

- record new vocabulary
- write down useful sentences for teleconferencing
- speak in English on the telephone with fellow students.

21 The Curious Incident of the Dog in the Night-time

What did we do last time?

Do a review of the last type 3 lesson (Unit 18). Remind students of what they worked on (see Teacher's notes for that unit) and do some quick revision as follows.

Social skills: Persuading

Ask students to give you strategies for persuading. Try to elicit the following:

- make it attractive
- make it personal
- repeat the message.

Then brainstorm possible ways of doing the above in English. In pairs get students to think of tasks related to their own work and then try to persuade their partner to do them.

Talking about holidays and holiday problems

Get students to think of nouns that go with the following to create compounds: *package*, *food*, *travel*, *money*, *tour*, *tourist*, *charter*.

On the agenda: Why are we doing this?

Tell students the objectives of this lesson:

- to practise talking about **books**
- to develop **social skills** for **dealing with people who are difficult to understand**
- to build **vocabulary** related to **books and reading**.

Reinforce this by writing the key words on the board or OHP.

Warm up

Ask students what makes it difficult to understand some people and try to elicit things like *fast speech*, *word linking*, *jargon*, *colloquial language*, etc. Ask what expressions students use to deal with these problems.

Dealing with people who are difficult to understand

What's the point?

See the Introduction (page 16): Type 3 units – social skills.

Answers

1 a She can't send emails or connect to the internet.
  b Roger doesn't bother to find out how much Liba knows about computers and assumes that she knows as much

about them as he does. He uses jargon which she doesn't understand. He needs to go through the instructions step by step, checking that she has understood. At the end of this conversation she still doesn't know what to do.

Track 21.1 tapescript ▶▶|

ROGER: How can I help you?

LIBA: Well, my computer's not working properly and I can't send emails or connect to the internet. It stopped working yesterday.

ROGER: Right. Are you on a modem or broadband?

LIBA: I'm on broadband.

ROGER: Right. It'll be the firewall. You need to check the permissions settings for your browser and email client, change the settings that are wrong, give full permission to both, and that should do the trick.

LIBA: Erm … permissions settings? I don't know how to do those things.

ROGER: Just go into the firewall options, see what the settings are, change them so they give full permission to your browser and email client, and you shouldn't have any problems after that.

LIBA: But I still don't know what to do …

Answers

2 a The firewall
  b The web page viewer, e.g. Internet Explorer
  c In this conversation, Roger starts off as before, assuming Liba can follow what he's saying, but she quickly explains that he needs to make things clear and answer her questions. She asks him to explain when she doesn't understand the jargon he uses. She asks him to explain the instructions step by step, and she checks that she understands what to do. As a result, he sorts out the problem and she understands what she needs to do.

3 a but I don't understand what you've just said
  b me through what to do exactly
  c that, please? What's the browser
  d And what did you mean about

Track 21.2 tapescript ▶▶|

ROGER: How can I help you?

LIBA: Well, my computer's not working properly and I can't send emails or connect to the internet. It stopped working yesterday.

ROGER: It'll be the firewall. You need to check the permissions settings for your browser and email client, change the settings that are wrong, give full permission to both, and that should do the trick.

LIBA: Look, I'm sorry but I don't understand what you've just said. Assume that I don't know that much about computers. Can you talk me through what to do exactly?

ROGER: OK. I'm fairly sure it's your firewall that's causing the problem. The firewall's a program that essentially stops someone accessing your computer over the internet. Is your router's ADSL light on?

LIBA: The router? What's that?

ROGER: It's the small box supplied by us which controls your connection.

LIBA: Yes, the light labelled ADSL is on.

ROGER: Good. Click on the icon for your firewall.

LIBA: Where's the icon? Is it at the bottom?

ROGER: Yes, it's in the bottom right-hand corner. Click that now to turn your firewall off. We'll turn it on again later.

LIBA: OK. I've done that. And I can see that the internet's working again.

ROGER: Good. That means it's definitely your firewall causing the problem. Now we need to check the permissions settings for your browser and email client.

LIBA: Can you explain that, please? What's the browser?

ROGER: It's your web page viewer. Most people use Internet Explorer.
LIBA: And what did you mean about permissions settings?
ROGER: You need to run the firewall from the Start menu. Click on Programs, look through the list, and give your browser full permission and your email client full permission.
LIBA: Can you talk me through it step by step?
ROGER: Sure. You need to look through the list until you find your browser. Have you got that?
LIBA: Yes, now what?
ROGER: Right click on browser, and left click on full permission.
LIBA: It's got a message saying Are you sure?
ROGER: Yes, that's fine. Click Yes and then …

Possible answers

4 Assumptions about subject
Sorry, but I'm not familiar with …
I'm new to this, could you explain it more simply?

Difficult words
What do you mean by …?
What does … mean?

Explaining too quickly
Could you go over that again more slowly?
Sorry, I didn't quite catch that.

Have a go

- See the Introduction (page 17): Type 3 units.
- It might be a good idea to demonstrate this activity before students do it in groups. This is a good way to get students to focus on using the right language, which you could write on the board or OHP. One possibility would be to talk about the basic rules of cricket, so for example, you could say the following:
  There are 11 players in each team.
  The objective of the batting team is to score as many runs as possible.
  The bowling team should try to get the batters out.
  They can do this by hitting the stumps with the ball.
  There should be a lot of things that students will not understand about this game and so it should encourage use of the target language.
- Give students a few minutes to prepare their subject; specify whether you want this to be work-related or not. Encourage them to use the language for dealing with people who are difficult to understand and remind them that Student A's topic should be difficult.

Background briefing: Autism

Autism is a lifelong developmental disability that affects the way a person communicates and relates to people around them. Children and adults with autism have difficulties with everyday social interaction. Their ability to develop friendships is generally limited as is their capacity to understand other people's emotional expressions. Asperger Syndrome is a type of autism.

People with autism can often have accompanying learning disabilities but everyone with the condition shares a difficulty in making sense of the world. They generally experience three main areas of difficulty.

- Social interaction (difficulty with social relationships, for example appearing aloof and indifferent to other people)
- Social communication (difficulty with verbal and non-verbal communication, for example not fully understanding the meaning of common gestures, facial expressions or tone of voice)
- Imagination (difficulty in the development of interpersonal play and imagination, for example having a limited range of imaginative activities, possibly copied and pursued rigidly and repetitively).

For more information about autism and Asperger Syndrome, go to the *English365* website: www.cambridge.org/elt/english365.

Read on

Books

While discussing the initial questions, also mention that people who read for pleasure become better readers more quickly, so encourage them to do this. Ask which books they have read and what they were about, but don't spend too much time on this as it will be covered later in the lesson.

1 Give a time limit for students to answer the questions. Tell students not to worry about the vocabulary in the text as this will be dealt with later.

Answers

1 Mark Haddon is the author of a book called *The Curious Incident of the Dog in the Night-time* about an autistic boy.
2 The book has won three prizes (the Whitbread best novel of the year award, the Guardian children's fiction prize and the Book Trust teenage fiction prize).

2 Get students to read through the questions and check the meaning of insane.

Answers

1 Almost everyone
2 The Whitbread best novel of the year award; £5,000
3 The Whitbread book of the year award; £25,000
4 Because he thought his work was inferior
5 He can't understand other people's emotions and he finds it difficult to communicate

3 • Stress that students will need to infer the answers to these questions, rather than find the direct answers in the text.
  • It would be good to recommend this particular book to students, especially if they haven't read a book in English before. It is written reasonably simply and is a very good read at the same time.

Answers

1 At the beginning of the book, he is 15 years, 3 months and 2 days old.
2 Siobhan is his teacher at the special school which he attends.
3 Christopher is an autistic boy – he observes human emotions but doesn't understand them.
4 Perhaps he is angry or upset because he doesn't understand why she laughs.
5 He likes prime numbers so he uses them to number his chapters.

The words you need ... to talk about books and reading

1 You might get students to look at the words to see if they are familiar with any of them before they look back at the text.

Answers

1 single out: choose one person or thing from a group to criticise or praise them
2 award: prize winner
3 intractable: very difficult – an intractable problem is one which is almost impossible to solve
4 sell handsomely: when a book sells handsomely, it sells very well
5 word of mouth: people learn about a book, a film, a product, etc. by word of mouth, not, for example, through advertising, but because they tell each other about it
6 fiction: literature and stories about imaginary people and events
7 empathy: the ability to understand what it is like in someone else's situation
8 entanglements: the entanglements of life are the difficult and complicated ties from which it is difficult to escape
9 gifts: natural abilities or skills
10 patterns: a particular way that something is often done or repeated

2 Get students to discuss possible meanings of the words in pairs before they try to fill the gaps.

Answers

1 bookshop, library   2 browse, flip through
3 paperback, hardback   4 fiction, non-fiction
5 plot, characterisation   6 novelist, poet

3 When you go through the answers, check the meaning of the phrases. For example, you might need to make it clear that *I couldn't put it down* means 'It was so exciting I couldn't stop reading it.'

Answers

1 down   2 set   3 about   4 characters
5 suspense   6 out   7 copy   8 recommend

It's time to talk

- Give students some phrases to help them talk about their book. For example:
  It's a ... (kind of book)
  It's set in ... (setting)
  The main characters are ... (characters)
  Basically, it's about ... (story)
  I liked it because ...
  What I liked about it was ...
- After students have discussed their books in pairs, you could ask individual students to present their book to the rest of the class.
- You may want to use the Extra classroom activity here (see pages 96 and 119).

What did we do today?

Check the Remember section quickly and remind students of the objectives of this lesson.

Follow up

Encourage students to:
- read books in English – perhaps graded readers or the book featured in this unit
- write down new vocabulary in their vocabulary books
- record useful phrases for dealing with people they don't understand.

22 Photo management

What did we do last time?

Do a review of the last type 1 lesson (Unit 19). Remind students of what they worked on (see Teacher's notes for that unit) and do some quick revision as follows.

The passive
Ask students for five different ways in which we use the passive. Elicit the following:
- to describe business or technical processes
- to report facts in formal written English
- to describe an action when it is not important who did it
- to politely avoid blaming a specific individual
- to focus our message by giving additional information about something we have just mentioned in a previous sentence.

See if students can give you an example for each use of the passive.

Pronunciation: Linking
Write the following sentences on the board:
Have you done it yet?
Have you ever been to Spain?
She always arrives early.
I waited for a few minutes.
She left Poland in 1997.
He had to go.
Get students to mark the different ways in which the words are linked. Then get them to practise saying the sentences in pairs.

On the agenda: Why are we doing this?

Tell students the objectives of this lesson:
- to improve **speaking skills: discussing possibilities**
- to revise the **first, second and third conditional**
- to improve pronunciation: **modal verbs with** *have* **in third conditional sentences.**

Reinforce this by writing the key words on the board or OHP.

Warm up

Also ask students what they take photographs of. Do they use a camcorder? Ask students what a corporate photographer is. If you have time, you could write the names of selected international companies on the board and ask them what kind of photographs they would take for them, for example McDonald's, Nike, BMW and Coca-Cola. What kind of image would they like to create for each company?

Background briefing: Statoil

Statoil is a Norwegian oil and gas company which is represented in 29 different countries, with its head office in Stavanger. About half of its 24,000 employees work in Norway. One of the world's largest offshore oil and gas operators, it is a major supplier of crude oil, and a leading supplier of petrol in Scandinavia, Poland, Ireland and the Baltic states as well as a major provider of natural gas in Europe. For more information about Statoil, go to the *English365* website: www.cambridge.org/elt/english365.

Listen to this

Taking pictures and telling stories

1 Tell students that they don't need to write full sentences – they can just writes notes for this exercise.

1 buys photos from agencies
2 It's part of public relations
3 1986
4 you can always meet different people
5 The new CEO
6 People who work for Statoil in the new service station

Track 22.1 tapescript ▶▶

INTERVIEWER: So, Harald, I know that you're Manager of Photo and Video in Statoil. Does that mean that you take pictures yourself or you manage and sub-contract the work?

HARALD: We have a photographer who travels around full time, but my main responsibilities are to take pictures myself and I buy a lot of photos from agencies.

INTERVIEWER: So you look at what's offered and then you say if it's right for Statoil or not?

HARALD: Yeah.

INTERVIEWER: And how many images do you have in your archive?

HARALD: Around 50,000.

INTERVIEWER: Wow! And this is, I guess, quite an important activity because it's part of public relations, very important to the oil industry, the energy industry, with pollution and environmental issues.

HARALD: Absolutely.

INTERVIEWER: So how did you move into this area, Harald? Did you always want to be a photographer?

HARALD: I started in Statoil in 1986 and always worked with pictures. It's always been an interest so I've taken quite a lot of courses with professional photographers in Norway.

INTERVIEWER: If you'd had the chance to be a professional photographer, would you have done that?

HARALD: Yes, maybe. Photography was always a hobby, but I really enjoy the work in Statoil. It's a big company, there are 24,000 different people in the company in 29 different countries. So it's nice, you can meet very different people in the Statoil family, as they say. Next week I have to take pictures of our new CEO, so it's an interesting job.

INTERVIEWER: Do you travel a lot?

HARALD: Not so very much. Next year I'll travel a little more. But one month ago I went to Estonia. My job was to take pictures of the new service station and take pictures of the people who work there and we also interviewed the manager of the Statoil office there. Tallin is a great place.

INTERVIEWER: So did the people in Tallin enjoy being photographed?

HARALD: Not everybody. Some of them, yeah. But some people just hate photographers.

2 1 He didn't have much time.
2 Getting closer to people, using more colour
3 On the front cover of the internal magazine
4 To be interested in people / sensitive to people
5 To tell an interesting story
6 Nelson Mandela, because he has a beautiful face and a fantastic story to tell

Track 22.2 tapescript ▶▶

INTERVIEWER: So, how many pictures did you take in Tallin?

HARALD: A few. If I'd had more time, I would have taken a lot more pictures of the old town, just sat there with a beer and photographed the people. It was minus ten but it's beautiful.

INTERVIEWER: OK. And when you take photos like this in Tallin, do you have to follow a certain business company style or can you take more artistic photographs?

HARALD: It's mostly business but we're also trying to give pictures a new image. We call it a 'new look' in Statoil. That means that you go a little closer to the people and that you use more colour in the picture.

INTERVIEWER: Interesting. And what's the best picture you've ever taken?

HARALD: The best ever picture I've taken, this was two weeks ago.

INTERVIEWER: What was it?

HARALD: It was a woman who works in finance. I'd asked her to wear clothes that had a good colour. And she had this scarf with a lot of different colours and very good eye contact with me ... you can see ... this picture will be published on the front cover of our internal magazine.

INTERVIEWER: It's really good. So, if you had to give me some advice about being a good photographer, what would you say? What's the secret?

HARALD: I think the main quality of a good photographer is to be very interested in people. If you want to take good photos of people, you need to be interested in people, you have to be sensitive to people.

INTERVIEWER: OK. And what's a good photograph for you? What essential ingredient do you try to capture in your photos?

HARALD: I always want my pictures to tell an interesting story. So I try to communicate with people and let them tell me their story. And then I take the picture. So it's a lot of psychology. Even when I meet a drunk in the street, it's the same. I think everybody has a good story to tell.

INTERVIEWER: And if you had the chance to meet and photograph somebody famous, who would you like to do? Who's the best subject for a photograph?

HARALD: That's a very difficult question. Perhaps ... Nelson Mandela. The photographer that did a workshop for me in Norway, he'd taken some pictures of Nelson Mandela. And I think of all the people, if I'd had the chance, I'd have taken Nelson Mandela – a beautiful face and a fantastic story to tell.

What do you think?

Also ask students why they would like to take pictures of that famous person. To stimulate discussion, you could ask if students have a hobby now. What is it? Why do they enjoy it? How often do they do it?

Check your grammar

Revision of first and second conditional; third conditional

1 Ask students what they can remember about the first and second conditional before you look at the sentences. Can they make any sentences themselves? Students will probably have studied this at some stage before, if not in *English365* Book 2, so stress that this is a revision section and that you want to focus on accuracy and range of use.

Answers

In the first conditional sentence, the speaker feels it is possible that he/she will have time to show the pictures.
In the second conditional sentence, the speaker is obviously very busy and doesn't think he/she will have the time to show them.

2 Students may well have problems with the fluent pronunciation of these sentences, so tell them that you will look at the pronunciation later in the lesson.

Answers

2 b
3 *If* + past perfect tense + modal verb + *have* + past participle
4 1 would   2 had

5 Thinking of the functions of conditional sentences may be more useful than thinking of them as just a grammatical structure. See if students can think of another sentence for each function.

Answers

1 e   2 c   3 a   4 b   5 d

Do it yourself

Students can do these exercises individually or in pairs.

Answers

1 1 If she phones, I'll ask her to contact you.
2 It would save a lot of money if we did this.
3 If you rent the office space for 12 months, we will offer you a 10% discount.
4 If you sent me the invoice, I would pay you.
5 You wouldn't have lost it if you had saved the data before you sent it.
6 I would have helped immediately if he'd told me about the problem.
2 *Suggested answers*
1 ... I'll help you prepare your presentation.
2 If you worked a bit more carefully, you wouldn't make mistakes.
3 If you don't stop doing this, I'll report you to the management.
4 If I were you, I'd buy some spare keys.

3 1 If sales had been better / If sales hadn't been so bad, the company wouldn't have fired me.
2 If my English had been better / If my English hadn't been so poor, I would have understood my colleagues from London.
3 If the traffic hadn't been so bad, I wouldn't have missed my flight.
4 1 will include   2 had sent   3 arranged
4 won't include   5 had known   6 made   7 will stick
8 email
a a criticism: If you had sent it to me ... (2) / If I had known ... (5)
b a threat: Please note that if your article is late again ... (4)
c advice: Just as an idea, if you arranged ... (3)
d an offer to help: In future, would it be useful if I made sure ... (6) / I promise that if we agree a deadline ... (7)

Sounds good

Modal verbs with *have* in third conditional sentences

1 Tell students that you are now going to look at the fluent pronunciation of this structure. Remind them that although they may find it difficult at first, the most important thing initially is to be able to understand what is being said, rather than being able to reproduce the pronunciation perfectly themselves.

Answers

1 I'd   2 She'd   3 couldn't   4 might   5 wouldn't   6 we'd

Track 22.3 tapescript ▶▶|

1 If you'd told me about the problem, I'd have helped.
2 She'd have come to the meeting if she'd had time.
3 If I hadn't gone to the interview, I couldn't have got the job.
4 They might have got it by now if you'd sent the package a day earlier.
5 If you'd saved the file first, you wouldn't have lost it.
6 If we'd reached our targets, we'd have got a very good bonus.

2 You might need to demonstrate this yourself several times and give students time to practise on their own.

3 Also demonstrate these sounds for students and get them to practise in pairs.

It's time to talk

- The key facts should be decisions that students made and things that they did. You could demonstrate this yourself before students go on to work in pairs.
- You could develop this by getting students to make a comment about their partner's key facts. In this way, students will have to listen carefully to what their partner says before they make a third conditional sentence.
- You may want to use the Extra classroom activity here (see pages 96 and 120).

What did we do today?

Check the Remember section quickly and remind students of the objectives of the lesson.

Follow up

Encourage students to:
- write sentences about themselves using conditionals
- write up what they talked about in *It's time to talk* and hand it in to you.

23 Children's world

What did we do last time?

Do a review of the last type 2 lesson (Unit 20). Remind students of what they worked on and do some quick revision as follows.

Talking about marketing and market research
Brainstorm as many words as possible connected to marketing and market research. You could help students by giving the first part of some of the common collocations in Unit 20. For example: *mass, direct, brand, consumer, market, after-sales.*
In pairs, get students to talk about the marketing in their organisation using some of the words above.

Meetings: Teleconferencing
Ask students for some of the rules for teleconferences. Try to elicit the following:
* use names when you want to speak to someone
* leave a pause before responding
* don't speak over people
* speak slowly and clearly.
Ask students how to do the following in English:
* begin with small talk
* ask for repetition
* summarise at the end.
If you have time, you could set up a quick teleconference role-play. Put students into small groups and get them to, say, arrange a face-to-face meeting together.

On the agenda: Why are we doing this?

Tell students the objectives of this lesson:
* to talk about **setting up meetings**
* to build **vocabulary** related to **meetings and conferences**
* to develop skills for **negotiating: bargaining and reaching a compromise.**
Reinforce this by writing the key words on the board or OHP.

Background briefing: UNICEF

The United Nations Children's Fund is a global organisation dedicated to the protection of children and aims to overcome the poverty, violence, disease and discrimination that can affect them worldwide. UNICEF helps children get the care and stimulation they need in the early years of life and encourages families to educate girls as well as boys. It strives to reduce childhood death and illness and to protect children in the midst of war and natural disaster, including those affected by HIV/AIDS. It was set up in 1946 by the United Nations to care for the children in Europe affected by the Second World War. It now works in 157 countries around the world. For more information about UNICEF, go to the *English365* website: www.cambridge.org/elt/english365.

You may want to use the Extra classroom activity here (see pages 97 and 121) as a lead in to the unit.

Warm up

Also ask what kind of meeting it was. Was it formal or informal? What was its purpose?

Listen to this

Working for the international community

1 Before students look at the issues, ask them what they think might be involved in setting up a meeting. Can they predict anything that Yoshihisa Togo talks about?

Answers

1 He mentions:
  1 distance   2 accommodation   3 transportation
  4 time zones   5 language
  He does not mention: weather, administration, too many meetings
2 1 Distance is problematic because delegates come from Europe and North America.
  2 Accommodation is expensive.
  3 Transportation is expensive.
  4 Delegates come from different time zones on long haul flights and so there's the problem of jet lag.
  5 The language can cause some difficulties (they usually use English at UNICEF meetings).

Track 23.1 tapescript ▶▶|

INTERVIEWER: Is your office involved in planning and setting up international meetings?
TOGO-SAN: Yes. For instance, next year our Committee will celebrate its 50th anniversary, so we are now sending out invitations for next year's National Committees Annual Meeting, to be held in Japan. So that is, you know, a big event.
INTERVIEWER: It certainly will be. So what are the practical problems about setting up such an event?
TOGO-SAN: Well, mainly distance. Distance from the major national committees because most of the national committees are located in Europe ...
INTERVIEWER: Yes.
TOGO-SAN: ... and some in North American countries, but mainly from Europe. And part of this is two related difficulties, perhaps the major ones: how to get inexpensive accommodation and inexpensive transportation – the costs are important in both these areas. We don't want to spend a lot of money on these things.
INTERVIEWER: Yes, I understand. And obviously you have time differences and that sort of thing to contend with?
TOGO-SAN: Yes, of course, that too. Delegates come from different time zones. That affects the time to acclimatise after a long haul flight. Maybe a day – a day of jet lag.
INTERVIEWER: Yes, I'm sure. So what about language? Is translation a significant barrier in international meetings?
TOGO-SAN: Yes, it can be, we have had some difficulties, but it's not a big problem for UNICEF.
INTERVIEWER: Why? Do you use translation facilities or interpreting? Simultaneous interpreting?
TOGO-SAN: No, we don't normally do that.
INTERVIEWER: Right. So ...
TOGO-SAN: For the annual conference of national committees, and at headquarters meetings, we only use English.
INTERVIEWER: So English is the official language of the organisation?

TOGO-SAN: Well, actually UNICEF is a United Nations organisation so the official languages are not limited to English. But mostly English is used, only rarely translation. Using English usually avoids the need for translation.

3 Students do not need to write full sentences here.

Answers

1 Security has been discussed (UNICEF is a UN organisation) but it is not a major issue.
2 To help the children in countries where they really need help (the supply of water, vaccinations, education).
3 Teleconferencing is sometimes useful if someone cannot attend a meeting.
4 Video-conferencing is useful and the technology is improving.

Track 23.2 tapescript ▶▶

INTERVIEWER: Togo-San, I have another question about international meetings. Has the issue of security become much more evident in the planning and execution of UNICEF meetings?

TOGO-SAN: Not really. We are a UN organisation so evidently there must be some serious discussion about how to protect delegates, or country representatives, at meetings. But our main priority is to help the children in countries where they really need help, you know the supply of water, vaccinations, education.

INTERVIEWER: Yes, these are the priorities, of course. And for meetings, have you much experience of video-conferencing or teleconferencing?

TOGO-SAN: These facilities are sometimes useful, yes, if someone is unable to attend in person. Mainly this might happen for headquarters meetings, meetings in New York.

INTERVIEWER: So you use teleconference facilities?

TOGO-SAN: Yes, where the rest of the people are in one room and you are connected with a telecom line.

INTERVIEWER: Yes. And is that satisfactory?

TOGO-SAN: Well, yes, so far no problems. And video-conferencing is also possible and the technology is improving.

What do you think?

Some students, of course, may not have any experience of setting up meetings, so you could ask them how meetings they have been to were organised. Who organised them? How were they invited?

The words you need ... to talk about meetings and conferences

Students can do these exercises individually or in pairs. After they have finished the exercises, get them to make sentences about their own organisation using the vocabulary.

Suggested answers

1
Before the meeting   planning   send out invitations
plan agenda   arrange venue   fix accommodation
registration
During the meeting   video link   networking
simultaneous interpreting   provide refreshments
provide technical support
After the meeting   study feedback   write report
plan next meeting
People   chair   administrative support   delegates
organising committee   PA

2 Students can talk through the meaning of these words with a partner before they do the matching.

Answers

2 1 networking   2 video link   3 conference   4 translation
5 security   6 teleconferencing   7 registration
8 congress   9 delegates   10 interpreting
3 1 d/f 2 e 3 a 4 h 5 c 6 b/f/c/e 7 f 8 g
4 Suggested answers
1 send out invitations
2 complete the registration process
3 pay attention to security
4 keep to the agenda
5 fill in a feedback form
6 study the feedback
7 write up a report
8 arrange another meeting

It's time to talk

- Get students to build up a picture of the business by brainstorming a possible profile. Ask questions like: *Where is the meeting going to take place? Where are the subsidiaries? How many departments are there?*
- Encourage students to use vocabulary from the unit. Give them some useful phrases that will help during the discussion. For example:
  We'll need to ...
  We'll have to ...
- After they have finished the group activity, selected groups could feed back to the rest of the class.
- If you haven't already done so, you may want to use the Extra classroom activity here (see pages 97 and 121).

COMMUNICATING AT WORK

Negotiating 2: Bargaining and reaching a compromise

- Explain that you are now going to continue looking at useful language for negotiating and remind them of the work they did earlier on stating preferences. Reaching agreement is the next stage of negotiating.
- Before you start, see if students can tell you the structure of a negotiation without looking at the diagram in the Student's Book.

Answers

1 1 The second speaker can't write the whole report.
2 They agree to write half of the report each.

Track 23.3 tapescript ▶▶

A: Hi, Rob, have you written the report on the meeting last week?
B: No, I haven't.
A: Can you do it? We need it this afternoon.
B: Well, I can't do all of it. I tell you what, if I write the first part on the new partnership and you write the second part on the marketing plan, we could do it together and get it finished.
A: Yes, OK. Then we can check each half and put it together ... I'll email you my bit when I've done it.
B: Fine. Talk to you later.

3 Play the track again and stop after each sentence if necessary.

Track 23.4 tapescript ▶▶|

A: Now, we need to agree on the unit cost. We would like to suggest €550 per unit, plus delivery and training costs on top.

B: Well, I think that's rather high. Perhaps if you include the cost of the delivery and training costs we can accept that.

A: Delivery and training? I don't think we can agree to that, not the training. But we'll take care of the delivery if the unit cost is €550. The training is an additional cost, I think you can see that.

B: OK, we'll accept that.

A: Thanks. I'm sure that's a fair position. €550 per unit, we pay delivery and you pay the costs for training.

4 • Set the scene. Give students a few minutes to look at their file cards and prepare what they are going to say. Remind them to use the language from the unit.
• When they have finished the role-play, get students to feed back to the rest of the class to see who got the best deal.

What did we do today?

Check the Remember section quickly and remind students of the objectives of this lesson.

Follow up

Encourage students to:
• keep a record of useful vocabulary
• record useful language for negotiating in a separate part of their vocabulary books.

24 Going up?

What did we do last time?

Do a review of the last type 3 lesson (Unit 21). Remind students of what they worked on (see Teacher's notes for that unit) and do some quick revision as follows.

Social skills: Dealing with people who are difficult to understand

Elicit ways of dealing with people who are difficult to understand:
• make sure the person understands how much you know about the subject

• ask them to explain difficult words
• ask them to explain step by step
• ask questions to check you've understood.

Ask students for ways of doing these things in English. Quickly get students to explain an aspect of their job to a partner. Encourage the use of these techniques.

Talking about books and reading

Ask students to give you words for the following definitions:
• a book with a cover made of thin card
• a book with a stiff cover
• a book about real events
• a book about imaginary characters
• the writer of a book about imaginary characters
• the main story in a book
• to look quickly at the pages of a book.

On the agenda: Why are we doing this?

Tell students the objectives of this lesson:
• to practise talking about **career coaching**
• to develop **social skills** for **dealing with conflict**
• to build **vocabulary** connected to **your education**.
Reinforce this by writing the key words on the board or OHP.

You may want to refer students to the unit title and explain that you might hear this in a lift.

Warm up

Ask students what is meant by *conflict*. Try to elicit that it can just be differences of opinion or people wanting different things, and not necessarily arguments. If students don't want to talk about themselves, they could talk about a situation they are aware of.

Dealing with conflict

What's the point?

See the Introduction (page 16): Type 3 units – social skills.

Track 24.1 tapescript ▶▶|

HANNAH: Where've you been? I've been waiting for ages. I was about to go …

PABLO: Sorry. I had a meeting which went on for ever and then Marie stopped me as I was rushing out, and finally when I got out it was raining and the traffic was dreadful because the rain was so heavy and it took three times as long as usual …

HANNAH: I just hate starting late. It's just such a waste of time and effort. It almost seems not worth starting at all.

PABLO: Look, I'm sorry. You don't have to go on about it. It wasn't my fault …

HANNAH: Well, if it happens once more, I'm going to give up playing tennis with you. I'll find another partner. OK?

PABLO: Well, you don't have to react like that. It's not my fault that the traffic was absolutely terrible. And it's not always me. What about the time you …

Answers

2 a Because it's a waste of time and effort
   b 7 o'clock
   c Hannah is still angry and aggressive but Pablo is more conciliatory. He makes it clear how sorry he is and makes sure she can see his point of view. By the end he has managed to deal with the conflict successfully.
3 a make sure it doesn't happen again
   b and see it from my point of view
   c agree that it's not always possible
   d you accept my point

Track 24.2 tapescript ▶▶|

HANNAH: Where've you been? I've been waiting for ages. I was about to go …

PABLO: I'm sorry I'm so late. I had a meeting which went on for ever and then … oh well, I guess I should have tried to leave the meeting earlier.

HANNAH: I just hate starting late. It's just such a waste of time and effort. It almost seems not worth starting at all.

PABLO: OK, I really am sorry. I'll really try and make sure it doesn't happen again. OK?

HANNAH: It's just that I can't stand not starting on time. If you can't promise to be on time, I'm going to give up playing tennis with you. I'll find another partner. OK?

PABLO: Oh, Hannah, I'm sorry you're so upset. It would be a real pity to stop just because I got delayed this once. But try and see it from my point of view. It's sometimes very difficult to get out of important meetings and …

HANNAH: If you say you're going to be here at 7 o'clock then I think you should be here at 7 o'clock, that's all.

PABLO: Yes, you're right in principle and I do normally try and get here on time but you have to agree that it's not always possible. Everyone's late sometimes, aren't they?

HANNAH: Well, I try hard not to be. But yes, I guess sometimes there's not much you can do about it.

PABLO: OK, I'm glad that you accept my point. Now let's go in and enjoy it. That's why we've come. OK?

HANNAH: OK.

Possible answers

4 An irritated friend
   Sorry, but I've been really busy recently.
   We could see if there are still some available.

   A member of the family
   I'll do it now.
   Well, I did it last time.

   A work colleague
   I said I'd try to make the call but I've been very busy today.
   Sorry, I didn't realise that it was so important.

Have a go

- See the Introduction (page 17): Type 3 units.
- Set the scene and give students some time to prepare for the role-play.
- Afterwards, selected students could feed back to the rest of the class. Who dealt best with the conflict? Why?

Read on

Careers

- Ask students what *career* means. Get them to explain the difference between a *career* and a *job*. (The *Cambridge Advanced Learner's Dictionary* definition of *career* is: the job or series of jobs that you do during your working life, especially if you continue to get better jobs and earn more money.)
- You could also ask why people change their jobs. Ask if the trend in their country has changed recently.

1 Make sure students are clear about the task here. They are not expected to find the answers to the questions in the texts. You could get students to read the texts quickly and ask them to summarise the situation for each person before they do the task.

Answers

1 Kevin Walters   2 Bruno Lundby   3 Clara Hart
4 Andrew James   5 Kevin LeRoux

2 • Give a time limit for this.
   • When students look again at the questions in exercise 1, stress again that they should infer the answers from the contexts.

Answers

1 He runs *Better Business* magazine with his wife
2 Colleagues, holidays and company pension schemes
3 He might find it more difficult to get a job in accountancy
4 Working in a CD shop for a few months
5 Because he didn't have any formal qualifications
6 There is a policy of career progression
7 She's an operations director with UBS; she expects more international postings
8 Because there are only a few other house-husbands where he lives / socialising with the mothers can be awkward
9 It has nothing to do with her current job
10 Negotiating and persuading people

3 Remind students that understanding how different parts of a sentence relate is an important skill for understanding texts more easily and being able to use more complex sentences in their writing.

Answers

1 where: a converted mill in a valley in Wales
2 which: *Better Business* magazine
3 when: in the new year
4 this: taking a job as a cashier in a high street bank
5 it: the fact that he had once worked in a CD shop
6 which: ISS
7 here: in Connecticut
8 it: socialising with mothers
9 It: being a house-husband
10 The ones: the skills

Reading tip

Stress how important reading is for pleasure. Ask students if they have started reading the book from Unit 21 yet.

The words you need ... to talk about your education

1 Explain that learning suffixes will help students say things in different ways and so extend their range of expression.

1 pension, succession, progression, qualification, operation, organisation, production, negotiation
2 pension (no verb), succeed, progress, qualify, operate, organise, produce, negotiate
3 operational (the word in the article is *organisational*)

2 When students talk to their partners about their education, encourage them to expand where possible. Tell them to talk about the age they did each thing, where it was, what subject(s) they studied, etc. Encourage the listener to ask questions to get more details. You could start things off by talking about your own education.

1 Went to nursery school / kindergarten
2 Started primary school
3 Moved to secondary school
4 Applied to university
5 Sat university entrance exams
6 Went to university
7 Graduated from university
8 Began to study for higher degree
9 Successfully completed Master's degree
10 Began doctorate
11 Wrote doctoral thesis
12 Awarded doctorate

It's time to talk

- Make sure that students are clear about what is meant by *brand* (how the students would present themselves).
- You may want to use the Extra classroom activity here (see pages 97 and 122).

What did we do today?

Check the Remember section quickly and remind students of the objectives of the lesson.

Follow up

Encourage students to:
- read for pleasure – you could ask them to read articles or books in English and then get them to report back to a partner every other week on what they have read
- record useful vocabulary
- write down phrases for dealing with conflict.

25 International education – planning for the future

What did we do last time?

Do a review of the last type 3 lesson (Unit 22). Remind students of what they worked on (see Teacher's notes for that unit) and do some quick revision as follows.

First, second and third conditionals
Ask students to give you examples of first, second and third conditional sentences. For example:
If you work harder, you'll finish on time.
If you worked harder, you'd finish on time.
If you'd worked harder, you'd have finished on time.
Get students to tell you the difference between the sentences and quickly go over the grammatical forms. Then ask for the various functions of conditionals (i.e. regret, criticism, advice, threat and offer to help) and get them to give you an example of each. Students could work in pairs for this.

Pronunciation: Modal verbs with have in third conditional sentences
Focus on the third conditional sentences that came up in the revision activity above and go over the pronunciation. Ask students to practise saying the sentences with a partner.

On the agenda: Why are we doing this?

Tell students the objectives of the lesson:
- to improve **speaking skills: discussing future plans**
- to review the grammar of **future reference: present tenses,** *will*, *going to*, **the future continuous**
- to improve **pronunciation: chunking and pausing.**

Reinforce this by writing the key words on the board or OHP.

Warm up

To stimulate discussion, you could also ask students what training they have done recently. What was it? What did it involve? How useful was it?

Background briefing: Amigos sem Fronteiras and FöreningsSparbanken

Amigos sem Fronteiras
Amigos sem Fronteiras or 'Friends without Frontiers' is a Portuguese charity dedicated to helping young people in underdeveloped countries such as Mozambique. Their activities include finding penpals for young people in Mozambique as well as raising money to go towards their education. The charity also aims to renovate buildings in order to create a study and support centre for young people, to organise a variety of training programmes and train teachers.

FöreningsSparbanken
FöreningsSparbanken (FSB) is a banking business that serves over ten million customers, corporate and private,

across Scandinavia and in the Baltic region. The bank offers customers classical banking services including savings accounts, credit cards, electronic banking and loans, but it also provides investment business in the commodity, stock, and money markets. The company has over 15,000 employees, of whom 8932 are in Sweden.

For more information about Amigos sem Fronteiras and FöreningsSparbanken, go to the *English365* website: www.cambridge.org/elt/english365.

Listen to this

Developing people

1 Get students to read through the profiles before you play the tracks.

Track 25.1 tapescript ▶▶|

INTERVIEWER: Marcus, why did you set up Amigos sem Fronteiras?

MARCUS: I was invited to Mozambique in the 80s and when I went there and saw the poor areas, I had to help. And so my idea was to set up this organisation.

INTERVIEWER: And what's the main objective?

MARCUS: We work in poor or developing countries in education. So at the moment we're working in Mozambique to help local people and the government set up secondary schools, to help development.

INTERVIEWER: How do you raise money?

MARCUS: Well, we have on the website the possibility for anyone to help. We give information about a person studying, and then you partner or sponsor them. For the future, we're trying to get governments involved in Brussels.

INTERVIEWER: OK. Interesting. So what's your next project?

MARCUS: We're going to start rebuilding or repairing a library soon with over 25,000 books ... that will be opening in January next year so that a primary school and secondary school can use it ... that's over 4,000 students.

INTERVIEWER: What's the deadline?

MARCUS: It should open in January next year.

Track 25.2 tapescript ▶▶|

INTERVIEWER: Dani, you're a management trainer, a competence manager. What does a competence manager do? Plan training and personal development for people?

DANI: Exactly, but we do it together. I'm a competence manager for around 25 people. And we talk once a month and get an agreement on how people want to develop ... some want training in presentations, team building ... everyone's different.

INTERVIEWER: What training programmes will you run in the future?

DANI: I only have one course planned ... the next is ... we're running a team-building seminar in Stockholm, in a hotel ... the important thing is not to be at the company.

INTERVIEWER: You have another job as well, I think?

DANI: Yes, I own my own company called JKM – organisation and team development ... for leadership, management and team building.

INTERVIEWER: Are you going to go 100% with that in the future?

DANI: That's what I want. But I work a lot with older managers and when I tell them how they should manage, they always ask me what my experience is. So I have to work as a manager for five years at least, then maybe I can go 100% as a management trainer. It's a question of credibility.

2 Play the tracks before students look at the questions. When they have listened once, get students to try to answer the questions. You may need to play the tracks again.

Track 25.3 tapescript ▶▶|

INTERVIEWER: What plans do you have for next year, for future development?

MARCUS: We bought some old army barracks and we're going to rebuild those into a new school – for both secondary level and also to teach professional skills.

INTERVIEWER: What kind of impact will this have both short and medium term?

MARCUS: The problem is that after secondary school it's difficult to go on to another school because they are too far away ... about 3,000 kilometres. So what we want is that they study in the area where they're living, and can learn a profession and, the next but most important objective in a way, is to help people to start working in their own region too.

INTERVIEWER: Like a catalyst for the local economy – to stop migration to the big cities?

MARCUS: Exactly. So I'll be spending a lot of time here ... to rebuild the army barracks ... and also to look at other countries, what we can do to support education development elsewhere in Africa.

INTERVIEWER: Where will you be five years from now? What's the long-term vision?

MARCUS: We'll need about three more years for this project, then the vision is to expand into other provinces in Mozambique and then maybe also Zimbabwe. But that means we'll have to grow because we're still a very small organisation.

Track 25.4 tapescript ▶▶|

INTERVIEWER: Do you think you'll ever move back to Iran, Dani?

DANI: I don't think to live there. You know, when I'm in Iran they don't accept me as a real Iranian, they say I'm a foreigner ... so it would be strange to begin again in a country where you don't even know how to act. But there's a pragmatic family reason – my wife and children are Swedish and don't speak Farsi.

INTERVIEWER: I guess there are many interesting cultural differences between Sweden and Iran, how people act?

DANI: Oh, yes. Some very obvious differences. For example, it's very common if you know somebody well that they want to kiss you on the cheek, three times. In Sweden, you don't do that as a man.

INTERVIEWER: OK. Interesting.

DANI: And another interesting thing, in Europe when you look down, you think someone is lying. In Iran when a person doesn't look in your eyes, they're showing respect – maybe you're older or have a higher rank. So I had that problem when I moved from Iran as a child. At school when a teacher is angry with you in Iran, you have to look at the floor – in Sweden they want you to look at them – and then my father would get angry with me ... why are you looking at me?

INTERVIEWER: So will you be doing more of this kind of cultural coaching in the future?

DANI: Yes, I hope so ... two reasons for that. First, I know I like it. When I worked at the tax department in Sweden, I actually gave courses to help Swedes manage immigrants. And, also, I think it's important for managers working in Sweden or in other countries which have contacts with the Middle East to learn about culture, to be competent in this.

What do you think?

You could also ask students what differences they are aware of between their culture and another culture they know.

Check your grammar

Future reference: present tenses review, *will*, *going to*, the future continuous

Students will probably have studied these forms before. It is a good idea to acknowledge this and stress that this is a review with a focus on using them correctly.

Mention that the speakers in the listening exercises referred to the future using different tenses.

1 • Quickly check the names of the tenses when you go through the answers.
   • Remind students to look at the Grammar reference section, particularly if they are having problems with future reference.

Answers

1 1 c   2 a   3 d   4 b
2 1 *will* expresses a general prediction about an unspecified moment in the future; it is a prediction based on opinion rather than present evidence
  2 *going to* expresses a prediction based on present evidence, with the speaker describing an event happening in the near future
3 *will + be + -ing*
4 1 An action in progress at a specific point in the future
  2 A future arrangement

Do it yourself

Answers

1 1 Don't worry. I'll send you the information this afternoon.
  2 Friday is no good for a meeting. A client is coming to my office on that day.
  3 My computer is doing strange things. I think it's going to crash.
  4 The train leaves / is leaving at five today, according to the timetable.
  5 This time next week I'll be sitting on a beach somewhere in Mexico.
  6 Where are you going (to go) on holiday this year?

Answers

2 1 I'll do   2 departs   3 'll   4 are meeting
  5 is going to be   6 Will you be using   7 won't do
  8 I'm going to go
3 *Suggested answers*
  1 I'll still be driving back to the office from a training seminar at that time.
  2 This time on Saturday I'll be landing on a Caribbean island.
  3 I'll be leaving for the airport at five o'clock so it will have to be brief.
  4 But I'll be seeing him at two o'clock so I'll ask him.
  5 Will you still be using the digital projector at three o'clock because I need it for an afternoon meeting?
  6 I'll be starting a seminar at nine o'clock so could you call before that?

4 When students have asked their questions in pairs, ask selected students to put some of their questions to the whole class.

Answers

3 I'm leaving   4 I'm seeing   6 I'm starting

Sounds good

Chunking and pausing

Tell students that you are now going to look at some features of natural speech in English.

1 Tell students that chunking and pausing are helpful for reading aloud and that pausing can add emphasis to what you are saying.

Answers

The lines in the text represent the natural breaks (pauses) made by the speaker.

Track 25.5 tapescript ▶▶|
See the Student's Book.

Answers and Track 25.6 tapescript ▶▶|

2 Friends / comrades / and fellow South Africans. / I greet you all / in the name of peace / democracy / and freedom for all. / I stand here before you / not as a prophet / but as a humble servant / of you / the people. / On this day of my release / I extend my warmest gratitude / to the millions of my compatriots / and those in every corner of the globe / who have campaigned tirelessly / for my release.

It's time to talk

• Set the scene. Before you start the activity, pair up Student As and Student Bs to work together in order to prepare. Stress that they should try to use as many different future forms as possible – refer them to the Remember section, if necessary.
• As they prepare, go round and monitor them and check what kind of solutions they are going to suggest and what language they intend to use.
• Then pair up Student As with Student Bs to complete the pairwork activity.
• After they have finished, get selected pairs to feed back to the whole class about their solutions.

- You may want to use the Extra classroom activity here (see pages 97 and 123).

What did we do today?
Check the Remember section quickly and remind students of the objectives of the lesson.

Follow up
Encourage students to:
- write sentences about the future using the forms from this lesson
- prepare carefully for telephone calls that they are going to make in English
- practise chunking and pausing by reading aloud for homework.

26 Public relations

What did we do last time?
Do a review of the last type 2 lesson (Unit 23). Remind students of what they worked on (see Teacher's notes for that unit) and do some quick revision as follows.

Talking about meetings and conferences
Get students to look back at *The words you need* section in Unit 23. Working in pairs, get them to choose words and define them for a partner who has to listen and say what the word is. They can take it in turns to do this.

Negotiating: Bargaining and reaching a compromise
Ask students to give you phrases for:
- making suggestions
- bargaining
- reaching a compromise.

On the agenda: Why are we doing this?
Tell students the objective of this lesson:
- to talk about **organisations and public relations**
- to build vocabulary connected to **public relations**
- to develop skills for **meetings: summarising and closing**.
Reinforce this by writing the key words on the board or OHP.

Warm up
Also ask students exactly what is involved in PR. This kind of prediction activity will help students with the listening activity in the next section.

Background briefing: Samanea PR
Samanea PR is based in Ampang, Malaysia. The company was created in 1995 by its current owner and managing director, Aisha Rashid. Samanea PR supplies consultancy on public relations to companies, organisations and government departments. This work covers a wide variety of themes, including positioning, corporate image, reputation and any related issues that assist in building and maintaining a positive image. Media relations is an important dimension to this work. For more information about Samanea PR, go to the *English365* website: www.cambridge.org/elt/english365.

Listen to this

PR – process, culture and principles
1 Tell students not to worry if they are not sure what process, culture and principles mean at this stage. This will become clear in the listening activity.

> **Answers**
>
> relationships – building, maintaining and sustaining them

2 You may need to pause the track after the key words to give students time to write them down.

> **Answers**
>
> 1 objectives   2 communications strategy   3 audiences
> 4 tactics   5 Build, relationships

Track 26.1 tapescript ▶▶
INTERVIEWER: So Aisha, tell us about what a good PR strategy consists of.
AISHA: I think, first of all, you have to understand what it is you want to achieve, so you have to have clear objectives. Then secondly, you develop a good solid strategy, a communications strategy.
INTERVIEWER: Yes.
AISHA: And we need to plan according to whom it is that we want to talk – who our target audiences are, we call them audiences. We have to clearly identify the audience, or audiences.
INTERVIEWER: Right.
AISHA: And based on who we want to talk to and what kind of strategies we want to use, we come up with the actual tactics, actually *how* to reach our audience. It's important to choose the most appropriate tactics – it depends what we want to achieve.
INTERVIEWER: And then what? What comes next?
AISHA: Well, you know, it's all about relationships. If you look at the word PR, the second word is 'relations', and that's the most important thing – we should be focusing on building, maintaining and sustaining relationships. Relationships are the most important thing.

> **Answers**
>
> **3** 1 product   2 relationship   3 key stakeholders

Track 26.2 tapescript ▶▶
INTERVIEWER: Tell us something about the culture of PR as you see it. Has there been a shift away from an emphasis on product and towards what consumers want?
AISHA: Yes. Yes, you're correct. It's important to understand what the consumers want and to give them what they want, instead of, you know, saying, 'Here's the product, now come and buy it.' So there's less emphasis on product, and more on consumers.
INTERVIEWER: Yes, maybe that approach is more associated with mass marketing?
AISHA: Exactly, and it doesn't work any more. So instead of mass marketing it's more a case of identifying your customers and then building a relationship and giving them exactly what they want.
INTERVIEWER: More relationship marketing.
AISHA: That's right, exactly.
INTERVIEWER: Is this a trend that you see happening across Asia?
AISHA: Oh yes, right across Asia.
INTERVIEWER: Very much so?
AISHA: Yes. And I think for us the advantage is that relationship marketing is not a big issue for us because that's how we do business.

INTERVIEWER: Do you think western companies working in Asia, do you think western companies struggle with this concept?

AISHA: Yes. Here, it's a slow, gradual building process, but if you are successful, the shelf life is longer.

INTERVIEWER: Yes. Maybe in the west the expectation is that everything has to move more quickly.

AISHA: Yes, I think so. But I believe that you really have to work on the relationship.

INTERVIEWER: And how can businesses get the best out of their employees, to meet these PR objectives?

AISHA: Well, I think there's been a change in this area. Not very long ago, employees were just commodities, like things, not given much value. That's changed. Now work is more complex, more skilled. Employees are the most valued, the key stakeholders in an organisation. That's a very important feature of PR nowadays.

INTERVIEWER: Yes, companies are always saying 'Our employees are our most important asset.'

AISHA: They do say that. But now they have to live that too – they have to really care for the welfare of their employees.

> ### Answers
> **4** 1 integrity / honesty   2 ethics   3 transparency / openness / accountability

Track 26.3 tapescript ▶▶❙

INTERVIEWER: What would you emphasise as being the key principles of PR?

AISHA: Well, I would say above all integrity … that means honesty in relationships.

INTERVIEWER: Yes.

AISHA: … and secondly, and related to that, high ethics.

INTERVIEWER: Yes.

AISHA: I'm a great believer in those principles, you know, and that has got to come across, it has to be communicated.

INTERVIEWER: So ethics includes considerations of environmental impact?

AISHA: Oh yes, very much so, environmental impact, and whether we are, you know, an honest employer and whether we are an honest manufacturer. So the components of our products, are they really safe? And the way we produce our products, is it going to affect the environment? You know, that's what ethics is all about. I'm a great believer in ethics.

INTERVIEWER: And what else?

AISHA: I think transparency, by which I mean a greater openness and accountability. All these things together, integrity, ethics and transparency, they all mean responsibility.

INTERVIEWER: So in general there's more open communication with the public?

AISHA: Well, I've always believed that transparency has to be something inherent in what we do, but of course this is Asia, you know, and the way we do business is more of relationships and relationship building and so on, not so much on transparency.

INTERVIEWER: Yes.

AISHA: But there's no reason why they cannot work hand in hand, you know. We can have the best of both worlds.

What do you think?

Explain that *transparency* means openness, if students did not catch this in the interview. Develop discussion by asking how far the students' organisations are open with the public. Students could also think about an organisation that they know well. What kind of PR does it have?

The words you need … to talk about public relations

1 • Suggest that students look at the tapescripts to check their answers. This will encourage them to take on more responsibility for their own learning.

• When students have finished, get them to define the collocations in their own words. This is important as they may be able to match the collocation, but this does not necessarily mean that the meaning is clear or that students are able to use it in the future.

> ### Answers
> 1 d   2 g   3 f   4 b   5 c   6 f/d   7 e   8 c   9 a/g   10 f

2 You could add a competitive element to this activity by putting students in pairs and getting them to find the synonym as fast as possible. This should provide a change of pace.

> ### Answers
> **2** 1 strategy   2 stakeholders   3 welfare   4 integrity   5 ethics   6 accountability   7 transparency
> **3** build = create; maintain = keep; sustain = keep and continue for a period of time

4 Get students to read through the text quickly before they attempt to fill the gaps.

> ### Answers
> 1 relationships   2 stakeholders   3 strategies   4 marketing   5 transparency   6 accountability   7 ethical   8 environmental

It's time to talk

• Before you start the activity, you could discuss the issues surrounding such a scenario. How would it damage a company's image? What would students do if it was their organisation that something similar happened to? Are students aware of any real life situations like this?

• Give students time to assimilate the information. Note that Fred Wacko is a fictional character.

• Tell students that they should try to reach some sort of agreement about what should be done.

• When they have finished, get them to report back to the rest of the class about what they decided to do.

• You may want to use the Extra classroom activity here (see pages 97 and 124).

COMMUNICATING AT WORK

Meetings 3: Summarising and closing

• Explain that you are going to continue the work on meetings. Refer back to what was done in Units 11 and 20.

• Get students to discuss their answers to the questions in pairs. You could also ask them what the functions of different meetings are (i.e. progress reports, decision making, etc.). Ask what happens at the end of meetings and what kind of language is used to close them.

Answers

1 1 budgets   2 marketing   3 a complicated problem

2 You may need to play each track more than once to give students time to write down the key phrases. Elicit that the chairperson is the participant most likely to use these phrases.

Answers

1 the main point   2 We've agreed that the budgets
3 time's running out   4 lots of good ideas about marketing
5 any more questions   6 get in touch if you need
7 sum up the discussion   8 close the meeting
9 there'll be a report

Track 26.4 tapescript ▶▶

SPEAKER 1: OK, so the main point is this. We've agreed that the budgets will remain the same for the coming year. This is going to be a difficult period for us but I think in the circumstances the decision is the right one. Thank you all very much.

Track 26.5 tapescript ▶▶|

SPEAKER 2: Well, I think time's running out. Thanks everyone. We've had lots of good ideas about marketing this product, and we've had a few questions. If there are any more questions, that's fine. If not, I think we can finish. As I said, everything will be in the report, but please get in touch if you need any more clarification.

Track 26.6 tapescript ▶▶

SPEAKER 3: Well, I'd like to sum up the discussion. Everybody of course has a range of different opinions on this extremely complicated problem. The most important thing is transparency and openness. We have to take some difficult decisions. For now we're still at the discussion stage. Thanks for coming. We'll close the meeting here. Of course, there'll be a report on this meeting to follow.

Answers

3 Indicating the end of a meeting 3, 8; Summarising 1, 2, 7; Asking for questions 5; Looking ahead 6, 9; Positive message 4

4 This should be a relatively short activity, with the focus just being on using the phrases presented earlier.

5 Before you start this, brainstorm ways that the money could be raised. Get students to appoint a chairperson for each group and ask them to keep a note of the main points so that they can be summarised.

What did we do today?

Check the Remember section quickly and remind students of the objectives of the lesson.

Follow up

Encourage students to:
• record useful vocabulary for talking about PR
• write down useful phrases for meetings in categories, as in exercise 3 in *Communicating at work*.

27 When I'm 74

What did we do last time?

Do a review of the last type 3 lesson (Unit 24). Remind students of what they worked on (see Teacher's notes for that unit) and do a quick review as follows.

Social skills: Dealing with conflict
Elicit ways of dealing with conflict:
• try to make things better
• don't give in
• don't agree to things that aren't possible.

Talking about career coaching and education
Elicit the different stages in education and then get students to tell a partner quickly about their own education.

On the agenda: Why are we doing this?

Tell students the objectives of the lesson:
• to practise talking about **money management**
• to develop **social skills** for **giving feedback**
• to build **vocabulary** connected to **personal finance**.
Reinforce this by writing the key words on the board or OHP.

Draw students' attention to the unit title. Can they think what this might be a reference to? Tell them that the Beatles wrote a song called *When I'm 64*.

Warm up

Ask students to discuss the questions in pairs before discussion with the whole class. You could ask what the benefits and possible negative effects of feedback are. Try to elicit that feedback should be given sensitively and constructively. Ask students how they give feedback.

Giving feedback

What's the point?

See the Introduction (page 16): Type 3 units – social skills. See also the section in the Introduction on giving feedback (page 13); you may want to reflect on how you give feedback to the students.

Answers

1 a She has given a speech
b Not at all
c Francesca should ask Heidi how she felt about the speech and give her some useful advice and tips about how to give speeches successfully.

Track 27.1 tapescript ▶▶|

FRANCESCA: So, you've made your speech. I told you there was nothing to worry about, Heidi.
HEIDI: Yes, thank goodness, I was absolutely dreading it. I'm so glad it's over.
FRANCESCA: And you got through it. That's all that matters.
HEIDI: Did you think it was OK?
FRANCESCA: It was fine. You don't normally have to make speeches, after all.
HEIDI: Was it obvious it was my first speech? What mistakes did I make?

FRANCESCA: Well, there were one or two small things. But nothing to worry about. You've done it now!

HEIDI: Yes, and I hope it's a long time before I have to go through anything like that again. What do you think I should do so I do it better next time and don't feel so nervous? You give speeches quite often – how do you do it?

FRANCESCA: Well, I don't really know, I just do it as well as I can.

Answers

2 a Feeling nervous
b Breathing exercises
c Francesca asks Heidi how she felt about the speech and gives focused praise. Her feedback is useful as she asks about the difficulties, makes constructive suggestions for how it can be improved next time and offers to help.

3 a happy with it
b the way you remembered to
c you find most difficult
d you should work on for next time

Track 27.2 tapescript ▶▶

FRANCESCA: So, you've made your speech. Well done, Heidi. Were you happy with it?

HEIDI: I don't know. It's hard to tell. I was absolutely dreading it before I started but it wasn't too bad once I'd got going. I'm glad it's over though!

FRANCESCA: But how do you think it went on the whole?

HEIDI: Well, I suppose I was reasonably pleased. I think they appreciated some of the things I said. What did you think?

FRANCESCA: I thought it was good. I particularly liked the way you remembered to thank all the other staff as well. I think that made everyone happy and got them on your side as well.

HEIDI: Good, I wanted to say something to them as well.

FRANCESCA: And has it helped you for when you have to do another one? What did you find most difficult about it?

HEIDI: The worst thing was feeling so nervous. I don't know what you can do about that. Breathing exercises? That kind of thing?

FRANCESCA: I don't think your nerves showed very much, except maybe right at the start. I'm sure doing breathing exercises and breathing properly can help.

HEIDI: Yes, I'll remember that.

FRANCESCA: Is there anything else you think you should work on for next time?

HEIDI: Well, I was worried I'd forget what I wanted to say.

FRANCESCA: What I always do is make notes on small cards to remind me.

HEIDI: Yes, that's a good idea.

FRANCESCA: And practising out loud can be very helpful.

HEIDI: Maybe if I practised with someone …?

FRANCESCA: Yes, I'd be very happy to listen to the next one before you do it.

Possible answers

4 A family member who does not perform well
Well, you tried your best.
Keep practising and I'm sure that you'll get better.

A friend who shows you a story he/she has written
I really like the beginning.
I think there are some very good parts in it.

A colleague who fails to make an important point in a meeting
Next time maybe you should write notes about the things you need to say.
You made some good points, but why didn't you mention …?

Have a go

- See the Introduction (page 17): Type 3 units.
- Set the scene and perhaps remind students of some of the things that they could give feedback on. For example: use of language, body language, use of voice.
- You could ask selected groups to feed back to the rest of the class on their performance.

Read on

Personal finance

- Tell students that *demography* means the study of changes in the number of births, marriages, deaths, etc. in a particular area during a period of time. A *time bomb* is a situation which is likely to become difficult to deal with or control.
- Explain that in this part of the lesson students will look at a text on demographics and practise interpreting visual information in order to make predictions about the content. Predicting is an important reading skill as thinking about what topics and information may be in a text will help them to understand it more easily.
- Get students to discuss their answers to the questions quickly in pairs. Tell them that these questions will activate their knowledge of the subject and so help prepare them for reading the text.
- There may be some items of vocabulary that students are unfamiliar with. Tell them that the vocabulary will be dealt with after the reading exercise.

1 Before students look at the questions, get them to look at the graphs and ask them what the graphs tell them. You may be able to elicit sentences like the ones in the book.

Answers

1 up 2 down

2 • If necessary, tell students that *baby boom* means a large number of babies born at a particular time.
• Give students a time limit for this.

Answers

The article mentions:
retirement, birth rates, the baby-boom generation, government finances, pensions, the size of the workforce
It does not mention:
the leisure industry, older politicians, housing

3 • Give a time limit for this exercise. It is useful to encourage students to identify the main points in a paragraph.
• You could ask students to think of their own titles for the paragraphs before they do the matching exercise.
• When you go through the answers, get students to say why they chose a particular heading for each paragraph.

Answers

1 e   2 d   3 f   4 g   5 h   6 a   7 c   8 b

Additional exercise

Summarising a paragraph effectively means that students have to have a good grasp of the main points. You may want to give them this additional exercise to develop reading skills.

Summarising the content
Complete these sentences about each paragraph in the article.

1 The world's population is getting ....
2 A lot of people are going to .... in just over ten years.
3 Women are having ....
4 Old people are retiring .... and living ....
5 So .... working people will have to pay for .... people in retirement.
6 This will cost .... than governments can afford.
7 So governments will have to try and find ways to encourage older people to work ....
8 Flexible deals may make work more .... to old people.

The words you need ... to talk about personal finance

Background briefing: Mr Micawber

Mr Micawber is a character in the novel David Copperfield, written by Charles Dickens (1812–1870). Dickens is considered to be the greatest English novelist of the Victorian period. The character Mr Micawber is famous for always having financial problems. You may need to point out to students that the figures refer to pounds, shillings and pence (decimalisation was not introduced until 1970).

1 • Give a time limit for this and get students to compare their answers in pairs before you go through the answers.
  • There may be other words in the text that are new to students. Get them to underline the words and then compare them with a partner. Students could then explain any words that they can and compare with another pair. You could explain any words that are still not clear at the end of this process.

2 After the matching activity, you could give students an example sentence so that they are clear about what to do. For example: *The mortgage had a fixed interest rate.*

3 If you feel that students will struggle to complete the sentences, allow them to look at the words in the box from the start.

Reading tip

Refer students to this and point out that this can be a useful way to improve their range of vocabulary. Highlight also, however, that if students are reading to extract information from a text they should not concentrate on individual words but try to find the main points.

It's time to talk

• Make sure that students understand the task. Give them time to prepare and stress that Student Bs should invent their own character. Remind Student As that they should take notes so they can report back to the class.

• You may want to use the Extra classroom activity here (see pages 97 and 125).

What did we do today?

Check the Remember section quickly and remind students of the objectives of this lesson.

Follow up

Encourage students to:
• write phrases for giving feedback
• write sentences about their personal finance
• highlight useful vocabulary when they are reading a text.

28 Working in the USA

What did we do last time?

Do a review of the last type 1 lesson (Unit 25). Remind students of what they worked on (see Teacher's notes for that unit) and do some quick revision as follows.

Future reference
Elicit different ways of referring to the future. Get students to give you example sentences for the following:
• present simple
• present continuous
• *will*
• *going to*
• future continuous.
Ask them the differences in meaning.

Pronunciation: Chunking and pausing
Write the following on the board:
When speaking in English we often 'chunk' words together, that is, group words and use pauses around these groups. For example, at the moment.
Get students to say this with appropriate pauses.

On the agenda: Why are we doing this?

Tell the students the objectives of the lesson:

- to improve **speaking skills: reporting what people say**
- to revise **direct and reported speech**
- to improve **pronunciation: spelling and pronunciation.**

Reinforce this by writing the key words on the board or OHP.

Warm up

Explain that students are going to read a short text on the differences between working practices in the US and Europe. You could ask some questions to guide their reading, for example:

How many hours a year do Americans work?

How many hours a year do Germans work?

How much less work do French people do?

You could also ask if this surprises students. Do they agree with it? What cultural differences have students noticed?

Listen to this

An American success story

Background briefing: Barry Gibbons

In 1989 Barry Gibbons was appointed as Chairman/CEO of Burger King and moved to Florida. Within a year he achieved a phenomenal turn-around in company fortunes, ultimately resulting in two new restaurants opening every day somewhere in the world. He resigned from Burger King in 1993 and became a successful author, speaker, consultant and entrepreneur on both sides of the Atlantic. In addition to being the Chairman of a music retail chain, Barry has co-founded and invested in a variety of ventures including a branded food service business, a magazine/compact disc publishing company, speciality coffee bars and themed Mexican restaurants. In 1996, Barry published his first book, *This Indecision is Final.* His latest book, *If You Want To Make God Really Laugh Show Him Your Business Plan* (1998), covers the 101 universal laws of business. For more information about Barry Gibbons, go to the *English365* website: www.cambridge.org/elt/english365.

1. • Check the meaning of these words which occur in the listening:

   figurehead – someone who has the position of leader in an organisation but who has no real power

   restless – someone who is unwilling or unable to stay still or to be quiet and calm, because they are worried or bored

   stubborn – someone who is determined to do what they want and refuses to do anything else.

   You may also want to check students know what a *Palm Pilot* is.

   • Before listening, get students to note down what they think Barry will say about general differences between Europeans and Americans at work.

   • Then get students to write down the headings from the Student's Book and make notes about what Barry says. Refer to the section on note-taking in the Introduction (page 16).

Refer to the section on note-taking in the Introduction (page 16).

1. Stronger emphasis in US on activity, on being seen to be busy
2. American business life more strongly influenced by lawyers than in Europe
3. Americans are great talkers but not very good listeners, in comparison to Europeans

2. Get students to read through the questions before you play the track.

1. To be able to find the right people to support him
2. Burger King had 14 lawyers, showing the great importance of lawyers in American business culture
3. Leaders increasingly represent the company, supporting the brand
4. He is a good example of the figurehead style of leadership
5. Energy, curiosity and 'won't take no for an answer'

Track 28.1 tapescript ▶▶

INTERVIEWER: Barry, you worked in America very successfully as CEO of Burger King. What was the secret of your success in the USA?

BARRY: When people talk about my success at Burger King, I say: 'Stop, stop, stop, stop, stop – *their* success – the people I picked who I could rely on.' And it became so important to me, that key ability I've had in life to be able to find people who are fit for the task, and to convince them to come and join me.

INTERVIEWER: Did you find it easy to convert to the US environment?

BARRY: No. There's a much higher emphasis in the US on activity rather than effectiveness. So it's very important to be up at five o'clock in the morning. And while you're on the treadmill at the gym, to be on your Palm Pilot, have eight hundred things on your notepad to do today before you go to sleep ...

INTERVIEWER: It's different in Europe?

BARRY: Yes, I think in Italy, Germany, etc. it's more like 'Do one thing.' We may take our time over it, but it's done properly.

INTERVIEWER: People say American business is dominated by lawyers. Is that true and did you have problems adapting to that?

BARRY: Oh, it's horrendous, make no mistake. In the UK, when I ran Grand Met, with thirty thousand people, we had one lawyer. We got to Burger King and we had fourteen. You could run a corporation with fourteen managers; we had fourteen lawyers. This and the emphasis on hyperactivity are the two big differences with the US.

INTERVIEWER: And do you think leadership is changing now?

BARRY: Yes, I think more and more you'll find that leadership is about representing the company, or branding the organisation. I think Richard Branson does it very well in Virgin, in a way just being the figurehead for what you stand for, how you do business, the personality of the company, rather than the things you push out there.

INTERVIEWER: One important thing we haven't mentioned is communication. How about differences in communication style in the US compared to here?

BARRY: The Americans are terrible listeners! They are absolutely wonderful givers out. But do they listen? No, they don't. I use a joke: you've got two eyes, two ears and one mouth, that's four to receive and one to give out. That used to be my rule in terms of listening and giving out information, but it's probably the reverse in America.

INTERVIEWER: So, a final question: coming back to you, what are the personal qualities that made Burger King recruit you, your main personal qualities?

BARRY: Mmm, I asked a good friend once what my main qualities were, and I was expecting that he would say I had great decision-making powers or that I was one of the world's greatest communicators, both I agree very, very important, but he said that I was the most restless person and greatest risk-taker he'd ever met. I think he meant a combination of three things: energy, curiosity – I'm interested in everything – and won't take no for an answer – 'Come on guys, you haven't had a new product in here for eight years, let's have forty.' Of course, some people will just call me stubborn.

What do you think?

You could also ask students how they tend to deal with tasks. Do they do one thing at a time or try to juggle more than one? Which is the best method? How do they prefer to work? Barry mentions a *Palm Pilot*. How do students organise their tasks?

Check your grammar

Direct and reported speech

1 Ask students when we use *say* and when we use *tell*. Elicit that *tell* needs a direct object. Write the following on the board to make this clear:
tell somebody something
say something.

Answers

1 said   2 told

2 Stress that if a statement is still true there is no need to change the tense of the verb.

Answers

2 1 The verb tense should be appropriate for the actual situation. Sometimes the main verb 'goes one tense back', e.g. *will* becomes *would* in reported speech. *He said some people would just call him stubborn.*
In spoken language the tense may stay the same if the sentence is still true. *He said some people will just call him stubborn.*
If the reporting verb is in the present tense, the reported verb generally stays the same. *He says some people will just call him stubborn.*
2 The changes to pronouns and possessive adjectives depend on who the words are reported by, e.g. *I* may become *he/she* and *my* may become *his/her*. The changes to time expressions depend on when the direct speech is being reported, e.g. *today* may become *yesterday*, etc.
3 We use *if* (or *whether*) in a reported question when the direct question does not contain a question word such as *what*, *when*, etc.
Direct speech: *'Is leadership changing?'*
Reported speech: *The interviewer wanted to know if leadership was changing.*
4 In reported questions, the verb usually goes after the subject and we don't use auxiliary verbs like *do*, *did*, etc.
Direct speech: *Is leadership changing?*

Reported speech: *He asked whether leadership was changing.*
Direct speech: *'What do you do?'*
Reported speech: *The interviewer asked what he did.*
3 1 I went to Paris last week.
 2 I've been to China before.
 3 Where are you going next year?

4 Refer students to the Grammar reference section. They could either read it in class or for homework.
It is worth emphasising that students should simply choose the tense appropriate to the situation and avoid worrying too much about 'conversion rules'. The tense of the verb does not always need to change, as mentioned in the Student's Book.

Answers

1 explained/suggested   2 asked/invited   3 suggested
4 praised   5 asked

Do it yourself

Answers

1 1 He told me that he would confirm last month.
 2 She wanted to know when the meeting is / was.
 3 He said / told me that I had to send the report yesterday.
 4 She asked me if we would like any help.
 5 Do you know what we should do?
2 1 was taking / would be taking 20 great new ideas back to her workplace
 2 he now had / has a new blueprint for his own leadership style
 3 she found / had found it a great way to recharge her batteries
 4 she can / could apply much of what she has / had learnt at home too
 5 if we can / could have more workshops next year / the following year
 6 if anyone has / had any / some photos of the social evening
3 1 c   2 h   3 f   4 e   5 a   6 d   7 g   8 b

4 Before doing this exercise, quickly go over what prepositions could be used with each verb. For example:
*She praised me **for** doing a great job.*

Suggested answers

a He/she reminded me that the deadline is / was at the end of the week.
b He/she warned me not to touch that surface or I'd burn myself.
c He/she praised me for doing a great job again.
d He/she admitted that he/she made / had made a mistake.
e He/she insisted that I/we (should) take regular holidays.
f He/she asked me if I need / needed anything.
g He/she suggested doing / that I should do at least two training courses every year.
h He/she invited me to lunch.

Sounds good

Spelling and pronunciation

Explain that you are now going to look at some common pronunciation problems for learners of English – specifically, problems caused by the same letters having different pronunciations.

1. • Get students to underline the words that they think sound different when they listen. You might want to play the track more than once before they practise saying the words themselves. Alternatively, you could demonstrate the words yourself.
   • If students are not familiar with the phonemic symbols, it might be a good idea to spend some time going through them.

Answers

1 health   2 insurance

Track 28.2 tapescript ▶▶|
See the Student's Book.

2. When students have checked their answers, get them to say the words in pairs while you go round and monitor. Encourage students to make a note of any sounds that they have problems with and stress that this is an important learning strategy.

Answers

1 hope   2 whole   3 singer   4 film   5 heard   6 pudding
7 increase   8 all   9 signature   10 then

Track 28.3 tapescript ▶▶|
See the Student's Book.

Test yourself

Monitor this carefully to check that students are pronouncing the words correctly.

It's time to talk

- Set the scene. Tell students that the objective of this activity is to practise using reported speech.
- Give students plenty of time to read through the information. Make sure that they are clear about what to do – explain that they should ask their partner the questions and that they will find the answers on their file card. They should answer using reported speech. While students are preparing, remind them to think about how they can report what has been said.
- After the activity, get selected students to report back on their conversations. They could also use reported speech for this. For example: *My partner asked me if there were* any *plans to make major changes.*
- As there is such a lot of information for students to digest in this activity, you could get them to repeat it with another partner once they have finished.

- You may want to use the Extra classroom activity here (see pages 98 and 126).

What did we do today?
Check the Remember section quickly and remind students of the objectives of this lesson.

Follow up
Encourage students to:
- write sentences using reported speech
- learn the phonemic symbols
- focus on sounds that are difficult for them.

29 Talk to a lawyer

What did we do last time?
Do a review of the last type 2 lesson (Unit 26). Remind students of what they worked on (see Teacher's notes for that unit) and do some quick revision as follows.

Talking about organisations and public relations
Get students to give you words that collocate with the following: *shelf, target, mass, public, build.*

Meetings: Summarising and closing
Ask students to give you phrases to do the following:
- indicating the end of a meeting
- asking for questions
- giving a positive message
- summarising
- looking ahead.

On the agenda: Why are we doing this?
Tell students the objectives of this lesson:
- to talk about **organisations and the law**
- to build **vocabulary** connected to **legal issues**
- to develop skills for **clear writing**.

Reinforce this by writing the key words on the board or OHP.

Warm up
Some students may not have experience of company law and so, if not, ask them if they have had any contact with lawyers for any other reason. It could be when buying a house, for example. Ask them what their experiences were.

Listen to this

Take my advice

1. Get students to read through the list before you play the track. Check the meaning of any new vocabulary.

1 1 no   2 yes   3 yes   4 yes   5 yes, but not often
6 yes   7 no   8 yes, but not often
2 *Suggested answers*
  1 For bankruptcy proceedings
  2 The procedure takes a long time – it is formalistic
  3 Set up new companies that are subsidiaries
3 *Suggested answers*
  1 Consult a lawyer, especially before signing any contract
  2 Sort out any possible problems before they happen; avoid
    problems

Track 29.1 tapescript ▶▶

INTERVIEWER: Jitka, I guess companies need lawyers for just about everything?

JITKA: Yes, that's correct. It starts with the founding of a company, putting together all the documentation necessary for incorporation and then getting all the permits necessary for a specific business activity.

INTERVIEWER: Yes. So what are you mainly concerned with in your work? Are you involved with criminal law or just company law?

JITKA: No, no criminal law, only company law.

INTERVIEWER: What, mainly?

JITKA: Well, perhaps three things. First, the setting up of companies. And then secondly, usually companies consult us whenever they want to sign an important contract, or lastly if they have employment-related problems, so employment law.

INTERVIEWER: So you would advise on what should be in and what should not be in a contract?

JITKA: Yes.

INTERVIEWER: So you're involved much more with … consultancy or advice rather than actual court work?

JITKA: Yes, definitely. Not much court work. I go to court very rarely and if so it's usually connected with bankruptcy proceedings.

INTERVIEWER: So you do bankruptcy work?

JITKA: Yes, my partners – the company does a little of this kind of thing, but personally, I do bankruptcy proceedings only very rarely.

INTERVIEWER: What are the most common legal problems that companies have in your experience – is it to do with contracts?

JITKA: Yes, it's the contracts and also the formalities necessary for founding a business, for setting up an activity. The procedure is quite formalistic in the Czech Republic.

INTERVIEWER: Yes.

JITKA: To make all necessary arrangements for setting up a company takes quite a long time. Then in terms of contracts, it really depends. We try to draw up contracts in order to avoid any possible problems or legal proceedings in the future.

INTERVIEWER: I see. And are you also involved with things like copyright or property disputes? Do you help businesses to patent new ideas, for example?

JITKA: No. Well, copyright, no, not really, I used to do this … a few years ago I did some work on trademark licensing contracts. But this is not really my area now.

INTERVIEWER: I see. And would you work on joint ventures, for example, between two companies?

JITKA: Well, sometimes, but this is not – this doesn't happen that often. We usually set up new companies that are subsidiaries of French or France-based companies, or we do some merger projects, mergers between two businesses. We do some work on acquisitions sometimes. But no, joint ventures are not very frequent.

Track 29.2 tapescript ▶▶

INTERVIEWER: Right, is there anything in particular about company law?

JITKA: Well, I would say that one thing businesses should be aware of is that it's always better to consult a lawyer before doing something than to try to reduce the effects of a mistake later.

INTERVIEWER: So your advice is to consult a lawyer?

JITKA: Yes, before signing any contracts, see a lawyer. Otherwise you sign the contract and then you realise later that there are problems. So see a lawyer first.

INTERVIEWER: Yeah, I'm sure. Otherwise you can end up going bankrupt.

JITKA: Right. It always pays to prevent problems at the beginning rather than have to resolve them later. I think that's important. That way you can stay out of trouble.

INTERVIEWER: Good. So the most important thing is to talk to your lawyer before you do anything?

JITKA: I think so, yes.

What do you think?

You could expand this by asking students if there is a 'compensation culture' in their countries. For example, in the UK there is a concern that people increasingly seek the advice of lawyers and want to claim compensation for even minor accidents and disputes. Is this the same in the students' countries? What is their attitude to this?

The words you need ... to talk about legal issues

Look at the logos and get students to say which companies they belong to. You could also ask students what logo their organisation has.

The following organisations use these logos: Apple Computer Inc., Airbus, McDonalds, Shell.

1 Get students to see how many they can do before they look at the tapescript.

1 company law   2 employment law   3 contract
4 copyright   5 trademark   6 joint venture   7 merger
8 acquisition   9 patent   10 to draw up a contract

2 and **3** Get students to read through the texts quickly before they attempt to fill the gaps.

2 1 was cleared   2 breaching copyright   3 sued   4 claiming
compensation   5 take legal action   6 judge   7 court
8 bankrupt   9 lose the case   10 appeal
3 1 trademark   2 joint venture   3 drew up   4 breach of
copyright   5 take legal action   6 claim compensation
7 court   8 appealed   9 loses   10 bankrupt

It's time to talk

- An alternative way of approaching this would be to allocate the different scenarios to groups. They could discuss the issues and then report their ideas back to the rest of the class. Tell students they do not need to be legal experts to do this activity. It is not important if they are not sure what the consequences might be.

- Elicit what grammatical form (the second conditional) is most useful for talking about the problems. Write the following on the board: *If there was an accident at work, the company would have to pay compensation.*

- You may want to use the Extra classroom activity here (see pages 98 and 127).

COMMUNICATING AT WORK

Writing 2: Clear writing

- Quickly ask students what kind of writing they do in their work and what problems they have writing in English. Remind them of the work they did on writing in Unit 2 (writing emails).
- Stress how important writing clearly is.

1 Give a time limit for this.

Answers

The report is about the restoration of a castle. There are five recommendations.

2 Before you look at these questions, ask students if they think the report is clear or not. Get them to say why. Elicit the fact that there are clear, numbered headings, the writing is direct and to the point, etc.

Answers

2 1 The title is at the top; the date is on the right
2 In the paragraph headed Background
3 *Suggested answers*
1 Different issues listed (L): all the numbered parts of the report.
2 Recommendations (R): 3.1 'It is recommended that a consortium of business and heritage organisations purchase the castle.' Recommendations 4.1–4.5.
3 Actions needed (A): 1 'A budget, a detailed cost-benefit analysis and an action plan are needed.' 3.3 'A detailed budget must be worked out.' Recommendations 4.1–4.5.
4 Facts (F): 2 'The castle is a 13th century hunting residence, once used by Richard III.' 'The castle is privately owned and in poor condition.' 3.1 'Around £1.6m is required. This money has already been raised from national and local organisations.'
5 Opinions (O): 2 'It is of considerable historic interest. It has tourism potential but restoration is mostly of cultural importance.' 3.4 'We believe that a public–private partnership will ensure the castle's future.'

4
- You could get students to write the report in class. In this way you can ensure that all the students will do it and hand it in to you. It could also, of course, be set for homework. If you decide to do it in class, give a time limit and explain your rationale for doing it then, i.e. it gives you the opportunity to monitor the work as students write and it ensures that everybody does it.
- Give each student individual feedback on their work. You might also want to go over useful errors with the whole group at the beginning of the next class.

Model answer

Strategic Planning Meeting
20 September 2005
Summary Report
1 Background
It is clear that we have rising costs and strong competition. Market conditions are very difficult as we have falling domestic demand.
2 Costs
2.1 Wage costs are too high.
2.2 The costs of locally sourced materials are also very high.
3 Recommendations
3.1 The company should draw up new full-time contracts linked to productivity.
3.2 We should explore the possibility of buying materials abroad.
4 Conclusion
In summary, the outlook in the medium term is difficult. In the long term, the company needs to consider relocation to South America or Asia. More research is needed.

What did we do today?
Check the Remember section quickly and remind students of the objectives of this lesson.

Follow up
Encourage students to:
- record useful vocabulary for talking about legal issues
- write another report in English based on their work and hand it in to you.

30 Personal change

What did we do last time?
Do a review of the last type 3 lesson (Unit 27). Remind students of what they worked on (see Teacher's notes for that unit) and do some quick revision as follows.

Social skills: Giving feedback
Ask students for phrases to do the following:
- get feedback and give focused praise first
- identify obstacles
- define an action plan.

Talking about money management and personal finance
Brainstorm words connected to personal finance and get students to make example sentences using the words.

On the agenda: Why are we doing this?
Tell students the objectives of this lesson:
- to talk about **a personal action plan** – explain that students are going to talk about an action plan related to their own work and life
- to develop **social skills** for **getting important messages across**
- to build **vocabulary** related to **personal development**.
Reinforce this by writing the key words on the board or OHP.

Warm up

Also ask students what kind of messages they have to communicate. Who do they communicate them to? You could ask students to make a list of the people they have to talk to in their work and private life. Are there any different ways in which they talk to these people?

Getting important messages across

What's the point?

See the Introduction (page 16): Type 3 units – social skills.

Track 30.1 tapescript ▶▶▌

MARY: Andrea, I must talk to you!

ANDREA: Oh hi, well, actually I'm expecting an important phone call …

MARY: Did you see anything last night?

ANDREA: See anything? Where?

MARY: You know, in the road. Did you see anything funny?

ANDREA: I don't know what you mean. Listen, Mary, I'd love to talk but I'm expecting an important phone call as soon as I get in …

MARY: Didn't you see anything at all? Or hear anything in the road? I hoped you'd be able to help me!

ANDREA: Mary, can we talk about this later?

Track 30.2 tapescript ▶▶▌

MARY: Andrea, I must ask you something. Are you busy at the moment?

ANDREA: Oh hi, well, actually I'm expecting an important phone call …

MARY: Oh, is this a good time to talk? Have you got a few minutes now?

ANDREA: Well, I'm expecting a call from the office any minute but go ahead, they're always a few minutes late.

MARY: I'm sorry, but it's really important. It's about the car. It was broken into last night …

ANDREA: Oh no!

MARY: … and I want to know if you saw or heard anything. Did you see anything last night? Or hear anything?

ANDREA: Did I see anything? Where?

MARY: In the road. Did you see anybody looking suspicious?

ANDREA: No, I certainly didn't see anybody strange, but I don't think I looked out of the window.

MARY: Can you remember if you heard anything? They can't have done it completely silently. I parked it at about 10.30 and I remember locking it, but then I had a shower and went to bed.

ANDREA: No, I'm sorry, I didn't hear anything. What have they taken?

MARY: Well, this morning I found the driver's window smashed – there's glass everywhere – and the CD player has gone.

ANDREA: How annoying! Is anything else missing?

MARY: Well, it could have been worse. Luckily there wasn't much in the car anyway …

Have a go

- See the Introduction (page 17): Type 3 units.
- Set the scene and give time for students to prepare.
- Make sure the observer focuses on how Student A communicates the important part of the message, i.e. that the friend shouldn't know about the party beforehand.
- Encourage students to get into their roles. For example, Student B could pretend to be impatient and not have much time.

Read on

Lifestyles

- Tell students that you are going to revise the main reading strategies that you have looked at in Student's Book 3.
- Explain that *stand up for yourself* means to defend or support yourself, especially when you are being criticised or told what to do.
- Get students to discuss their answers to the questions in pairs.

1 As a way to create interest in the reading, you could get students to close their books and flash the Student's Book page in front of the students quickly to see how much they can see of the picture and title.

2 Give a time limit. When you go through the answers, get students to say what helped them to make their choice.

3 Again, give a time limit for this reading activity.

1 How many UK employees would rather leave their present job than raise a difficult subject with their employer?

2 What hours did Karen work in her first job?

3 What did she have to do when she failed to meet her sales targets?

4 How many people (in the survey) say their managers are too busy to listen to them?

5 What kind of culture do we need to develop (according to Michael Richards)?

6 How has life changed for Karen?

The words you need ... to talk about personal development

Ask students if they agree with Parkinson's Law. Explain that you are now going to look at words related to personal development and assertiveness.

1 Ask students how assertive they think they are. Also ask them what the difference is between assertiveness and aggression.

Answers

1 1 f   2 c   3 j   4 g   5 i   6 b   7 e   8 a   9 d   10 h
2 1 be   2 set   3 draw   4 think   5 develop   6 manage
   7 have (*or* be)   8 get   9 take   10 learn

It's time to talk

- Give time for students to think about their situation and their plans.
- You could give students prompts such as:
  What do you feel about your skills?
  What score would you give assertiveness?
  What are you plans for ...?
- When students have finished, you could get them to report back to the rest of the class.

- Take some time to discuss how students can continue to develop their English even after the end of the course. You could elicit some of the following:
- review *English365* Student's Book 3 and their vocabulary books
- review *English365* Personal Study Book 3
- read English newspapers
- watch English TV and films
- listen to the radio in English
- meet up with other class members and speak in English.

- You may want to use the Extra classroom activity here (see pages 98 and 128).

What did we do today?

Check the Remember section quickly and remind students of the objectives of this lesson.

Follow up

Encourage students to:

- record useful phrases for getting important messages across
- write down their action plan for continued learning of English
- review their vocabulary book
- have as much contact with English as possible – if they don't, they may forget what they have learnt!

4 Extra classroom activities

Teacher's notes

Introduction
There are 30 photocopiable activities designed to supplement each of the 30 units in the Student's Book in this section. Each activity is supported by some Teacher's notes. There are various possibilities as to when to do them:

- instead of the *It's time to talk* section
- in addition to and following *It's time to talk*
- as consolidation in the following lesson
- as consolidation later in the course: you may want to use one if or when a natural break arises in a subsequent lesson.

However, do bear in mind that unlike the Better learning activities (you will find these on the Website), there is a direct link between the Extra classroom activities and the 30 units in the Student's Book. Each Extra classroom activity should be used to reinforce and consolidate learning which has already been initiated and your lesson planning should take this into account.

Procedure
Most of the activities are pair or groupwork of some kind, so before you do any of these activities, you should read, in particular, the notes on:
- pair and groupwork and
- feedback and correction on page 13.

Timing
We have not indicated timings for individual activities because this will depend on you and your class. Do note, however, that:
- some of them are essentially supplementary exercises which will only take about 10 to 15 minutes
- others are communicative activities which could take longer
- you will need to assess how long you think an activity will take.

What to do
See the following Teacher's notes for each activity. Before the lesson, photocopy the activity page and cut up the input as required. All the students will need a copy of the top part of the sheet (with the objective, introduction and instructions about what to do) and also the relevant input for the activity.

1 Have you ever ...?
- Put students into groups of three or four and explain that this activity will help them to practise using different tenses correctly.
- Give each student a set of tense cards.
- Give each group a set of topic cards. These should be put face down in the middle of the group.

- Demonstrate the activity before you start.
- Monitor the groups carefully to ensure correct use of the tenses.
- When the groups have finished, elicit some of the best sentences and write them on the board.

2 The right decision?
- This is a maze activity. Students are directors of a small company. There is a problem with the workforce and they have to make choices about what to do to solve the problem. Each pair or group of three will need one set of cards.
- Divide students into pairs or groups of three and give each group a set of cards.
- Set the scene and tell students that they must discuss all the options and possible consequences on the cards before they make a choice.
- They should take the first card, discuss it and then decide which choice they would like to make, then take the next relevant card, and so on.
- You might want to give them some help by writing some prompts on the board, for example:
  I think we should ...
  Why don't we ...?
  If we ..., we will ...
- Stress that students should only read the card that they have been directed to read.
- After the activity, do some whole class feedback. Ask questions like: *What happened in the end? What would you have done differently?* Give some help by writing the following on the board:
  We should(n't) have ...
  I wish we had ...

3 Have you heard the news?
- Students should work in pairs for this reading and discussion activity.
- Hand out the articles and give students time to read through their article. Get them to ask you if they have any problems.
- You could start by putting all the As together and all the Bs together so they can compare their ideas about what the main points are.
- Then pair up Student As with Bs to discuss the articles, and add their own opinions. They should attempt to reach an agreement about what should be done about the problem. Write some useful language on the board to help them, for example:
  Did you see the article in yesterday's ...?
  It said that ...
  Apparently, ...
  According to this article I read ...

- After the activity, get students to feed back to the whole class on what they discussed and what agreements they came to.

4 A new business
- This pairwork activity will give students the opportunity to practise using verb grammar correctly.
- You could divide the class into As and Bs before they start the pairwork activity so they can work together on constructing the questions. You could do the first one of each on the board as a model.
- Then put the As and Bs in pairs so they can ask and answer the questions in order to complete the profile.
- After the activity, do some whole class feedback to elicit the complete story from the students.

5 A good problem
- This is a group role-play activity. Set the scene and hand out the role cards. If you have uneven numbers or smaller groups, make sure that each group has at least the union leader and one or two members of the board.
- Give students a few minutes to read their roles and think about what they might say in the meeting.
- Encourage them to expand on the information on the cards and to make specific suggestions.
- After the role-play, get students to say what they decided and why. If you have time, you could get pairs from different groups to talk together and compare their different outcomes.

6 Not in my backyard
- This is a role-play activity in pairs. Start by explaining that the problem of young people gathering in residential areas is increasing in the UK and is the subject of local and national debate, and that the complaints detailed in the role cards are authentic.
- Draw students' attention to the title of the activity. This is a reference to people not wanting a problem near them although they would be happy for it to be somewhere else. For example, people may agree that nuclear power plants are necessary, but they wouldn't want one 'in their backyard'.
- Hand out the role cards and give students time to look at the information and decide how they are going to put across their complaints and arguments.
- Brainstorm some useful telephone language and write phrases on the board to help students with the task. For example:
  I'm calling about ...
  Can you do something about it?
  It's making my life a misery.
  We're doing all we can.
  Why don't you ...?
- As this is an authentic situation there is no real answer, but try to get students to reach some sort of mutually satisfactory agreement.
  After students have finished the role-play, you could open

this out into a general discussion by asking them if this is a problem in their country. Ask them what they think should be done.

7 A remarkable success
- For this pairwork activity, you will need to give each pair of students their own input.
- Start by asking students if they know anything about Dyson cleaners. You might need to explain that they are innovative vacuum cleaners that do not need bags. Traditionally you have to replace bags in cleaners when they are full, and as they become fuller they lose power. For more information about Dyson cleaners go to the *English365* website: www.cambridge.org/elt/english365.
- In pairs, students ask and answer questions to complete the profile.
- Monitor carefully to check that students are using the correct tenses.
- When they have finished, get them to look at each other's profiles to check they have the correct answers.

Answers

Student A
Questions
1 Where was he born?
2 What did he study?
3 How many countries did the company expand into?
4 What had he won by 1977?
5 What was he developing in the 1980s?
6 Where did he take his innovation?
7 Where did he set up subsidiaries?
8 What had turnover risen to?

Answers
1 Norfolk
2 interior and furniture design
3 40
4 his first design award
5 the bagless cleaner
6 to Japan
7 in France and Australia
8 £320 million

Student B
Questions
1 When was he born?
2 Who was he working for in 1972?
3 When did he become a director?
4 What was he renovating?
5 Why were companies reluctant to invest?
6 What had turnover risen to by 1993?
7 Where did it become the best-selling cleaner?
8 Where had he opened subsidiaries by the end of the decade?

Answers
1 in 1947
2 Rotork
3 in 1974
4 his house
5 because his innovation threatened the traditional vacuum cleaner market
6 £9 million
7 the UK
8 Germany, Spain and Japan

8 I'm going to do something about it

- You will need one sheet for each student.
- Students could do this individually or in pairs if they prefer, as long as both students speak.
- The politics part of this links in to the Student's Book topic, but stress that this is not the most important aspect. Tell students that they should focus on signalling the structure of their presentation.
- Give them time limits for making notes and for their presentations.
- Give them some useful language for structuring presentations. For example:
  I'll only talk for ...
  First, I'm going to ... Then, ... Finally, ...
  Please ask any questions at any point.
- They could give their presentations in pairs, groups or for the whole class.
- Allow time for feedback after the presentations.

9 Sounds fantastic!

- You will need a sheet for each pair with the instructions and phrases, and you will also need to cut up the language cards so there are enough for everyone.
- This starts as pairwork and then becomes a mingling activity which will encourage students to use language for active listening.
- First, get students to discuss when they might use the phrases. For example:
  That's great! = when someone tells you about something good and you want to show you are pleased.
  Really, do you? = when you want the person to know you are listening and are perhaps surprised at what they have said.
- Emphasise that all the phrases are used to show you are actively listening. You could also go over correct pronunciation, especially intonation, at this point.
- Make sure students understand what they are going to do next and brainstorm possible small talk topics that they could discuss. For example: the weather, holidays, cinema, free time.
- Then give each student a language card. If you have a small group, you could give students more than one language card.
- Students then mingle and have short conversations with a partner for one minute. During the conversation they should try to use the phrase on their language card as naturally as possible. If students have more than one card, they could either try to use them both in a conversation or use them alternately.
- When both students have used their language they should exchange cards and then talk to someone else. Exchanging the cards means that students will have the opportunity to use most, if not all, of the phrases.

10 A game of two parts

- For this game, you will need one copy of the page for each group of students. You will need a die for each group and enough counters for each student.

- You should monitor carefully to check that the verbs and particles are being matched correctly and that correct sentences are being made.
- When the groups have finished, go through all the possible multi-word verbs and elicit example sentences.

11 So you mean ...?

- For this group activity, you will need a set of sentences for each group of students. Distribute them equally.
- Stress that students should not just repeat what their neighbour says but they should paraphrase what they say in their own words.
- Some students might find this challenging, so go over the example with them carefully and perhaps add a couple of your own.
- Give students some help with language for natural sounding paraphrasing. For example:
  So, ...
  ..., then?
  You mean ...
  So what you're saying is ...
  Note that 'so' is a common way of introducing new topics or paraphrases into a conversation.
- Monitor the groups carefully.
- At the end of the activity, go through the answers and write up possible paraphrases on the board. You could elicit these from the group.

Possible answers

I don't think we will need to worry about the new product. → So you mean you think it will sell well?
The advertising campaign is way over budget. → So it's more expensive than we thought?
The presentation seemed to go on for ever! → So it was a bit boring, then?
The flight took 13 hours and there was a five-hour delay in Amsterdam. → You must be tired after all that travelling.
I'm fed up with this job. → So are you going to look for a new one?
My boss keeps giving me all the worst jobs. → You don't get on well, then?
I'm going to see a concert at the weekend. → So you like music?
I really need a holiday! → You've been working too hard recently.
I'm going to see a film tonight. → So you like the cinema, then?
I need some help with this report. → So you mean you want me to help you?
I'm going for a drink after work with my colleagues. → Do you get on well with them, then?
We're taking on new staff at the moment. → So orders are up then?

12 TV takeover

- In this reading and discussion activity, you will need one sheet for each student.
- Write the headline on the board and ask students for predictions about the article.
- Check or pre-teach the following words:
  conquer: to take control or possession of a foreign land

hooked: addicted to
charms: attractions
glued to: unable to stop watching something
telly: television
tiff: argument
veers: turns in the direction of
scapegoat: something that is blamed for something that is caused by something else
bane: cause of continual trouble or unhappiness

- Get students to look at the questions and tell them not to worry about the correct pronunciation of the names. The questions are intended to give students a quick overview of the article.
- Put students into small groups for the discussion.
- You could also ask:
  How much television do you watch?
  Do you feel that it ever affects your social life?
  Some people don't have televisions in their houses. What do you think of this?
  Would you ever decide to throw out your television?

13 It can't be!

- In this group activity, you will need a set of situations for each group of students.
- Put students into groups of three or four and distribute the situations.
- In turn, each student should read out their situation and the others should listen and make deductions about what happened or is happening.
- Write the following phrases on the board to help them and explain that there are many variations:
  It must be ...
  There might/may (not) be ...
  It should be ...
  It can't be ...
  Somebody must have ...
  There might have ...
  It can't have ...
- Give an example:
  Situation: *You can't find your English dictionary.*
  Possible deduction: *Somebody must have borrowed it.*
- The student whose deduction is the closest to what happened or is happening gets one point.
- The student with the most points at the end of the activity is the winner.

14 Negotiating a contract

- Set the scene and give out the role cards for this pairwork activity. Student A works for an English university and Student B is a training manager for an international organisation. Student B would like to send a group of students on a professional English course in the summer.
- Give students time to assimilate the information and prepare what they are going to say.
- Get students to brainstorm useful language for negotiating. For example:
  We expect to have a good working relationship ...
  It would be good to include ...
  We think the best option would be ...

We'd like to consider an alternative ...
- Tell them that they have a lot of flexibility when it comes to dealing with their bottom lines but that they should try to get the best deal possible.
- When students have finished, get them to feed back to the rest of the class on what was agreed, and see who got the best deal.

15 Getting what you want

- In this pairwork activity you will need to give a situation to each pair.
- The pairs have to create a dialogue around the situation. Stress that they should not say explicitly what the problem is. Get them to decide who the people in the situation are.
- Get students to brainstorm useful language for complaining. For example:
  There's a problem with ...
  I'd like you to do something about ...
  It's still not working and ...
  I'm very disappointed with ...
  Thank you. Yes, I'd be happy with that.
- They then perform the role-play in front of another pair, group or the whole class, who should say what the problem is and who the people are.

16 Really rarely

- This pairwork activity recycles both the grammar and pronunciation featured in Unit 16. Each pair will need the dialogues and adverbs to start with, and then a topic card later in the activity.
- Put students into pairs and get them to think about how the dialogues can be improved. Draw their attention to the adverbs they should use and remind them of the features of pronunciation they can use to improve the dialogues.
- Get them to practise in pairs and then get selected students to perform for the rest of the class.
- After they have finished this, put students into new pairs and give each pair a topic card. Ask them to have short conversations about the topic cards and to talk for about a minute. They should try to use the adverbs in their conversations and use pronunciation to add impact and to make them sound more interesting.
- Again, get selected pairs to perform for the rest of the class.

17 Unethical marketing?

- For this group discussion activity, you will need a sheet for each student.
- Put students in groups of three or four. Get them to read the list of marketing techniques individually. Help with any vocabulary and give further explanation, if necessary.
- Get the students to discuss the techniques and their attitudes towards them. Use the questions as prompts.
- As a follow up, you could ask students if they have experienced or seen any of these techniques. What did they feel? Are they aware of any other similar techniques?

18 You know you want to …

- In this pairwork activity you will need to give each pair a situation.
- Put students into pairs and make sure they understand what to do.
- Give them a few minutes to prepare their role-play around the situation – stress that they should not mention exactly what the situation is.
- Elicit strategies for persuading. For example: make it attractive and interesting, make it personal, repeat the message.
- Then get the pairs to perform their role-plays in front of another pair, group or the rest of the class, who should listen and say what the situation is.
- Put students into new pairs, but this time get them to choose a situation from their own work and prepare a role-play around it. Try to ensure that the persuader from the first role-play is now being persuaded. In this way both students will get a chance to do the persuading.
- Again, get selected pairs to perform for the rest of the class.

19 A health and safety audit

- In this pairwork activity you will need to give each student a role card.
- Set the scene and explain that a health and safety audit is when someone comes to an organisation to check that health and safety procedures and policies are being followed. If necessary, explain that risk assessment means checking on possible dangers that could cause injury, for example, cables on the floor that people could trip over.
- Give students time to read their role cards and prepare what they are going to say. Stress that the passive is often used to sound more impersonal. Encourage them to expand on the notes and use their imagination to develop the conversation.
- Give an example to get students started:
  A: *When was the documentation written?*
  B: *It was written last year.*
- While students are doing the role-play, check that the passive is being used correctly.

20 It's for all of you

- You could draw attention to the title of this activity. 'It's for you' is what people traditionally say when a person calls and it is for someone other than the person who answers. 'It's for all of you' is a reference to the fact that a teleconference call involves more than two people.
- This is a group role-play activity. Start by setting the scene. Brainstorm some useful language for the role-play. For example:
  What do you think about …?
  What did you say about …?
  Can you repeat that, please?
- Highlight the language and techniques that students should use and refer students to the Student's Book for more help with language, if necessary.

- Put students in groups of four and give them each a role card. If you have uneven numbers, you could leave out the role of the marketing executive. Give students a few minutes to read their roles and think about what they might say in the teleconference. You may want to tell the project managers that a screen reader is a system for blind or partially-sighted computer users which speaks the text content of a computer display.
- As this is a teleconference role-play, it is important that students do not look at each other. Get them to sit with their backs to each other or make use of internal telephones or a teleconference system, if available. You could give students names to use, or they could use their own real names. Remind them that it is important during teleconferences that people know who is being addressed.
- Encourage them to expand on the information on the cards and give more information based on their own experiences of using the internet.

21 Have you read that one about …?

- Students should work in pairs for this reading and discussion activity. Each student will need the questions and bestseller list.
- For the first part of this activity, you could add a competitive element by getting students to try to answer the questions as quickly as possible and see which pair answers them the fastest.
- For the second part of the activity, students should talk about which books most interest them and why by referring to other books on their bestseller list.
- Do some whole class feedback at the end to see which books are the most popular. This would also be a good opportunity to recommend the use of readers.

Answers

Student A
1 Judith Holder
1 *French Women Don't Get Fat* by Mireille Guiliano
2 *Red Herrings and White Elephants* by Albert Jack
3 Two
4 *The Little Prisoner*

Student B
1 Four
2 *Emperor: The Field of Swords* by Conn Iggulden
3 *Always and Forever* by Cathy Kelly
4 Wendy Holden
5 *The Journey*

22 If I were you …

- Students play this game in groups of three or four. Each group will need a set of conditionals and a board and die, as well as a counter for each student.
- Before you begin, go over the different types of conditional and elicit possible sentences. For example: Offer to help: *If you need any help, I'll do it.*
- Set the scene. Note that this is intended to be humorous.

- Your main role will be to monitor the groups to check that the conditionals are being used correctly.
- When you have finished the activity, ask selected students for advice, etc. that they gave Miranda for some of the situations.

23 Big hair

- This is a group discussion activity starting with questions about a text and moving on to a discussion about ways of raising money for charity, thereby linking with the work done by UNICEF. Each student will need a sheet.
- First, you will need to deal with some of the vocabulary from the article. You will need to explain that dosh is an informal term for money. Once you have explained this, you could get students to try to work out what the article is about from the headline.
- Get students to read the article and answer the initial questions quickly before they go on to discuss their answers to the questions which follow the text.
- Get students to choose one method of raising money and then to present it to the rest of the group. They should explain what the benefits of it might be and what kind of charity it might be suitable for.

Background briefing: Comic Relief

Comic Relief was set up in 1985. It was started by comedians who wanted to use comedy and laughter to let people know about poverty in the UK and in Africa. It is about having fun and making the world a better place. The organisation raises money and then uses it to help end poverty and unfairness. It works in the UK and also in the poorest countries in the world. It raises money from the public in the UK by getting them involved in fun special events. It does a lot of research to find out which charities to support and then carefully decides how best to spend the money donated by the public. It explains the causes of poverty in Africa and problems faced by groups and communities in the UK. It also lets people in the UK know how they can change things for the better.

24 It's my life

- This activity starts with students working individually and then becomes a pairwork discussion. Each student will need a sheet.
- Set the scene and go through the areas that students need to think about. Remind them that this practice could help them in a future job interview.
- Give students time to complete the information about their own education and career before they start asking each other questions. Encourage them to expand on the topic and not just to ask single questions. They should also make notes on what their partner says rather than writing the answers down word for word. You may want to refer to the section on taking notes in the Introduction (page 16).
- When they have finished, ask selected students to present their partner to another pair or the rest of the class.

25 I will

- This group speaking game leads on to a conversation. Each group will need one set of cards with future forms on them.
- Hand out the cards and place them face down in the middle of the group.
- Each student in the group should take it in turns to pick one up and read it out. The others should try to make a sentence using a future form as quickly as possible. The sentence should be true for them.
- The first person to make a correct sentence gets a point.
- Play this game at least twice so that each student has a good chance of using a few of the different forms.
- When students have finished, get them to have a conversation about the coming week using as many of the forms as possible. Encourage them to have a natural conversation, rather than just saying individual sentences. For example, you could give them the following prompt: *So, what are you doing over the next week?*
- When students have finished, get them to report back to the class on their plans.

26 This has been really useful

- This group activity is similar to the one in It's time to talk in the Student's Book, but here each student has a chance to introduce the issue and lead the discussion on a different topic. Each group will need a set of items on the agenda.
- In groups of three, students take it in turns to pick up an item, introduce the issue and lead a short discussion on it before summarising the recommendations and closing the meeting.
- Remind them to use the language for summarising and closing meetings. Elicit some useful phrases. For example:
Let's close the meeting now.
Any other points anyone wants to make?
This has been really useful …
So, we've agreed to …
I think we should fix a date for next time.
- If you have a weaker group, you could hand out the items and give students time to think about the issues and what they might say about them before the role-plays start.
- When students have finished, ask them to summarise selected items and the recommendations they made to the rest of the class.

27 The money doctor

- Set the scene and give out the role cards for this pairwork activity. Student A is a financial adviser who is doing a complete financial health check on Student B.
- Start by drawing students' attention to the 'Did you know?' statistic. What is their reaction to it? Is the situation similar in their country? Stress that personal debt is very common in the UK and that the scenario here is very realistic.
- Set the scene and give students time to read the information and prepare what they are going to say. You

might need to help students with the following vocabulary:

consolidate a loan: to put all your loans together into one big loan

ATM: abbreviation for *automated teller machine* – a machine, usually in a wall outside a bank, from which you can take money out of your bank account using a special card.

- As this activity is rather open-ended, encourage students to use language from Unit 27 and add as many of their own ideas as possible. You could help by writing some useful language on the board. For example:

What are your outgoings?
Could you tell me about ...?
You could/should ...
I suggest (that) you ...
I'd advise you to ...

28 She said ..., he said ...

- This group activity is intended to be light-hearted and to encourage students to practise using the forms of reported speech correctly. Each student will need a sheet.
- Put students in groups of three and ask them to complete the information about themselves first.
- You might want to remind students of the key points to remember when reporting speech. Refer them back to Unit 28 of the Student's Book, if necessary.
- Before they start, make sure they have decided who is interviewing whom and who is doing the reporting. Tell them that they do not have to be truthful. Try to ensure that each student has a turn at reporting.
- At the end, you could ask what some of the most interesting reported facts were.

29 Business and the law

- Students should do this reading and discussion activity in groups of four. Give each student in the group one article. If numbers are uneven, some students could have two stories.
- Students should read their story and be prepared to summarise it to the rest of the group. While they are doing this, go round and help with the vocabulary and encourage students to use dictionaries. You may find that there is quite a lot of new vocabulary, so perhaps set a limit of three words that students can look up. Encourage them to make sure they understand the main points and not necessarily every word. You could pool these words at the end to build on the vocabulary in Unit 29.
- Ask students to summarise their story and lead a short discussion on the main issues. Remind them to answer the questions given. You could write up the following to help them:

According to this article ...
My article is about ...
The main point is ...
I think ...
In my opinion ...
The company should have ...
The company shouldn't have ...
What do you think?

- At the end of the activity, get a spokesperson from each group to summarise what they discussed.

30 I need to talk to you

- Set the scene and give out the role cards for this pairwork activity. Student A and Student B work for the same organisation and have just been to a meeting with some important, longstanding clients.
- Give students time to think about what they are going to say. Remind them that they can add extra information if they want.
- Elicit useful language for getting across an important message. For example:

Are you busy at the moment?
I'm sorry, but this is really important.
I really need to talk to you ...
It's about ...
Can you remember ...?

- After they have done the role-play, ask students to think of a situation from their own working or personal life in which they might have to get across an important message.
- Get them to prepare it and perform it for another pair or the rest of the class.
- You may want to refer to the work on giving feedback in Unit 27 and ask students to comment on each other's performances.

1 Have you ever ...?

Objective
To practise using the present simple and continuous and the present perfect simple and continuous.

Introduction
In this activity, you will play a game which will encourage you to talk about a range of topics using different tenses.

What to do
1 Work in groups of three or four. Each person should have a set of tense cards.
2 Put the topic cards face down in the middle of the group.
3 Turn over the first topic card.
4 The objective is to have a conversation about that topic for one minute using a range of different tenses.
5 Take it in turns to say a sentence about the topic using the tense on your tense card. For example: Present simple question → *Where do you work?* The sentences made must be correct and must fit naturally into the conversation. If the group thinks that a sentence is incorrect they can vote to make the speaker take back the card.
6 When you have made a sentence using the tense on the card, put the card down.
7 After one minute you should start again with the next topic.
8 The winner is the first person to put down all their tense cards.

Input

Tense cards	Topic cards
Present simple statement	A current project
Present simple question	A previous job
Present simple negative	Your organisation
Present continuous statement	Your organisation's products or services
Present continuous question	Your colleagues
Present perfect simple statement	Your daily working life
Present perfect simple question	A problem at work
Present perfect continuous statement	Your greatest achievement at work
Present perfect continuous question	
Present perfect continuous negative	

2 The right decision?

Objective
To practise talking about management issues.

Introduction
In this activity, you will discuss and make management decisions.

What to do
1 Work in small groups or pairs. You are directors of a small manufacturing company. Unfortunately, you have a problem with the workforce. You have offered them a 2% pay rise, but because of the company's financial situation, you are unable to offer more.
2 Work together to decide what you are going to do to make your company succeed.
3 Your teacher will give you a set of cards.
4 Read card number 1 and discuss the options before you make a choice.
5 When you have made your choice, take the correct number card from the set and continue until you reach the end of the activity.

Input

Cards

1 The workforce is unhappy with this year's pay offer of 2%. The union requests a meeting. What do you do?
A Meet the union. Go to 2.
B Ignore the union. Go to 3.

2 In the meeting the union asks for a 3.5% increase. What do you do?
A Agree to its demands. Go to 4.
B Reject its demands. Go to 3.
C Continue to negotiate. Go to 5.

3 The union calls for a strike. What do you do?
A Arrange to meet the union leaders. Go to 2.
B Ignore it. The workers won't go on strike. Go to 6.
C Give the workers a 3.5% increase. Go to 4.

4 The pay increase costs a lot. You are over budget. What do you do?
A Increase the price of your products. Go to 7.
B Take out a bank loan. Go to 16.

5 Negotiations continue. The union sticks to its demands. What do you do?
A Explain the situation to the union and try to compromise. Go to 9.
B Ignore the union. Go to 3.

6 The workforce goes on strike. What do you do?
A Give them a 3.5% pay increase. Go to 4.
B Offer a 3% pay increase. Go to 9.
C Hold out. There's no way you can afford the increases. Go to 12.

7 The price increases result in a fall in sales. What do you do?
A Increase advertising. Go to 10.
B Find other ways of saving money. Go to 11.
C Take out a bank loan. The strike can't go on for ever. Go to 8.

8 The interest rates are very high. You are not producing any goods because of the strike. What do you do?
A Give the workers a 3.5% pay increase. Go to 4.
B Find other ways of saving money. Go to 11.

9 The union says they might accept a lower increase but want something in return. What do you do?
A Offer 3% and better working conditions. Go to 17.
B Offer 3% and an extra bonus to the union leaders. Go to 13.

10 The advertising campaign doesn't work and sales continue to fall. What do you do?
A Try to renegotiate the pay offer. Go to 9.
B Try to find other ways of saving money. Go to 11.

11 The only other way of saving money is redundancies. What do you do?
A Start making redundancies. Go to 3.
B Ask the union for its help. Go to 15.

12 The workforce stays on strike. Sales fall.
You go bankrupt.

13 The union accuses you of bribery. What do you do?
A Find other ways of saving money. Go to 11.
B Continue negotiations. Go to 15.

14 The workforce goes back to work but they are unhappy and productivity falls. What do you do?
A Enter negotiations once more. Go to 15.
B Offer the union leaders bonuses to keep the workforce happy. Go to 13.

15 You negotiate a deal for voluntary redundancy and can offer a 3.5% increase.
The strike ends. You have succeeded!

16 The interest rates are very high. You are losing a lot of money. What do you do?
A Withdraw the pay increase. Go to 6.
B Find other ways of saving money. Go to 11.

17 The union wants more time to think about it. What do you do?
A Let them have more time and hope everything will be OK. Go to 18.
B You're losing too much money. Tell them to take it or leave it. Go to 6.

18 The union accepts your offer and you've avoided a strike.
You have succeeded!

3 Have you heard the news?

Objective
To practise discussing a newspaper article.

Introduction
In this activity, you and your partner are going to read different local newspaper articles about the impact of banning smoking in public places in a small town. You are then going to discuss the issues.

What to do
1 First read your article and be prepared to summarise the main points.
2 Present the main points to your partner and add your own opinions.
3 Discuss the issue and try to reach agreement about what you think should be done.

Input

Student A

GOVERNMENT MOVES TOWARDS SMOKING BAN

The government indicated yesterday that it is seriously considering a complete ban on smoking in all workplaces. A blanket ban would cover not only offices but also all public places, including pubs and restaurants. This comes in the wake of new research that suggests passive smoking is much more harmful than previously thought and a recent survey which claims 75% of the population would support a complete ban. Peter Gregan, spokesman for anti-smoking groups welcomed the news: 'It really is about time that this issue was on the political agenda. The government has been dragging its feet for far too long on this issue.' This comes amid recent reports suggesting the government has been heavily influenced by the smoking lobby. 'Why should the health service have to fork out millions in healthcare for the victims of passive smoking? Why should people have to risk illness just doing their job? We can only accept a ban that would include pubs and restaurants,' Mr Gregan continued. Katie Pugh, a customer in the Rose and Crown pub yesterday said, 'I'm sick and tired of having to breathe other people's smoke – it stinks and it's bad for you. It's about time the government did something about it.'

Student B

SMOKING LOBBY FIGHTS BACK

Pro-smoking groups reacted strongly yesterday to news that the government might impose a ban on smoking in pubs and clubs, claiming that it was an infringement of people's individual freedoms. Sue Walton, a spokeswoman for one of the pro-smoking groups said, 'This government has been chipping away at people's rights for too long and this is just another example. If I want to enjoy tobacco I should have the right to do so.' Pub and club owners have also expressed fears that a ban would discourage smokers from drinking in their establishments. Norman Richardson, landlord of The Swan said, 'A lot of my customers are smokers – they come here for a sit down, a drink and a smoke with their friends. If they couldn't smoke I think they'd all stay at home. That's what they tell me anyway.' Sue Walton also pointed to little known research which suggests that in actual fact passive smoking is not harmful. She said, 'It seems to me that these reports have been suppressed – it's all political. The government is just trying to win a few votes at the expense of a minority.' Jason Wright, a smoker in The Swan yesterday, said, 'They say that they don't like the smoke in pubs, well it's their choice, isn't it? They don't have to come here, do they?'

4 A new business

Objective
To practise using gerunds and infinitives.

Introduction
In this activity, you will work in pairs to complete a profile of Sally Hulse who decided to set up her own business.

What to do
1 Work in pairs. Complete the skeleton questions and read the information.
2 Student A should ask Student B the questions first. Student B should answer the questions using the information provided.
3 Then Student B should ask Student A the questions. In this way you will both complete Sally's profile.

Input

Student A

Questions
When / she start / work / for ABG?
What / she hate / do?
What / she / want?
What / she decide / do?
Who help / her / set up the business?
What / she forget / do?
What / her friend / tell her / do?

Information
Sally wasn't allowed to continue trading and soon the tax office made her close the café down. She was losing money fast and she tried discussing the problem with the tax people but they refused to negotiate – she suggested paying the money in instalments at first but they wouldn't listen. Sally then promised to pay the tax bill in full but the tax office wouldn't let her open up the café. Eventually she had to give up the idea and, thousands of pounds in debt, she started working for ABG again. She hates it.

Student B

Questions
What / not allowed / do?
What / the tax office / make her / do?
What / she / try / do?
What / she / suggest / do?
What / she promise / do?
What / the tax office / let her / do?
Where / she start / work?

Information
Sally Hulse started working for ABG Electronics in 1995. She liked it at first but after a few years she found she hated working for a big company. She wanted to own her own business and so she decided to leave ABG in 2002. A few months later she opened a café. A friend of hers, an accountant, helped her to set up the finance side. Unfortunately, some months later, she forgot to pay her tax bill. Her friend told her not to worry.

5 A good problem

Objective
To practise talking about finance.

Introduction
In this activity, you are going to role-play a meeting and decide how to spend a sum of money.

What to do
1 Work in groups of five. Four of you are on the board of directors of a medium-sized company, and one person represents the union. The company made a profit of €50,000 in the last financial year. This is over and above what had been forecast. You are going to meet to discuss what to do with it.
2 Your teacher will give you a role card. Read it and prepare to put forward your point of view with reasons to support it.
3 Discuss possible options and try to agree on what to do with the money.

Input

Role cards

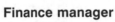

Marketing manager	Finance manager
You want to spend the money on a new advertising campaign. You feel that this will help to boost profits over the next year as sales increase. You feel that there is no guarantee that money spent on research will bring any results.	You feel that the company should play safe and deposit the money in a bank with a good rate of interest as this will guarantee a safe, if small, return. You feel that the company will not always have such good years and so it makes sense to put the money away for the future when it might be needed.
Research and development manager	**Union leader**
You want to put the money into research into new products. You feel that developing new product lines will help to keep the company ahead of the competition. You feel that there will be no gains for the company in the longer term if you don't invest more in R & D now.	You have been invited to participate in the meeting. You want to give the workers a bonus. You feel that it was the workers who made the profits possible. You feel that a happy workforce leads to greater efficiency and loyalty and that this move would improve relations between the management and the workforce.
Human resources manager	
You want to invest in staff training. You feel that the workforce is the company's most important asset and that having better trained staff leads to higher productivity and increased loyalty. You would also like to raise the idea of a profit sharing scheme for all the staff.	

6 Not in my backyard

Objective

To talk about a problem in a community and to practise making a complaint by telephone.

Introduction

In this activity, you are going to role-play a telephone conversation between a resident who is worried about the quality of life in the neighbourhood and someone who works for the local council.

What to do

1 Work in pairs. Your teacher will give you each a role card. Study it and prepare to talk about the issues raised with your partner.
2 Have the telephone conversation with your partner and try to reach agreement.

Input

Student A

You are a resident in a relatively good area of your city. Recently, groups of young people have started to gather near your house and you feel this is having an effect on your quality of life and on the neighbourhood in general. You telephone the local council to make a complaint about this and to enquire about what can be done.
You have the following complaints.

- The young people seem to start gathering after the youth club closes.
- They often make a lot of noise and leave litter in the street.
- They have started to commit low-level crime – damaging walls and fences and spraying graffiti, as well as abusing neighbours.
- You have called the police but as far as you know they have never come.
- Local community wardens have come but the young people ignore them.
- The young people seem to gather under streetlights.

Student B

You work in the local council and receive a telephone call from a resident complaining about groups of young people causing problems in the area. You are aware of this problem and it is becoming a widespread problem in the city. Try to reassure the resident and give the impression that the problem will be solved. These are the points you need to make.

- The council is aware of the problem and is doing all it can.
- There are plans to keep the youth club open until later in the evenings but there is a funding problem.
- The council has been in touch with the police but they say that such matters are low priority and they can only respond if a crime is actually committed.
- Local community wardens are very important. It is their job to patrol communities and try to prevent anti-social behaviour.
- There are plans to increase the street lighting in the area.
- Residents should install burglar alarms.

7 A remarkable success

Objective
To practise using the past simple, past continuous and past perfect.

Introduction
In this activity, you will ask and answer questions to complete a profile of James Dyson, the inventor of the bagless vacuum cleaner.

What to do
1 Work in pairs. Your teacher will give you a profile with some key information missing.
2 Do you already know something about Dyson cleaners? Read the profile and prepare questions to ask your partner in order to find out the missing information. You will need to think carefully about which past tense to use.
3 Ask and answer the questions in order to complete the profile.

Input

Student A

Ask questions using these question words to complete the profile of James Dyson.

1 Where?	5 What?
2 What?	6 Where?
3 How many?	7 Where?
4 What?	8 What?

James Dyson – inventor of the bagless cleaner

James Dyson was born in (1) .... , UK, in 1947 and went to the Royal College of Art in 1966 where he studied (2) .... In 1972, while he was working for Rotork, the company expanded its operations into (3) .... different countries. He became a director of Rotork in 1974 but left a year later in order to set up his own business. By 1977 he had won (4) .... – for a wheelbarrow.

In 1978 Dyson came up with the idea of a bagless cleaner while he was renovating his house.

While he was developing the (5) .... in the 1980s, he found that the big companies were reluctant to invest because it threatened the traditional vacuum cleaner market. As a result, he took his innovation to (6) .... and in 1986 it first went on the market there. Sales grew and the cleaner penetrated other markets worldwide. It was a great success and by 1993 turnover had risen to £9 million. In 1995 it became the best-selling cleaner in the UK.

The following year he set up subsidiaries in (7) .... and by the end of the decade Dyson had opened subsidiaries in Germany, Spain and Japan. Turnover had risen to over (8) ....

Student B

Ask questions using these question words to complete the profile of James Dyson.

1 When?	5 Why?
2 Who?	6 What?
3 When?	7 Where?
4 What?	8 Where?

James Dyson – inventor of the bagless cleaner

James Dyson was born in Norfolk, UK, in (1) .... and went to the Royal College of Art in 1966 where he studied interior and furniture design. In 1972, while he was working for (2) .... , the company expanded its operations into 40 different countries. He became a director of Rotork in (3) .... but left a year later in order to set up his own business. By 1977 he had won his first design award – for a wheelbarrow.

In 1978 Dyson came up with the idea of a bagless cleaner while he was renovating his (4) ....

While he was developing the bagless cleaner in the 1980s, he found that the big companies were reluctant to invest because (5) .... As a result, he took his innovation to Japan and in 1986 it first went on the market there. Sales grew and the cleaner penetrated other markets worldwide. It was a great success and by 1993 turnover had risen to (6) .... In 1995 it became the best-selling cleaner in (7) ....

The following year he set up subsidiaries in France and Australia and by the end of the decade Dyson had opened subsidiaries in (8) .... Turnover had risen to over £320 million.

8 I'm going to do something about it

Objective

To practise talking about political policies and structuring a presentation.

Introduction

In this activity, you are standing for a seat on the local council and you are going to give a presentation on your policy.

What to do

1 Imagine that you have decided that you want to do something to help improve your local community and so you have decided to stand for a seat on the local council.
2 Think of ways in which you think your local community might be improved and one policy in particular you would implement to make this happen.
3 Make notes about your policy, why you have chosen it, how you would implement it and what the benefits might be. Prepare to give a presentation about it.
4 Give your presentation, ensuring you structure it clearly.

Input

Make notes here.

My policy
Why
How
Benefits
Other points
Conclusion

9 Sounds fantastic!

Objective
To practise techniques and language for active listening.

Introduction
In this activity, you are going to look at techniques and language for active listening and then have short conversations.

What to do
1 Work in pairs. Look at the phrases below and discuss when they might be used.
2 Your teacher will then give you a language card with one of the phrases written on it.
3 Move around the class and have a short conversation with one person for a minute. You can choose the topic.
4 While you are talking, you should try to use the phrase on your language card correctly.
5 When you have both used your phrases, exchange language cards and then move on to talk to another person.

Input

When might the following be used?
What do they mean?

> *Phrases*
>
> That's great!
>
> I'm glad to hear it.
>
> Really, do you?
>
> Sounds fantastic!
>
> Oh, I'm sorry to hear that.
>
> It sounds as if you had a good time.
>
> What a shame!
>
> So what exactly did you do?
>
> That must have been great.
>
> Sounds awful!

Language cards

> **That's great!**
>
> **I'm glad to hear it.**
>
> **Really, do you?**
>
> **Sounds fantastic!**
>
> **Oh, I'm sorry to hear that.**
>
> **It sounds as if you had a good time.**
>
> **What a shame!**
>
> **So what exactly did you do?**
>
> **That must have been great.**
>
> **Sounds awful!**
>
> **Ask a question.**
>
> **Summarise what the person said.**

Objective
To practise using multi-word verbs.

Introduction
In this activity, you are going to play a game which tests your ability to form and use different multi-word verbs.

What to do
1 Work in groups of three or four.
2 Take it in turns to roll a die and move the number of spaces on the board.
3 When you land on a verb you should make a multi-word verb by choosing an appropriate particle from the list. You should then make a sentence using that multi-word verb.
4 If you want to make a multi-word verb with three parts, choose two particles from the list.
5 If a person makes a mistake they do not move forward.
6 If a person throws a six, they do NOT move and miss their next turn.
7 Sometimes you just follow the instructions to move forwards or backwards on the board.
8 The winner is the first person to reach the Finish.

Input

at   forward   to   after   down   on   out   off   up   over   against

START ▶	follow ▶	look ▶	come
Move forward two squares. ◀	work ◀	turn ◀	grow ▼
finish ▼	pick ▶	Move back five squares. ▶	give
build ◀	back ◀	bring ◀	Move back two squares. ▼
set ▼	get ▶	Go back to the beginning. ▶	**FINISH**

11 So you mean ...?

Objective
To practise summarising or paraphrasing.

Introduction
In this activity, you are going to paraphrase what your neighbour says. This is a useful skill in meetings and means you can check your understanding of what people say.

What to do
1 Work in groups of three or four.
2 Your teacher will give you each two cards with sentences on them. Read the first one out and the person on your left should paraphrase it. That person should then read his/her sentence, and so on, taking it in turns. Continue until everyone has paraphrased two sentences.
3 Then make a sentence about your work and the person on your right should paraphrase it. Then continue that way round until everyone has paraphrased two sentences. For example:
Sentence: *With a bit of luck I will be the new production manager next year.*
Paraphrase: *So you're going to get promoted?*

Input

✂ -

I don't think we will need to worry about the new product.

The advertising campaign is way over budget.

The presentation seemed to go on for ever!

The flight took 13 hours and there was a five-hour delay in Amsterdam.

I'm fed up with this job.

My boss keeps giving me all the worst jobs.

I'm going to see a concert at the weekend.

I really need a holiday!

I'm going to see a film tonight.

I need some help with this report.

I'm going for a drink after work with my colleagues.

We're taking on new staff at the moment.

Objective

To practise discussing a newspaper article.

Introduction

In this activity, you are going to read an article about television and then discuss the issues it raises.

What to do

1 Look at the title of the article. What do you think it means? How do you think the people of Bhutan feel about television?
2 Look at the questions and then read the text quickly to find the answers.
3 Talk about the discussion questions in small groups.

Input

Reading questions
1 Why is television so popular in Bhutan?
2 Summarise what the following people feel about television in Bhutan.

- Choki Wangmo
- Ugyen Choki
- Ugyen Dorji
- Kinley Dorji
- Dorji Ohm
- Leki Dorji

TV conquers remote Bhutan

When television arrived in Bhutan in June 1999, the remote Himalayan kingdom was immediately hooked on its charms. This was not surprising considering that Bhutan offers very little in terms of entertainment. Residents of the capital, Thimphu, now say they are glued to the telly for several hours a day. Long-running and popular Indian soap operas beamed from across the border are hot favourites. Thimphu residents animatedly discuss the serials and follow the fortunes of their characters.

Addicted

One of the viewers is Choki Wangmo. She and her three children cannot take their eyes off a Hindi soap on the television set in their tiny living room. Her 13-year-old daughter, Ugyen Choki, says she never misses the serial *Kasauti Zindagi Ki* (The Measure of Life), broadcast four days a week. When the lead characters in the soap have a tiff, Ugyen says she feels very sad. Her brother, Ugyen Dorji is also addicted to television. "My sleep is reduced because of TV. I know it affects my studies," he says.

"I cannot concentrate and even in the classroom I keep thinking about what will happen in the story tomorrow." Television dominates family discussions these days, says Choki Wangmo. "The children go out and play less. Even conversation at home veers around television," she says.

Vulnerable

Kinley Dorji, editor of *Kuensel*, Bhutan's only newspaper, says television is 'splitting' Bhutanese society. He says young viewers are particularly vulnerable. "The most popular programmes are the wrestling entertainment. When TV first came in, students wrote to us saying they were shocked. They could not imagine why these big men were throwing each other around and fighting." Mr Dorji says his paper received letters from children and carried reports saying how these wrestling sequences were simulated. "But very quickly the kids started doing it themselves. We received a report that in one school in central Bhutan a student broke his arm because his friend threw him on the ground, emulating these wrestlers."

Scapegoat

But many say that television is not the bane of Bhutanese society. Dorji Ohm, who works with a Thimphu-based NGO, Youth Development Fund, says TV is being made a scapegoat for Bhutan's problems. "In fact, most TV programmes are safe," she says. Most agree that people are watching too much television. The government is working on a law to set and monitor programme standards. But Communication and Information Minister Leki Dorji says there is only so much the government can do. "You cannot stop anything coming from abroad. The internet's spreading fast. There's radio and TV available on the net," he says. "So it's the responsibility of the parents to advise their children what to watch, when to watch and how much to watch."

Back at the Wangmo household, all eyes are still on the TV. Choki Wangmo admits family life can come second to television. "We eat dinner while watching TV and if we talk during a show, the children tell us off. They say they can't follow the dialogue."

Discussion questions
- Do you feel that television affects communication in your home? In what way?
- What are the possible harmful effects of this?
- Do you think that television can influence people's behaviour? How far do you feel it causes problems in society?

13 It can't be!

Objective
To practise using modal verbs for deduction in the past and present.

Introduction
In this activity, you are going to look at some situations and make deductions about what caused or is causing them.

What to do
1 Work in groups of three or four.
2 Your teacher will give you some situations and a description of what happened for each one. Take it in turns to read yours to the group without saying what the cause was/is.
3 The rest of the group should listen and try to say what caused the situation. The person who is closest gets a point.
4 The person with the most points at the end of the activity is the winner.

Input

Situation 1
The photocopier isn't working. You can't make any copies.
Cause: It has run out of paper.

Situation 2
Your colleagues from another city haven't arrived for a meeting you arranged last week.
Cause: You made a mistake with the time.

Situation 3
You can't find your diary.
Cause: You left it at home.

Situation 4
You can't get access to the internet.
Cause: Your phone line isn't working.

Situation 5
The finance department has rejected your expenses claim.
Cause: You forgot to send the right receipts.

Situation 6
Your bonus is much bigger than you expected.
Cause: Your boss thinks you deserve it. You've worked very hard this year.

Situation 7
Your mobile phone doesn't work.
Cause: It needs charging.

Situation 8
The door to your office is unlocked when you arrive for work.
Cause: The cleaners forgot to lock it.

Situation 9
Your boss isn't in her office.
Cause: She's been called away on urgent business.

Situation 10
You arrive at your hotel in another country. There are lots of people in the street.
Cause: There has been a small earthquake.

Situation 11
Your train doesn't arrive.
Cause: Some repairs are being done to the railway line.

Situation 12
An important letter hasn't arrived by post.
Cause: There has been a postal strike.

14 Negotiating a contract

Objective
To practise negotiating.

Introduction
In this activity, you will negotiate a contract and try to get the best possible deal for your organisation

What to do
1 Work in pairs. Student A works for an English university and Student B is a training manager for an international organisation. Student B would like to send a group of students on a professional English course in the summer.
2 Talk together to negotiate the best deals for your respective organisations.
3 Before you start, brainstorm language for the following:
   • stating positive expectations
   • stating preferences
   • suggesting alternatives.

Input

Student A

You are in charge of professional English courses at your university.
You want the following:
• A group of at least 24 students
• The group to arrive on a Sunday
• A four week course
• One study trip each week
• Four weeks accommodation on the university campus with shared facilities
• Confirmation by the end of the month and the non-returnable deposit to be paid at the same time

You can accept:
• If there are fewer than 24 students you will have to charge more
• The group can arrive on a Saturday but this is inconvenient for you
• A three week course – but not, for example three and a half weeks
• You could offer two half-day trips each week
• Accommodation with en-suite facilities, but this will cost more
• You can extend the confirmation deadline by a few days but no more
• You can be flexible about the dates for the deposit but would prefer it to be based on student numbers

Student B

You are in charge of training for your organisation. You want the following:
• The costs to be as low as possible
• You have 20 students who are interested so far – find out if it is possible to send this number
• The group to arrive on a Saturday to give students time to recover from the journey
• A four week course means that flights are more expensive – try to get a three and a half week course
• More than one study trip each week
• Accommodation on campus with en-suite facilities
• Confirmation of student numbers by the end of next month – you can pay the deposit then

You can accept:
• Paying slightly more for the students, but you want this cost as low as possible – you can try to get more students interested or try to get a deal on costs if there are only 20; try to get a discount if there are more than 24 students
• Half day trips
• You can't confirm student numbers any earlier, but you can pay the deposit if it is fixed rather than based on student numbers

15 Getting what you want

Objective
To revise useful language for complaining.

Introduction
In this activity, you will create a short dialogue around a situation in which a complaint is made.

What to do
1 Work in pairs. Your teacher will give you a situation. With your partner, create a role-play around the situation without saying exactly what the problem is.
2 Before you start, brainstorm some language for complaining.
3 Then perform the role-play in front of other students. They have to say what the situation is, what went wrong and who the speakers are.

Input

- -

✂

The TV doesn't work in your hotel.

One of the wheels on your suitcase fell off after your first trip abroad.

Your new laptop keeps crashing.

There is a mistake in the report you asked a colleague to write.

One of the buttons on your new MP3 player doesn't work.

Your hotel room hasn't been cleaned properly.

A company you do business with has put the wrong figure on an invoice.

You can't log on to the internet.

A CD you bought has a scratch on it.

You are in a restaurant – the chicken is not cooked enough.

16 Really rarely

Objective

To practise using adverbs and intonation to give spoken English more impact and interest.

Introduction

In this activity, you are going to look at some basic dialogues and try to improve them by making them more natural and interesting.

What to do

1 Work in pairs. Look at the dialogues and list of adverbs. Try to improve the dialogues by making them sound more natural by adding adverbs from the list and by using intonation, volume, stress and pauses. You can add extra information, if you wish.

2 Then work with a new partner. Your teacher will give you a topic card. Practise talking about the topic, using some of the adverbs listed and using intonation, volume, stress and pauses.

Input

Dialogues

Dialogue 1

A: So how was the meeting?

B: Not good. We didn't get what we wanted.

A: Why was that?

B: Well, when we mentioned the price they wanted to stop the meeting.

Dialogue 2

A: Did you have a good holiday?

B: Yes, I enjoyed it.

A: Where did you go?

B: Spain. The food was good and it was hot.

Dialogue 3

A: Have you met the new boss?

B: Not yet. What's she like?

A: She seems nice and she speaks French.

B: I'll be interested to meet her.

Adverbs

quickly	fluently	carefully	often
rarely	never	there	yesterday
now	then	really	very	absolutely
highly	unfortunately	luckily	

Topic cards

✂

A holiday

Something that has gone well at work

A problem at work

Your hobby

A recent news story

Your English

17 Unethical marketing?

Objective
To discuss marketing practices.

Introduction
In this activity, you will look at some controversial marketing techniques and discuss your attitude towards them.

What to do
1 Work in groups. Look at the list of marketing techniques below and discuss your attitudes to each one.
2 Think about these questions.
   • Is the marketing technique fair?
   • What might the negatives be?
   • How serious is it?
   • What benefits might there be for the company?
   • What should be done about them?

Input
....

Marketing techniques

Cold calling Some companies telephone people at home without being asked to do so and try to sell or promote their products or services.

Internet pop ups Advertisements 'pop up' on the internet, blocking what you are looking at.

Favourites list Some websites automatically add their address to your favourites list.

Spam Some companies send unsolicited emails advertising different products and services to your inbox.

Fly posters In an attempt to have a fashionable image that appeals to young people, some companies put up posters on walls and buildings rather than using advertising hoardings.

Targeting schools Some soft drinks companies give away free samples in schools.

Targeting children Some confectionary companies sponsor 'get fit' programmes for children.

SMS text messages Some companies advertise by sending out unsolicited text messages about their products or services.

Answering machine messages Some companies leave messages saying you have won a major prize and should phone back on a premium rate line to claim it.

18 You know you want to …

Objective
To practise persuading people to do things.

Introduction
In this activity, you are going to look at some situations and take it in turns to persuade your partner to do something for you.

What to do
1 Work in pairs. Your teacher will give you a situation. Look at the situation together and prepare a role-play. Student A should try to persuade Student B to do something. Try to use strategies for persuading.
2 When you have prepared your role-play, perform it for other students, who should try to work out what the situation is.
3 Then work with a new partner. Prepare a role-play about a situation in your workplace. Try to persuade your partner to do something for you.
4 Again, when you have finished, perform your role-play for other students, who should say what the situation is.

Input

Situations

You want a colleague to go to a meeting you are supposed to go to. You have been very busy and haven't prepared for it properly.

You want a colleague to go out and buy you some lunch from the shop.

You want a colleague to change the toner in the photocopier.

You are expecting a phone call from a difficult customer. Ask your colleague to take the call for you.

You would like your colleague to explain how to use some new, complicated software on your computer.

You haven't done your filing for weeks. Ask a colleague for some help.

You really want to play badminton tonight but your original partner can't make it. Persuade your colleague to play with you instead.

Objective
To practise using the passive.

Introduction
In this activity, you are going to talk about a health and safety audit.

What to do
1 Work in pairs. Your teacher will give each of you a role card. Look at it and prepare what you are going to say. Remember to use the passive so that what you say sounds more impersonal.
2 Role-play the conversation with your partner.

Input

Student A

You have been carrying out a health and safety audit in an organisation. After the audit, you talk to the person who is responsible for making sure that the health and safety guidelines are followed. You have made the notes below. Ask the person responsible some questions to clarify and check that things are being done properly. Give advice where necessary.

Notes

Written documentation – when? – who by? (not complete)

Distribution of information – who by? (not all staff aware)

Practice fire alarm – when last carried out? (should be every week)

Fire information in rooms – when last checked? (should be every year)

Risk assessment of all offices – when last done? (should be every year)

Workstation assessments – does everyone have a good chair? – does everyone have their chair, computer, keyboard, mouse, etc. in the right position?

Student B

You are the person in charge of health and safety in your organisation. An audit has just been carried out and the auditor wants to meet you and talk about your policy. You have been very busy and know that you have not kept some things up to date, and so you have prepared the notes below. If there are any problems, say what will be done to solve them.

Notes

Written documentation – last year – me

Distribution of information – my secretary (been off sick)

Practice fire alarm – last month

Fire information in rooms – checked last month – me

Risk assessment of all offices – two years ago

Workstation assessments – new chairs ordered last week; position of everyone's computer, keyboard, mouse, etc. to be checked next month

20 It's for all of you

Objective

To give students the opportunity to practise having a conference call.

Introduction

In this activity, you are going to have a teleconference to discuss setting up a new website for a small management training company. The website should attract potential customers and allow them to view services and training packages over the internet.

What to do

1 Work in groups of four. Your teacher will give you each a role card. The roles are: project manager, marketing executive, freelance web designer and systems administrator, and the characters are all currently in different cities. Read your card and prepare to put forward your point of view with reasons to support it.

2 Then have a teleconference to discuss possible options and try to agree on how to proceed with the website. Sit with your back to the group or use separate telephones if possible, and try to use language and techniques appropriate for a teleconference.

Language
Begin with small talk
Ask for opinions
Ask for repetition

Techniques
Use people's names
Leave a short space before responding

Input

Project manager (in Berlin)
You are in charge of the budget and schedule. While you realise the importance of improving your organisation's website, you are aware that costs must be kept as low as possible. These are your main concerns.

- Cost – you know web designers can charge a lot of money but you know the website has to be good
- Timing – you would like the website to be completed as soon as possible
- Accessibility – there is a legal obligation to make the website accessible to disabled and blind users; animations, lots of images and video cannot be read by screen readers
- Minimising risk – you want the website to be simple and safe

Freelance web designer (in Toronto)
You have been asked to design the organisation's website. These are your main concerns.

- You can design a non-interactive website at a low cost
- You are very keen on interactive websites and the use of moving images, video and music; you think it looks good and will attract people to the organisation's website (also it will look good in your portfolio, but you don't want to tell the organisation this)
- You think that download time is no longer an issue as people have broadband connections
- Clients think that online forms can take a long time to design and so are very expensive
- You are very busy at the moment; although you are keen to do the work, you cannot start it for two months
- You want to make as much money as possible

Marketing executive (in London)
You are from the marketing department and have prepared a report on user preferences. These are your main concerns.

- Ease of use – the website must be easy to navigate around
- Forms – you would like people viewing the site to be able to fill in a form online if they want more information rather than emailing you
- Interactivity – you feel the current website is not very interactive and not very appealing. It needs more pictures, animation, video and audio
- The website must download quickly for users without broadband

Systems administrator (in Dublin)
You will be responsible for maintaining the website and setting up any new hardware and software. These are your main concerns.

- Your current server is almost full – it cannot hold any more material than there is at present and you do not want to pay any additional costs to upgrade it
- Accessibility – you are worried that video, music and moving pictures will take too long for many people to download: the site has to be available for people who might not have broadband yet. Also, lots of video takes up server capacity so a more powerful server would be needed. Media rich websites also take up a lot of band width, which is very expensive
- Security – it is easier to make a non-interactive website secure

21 Have you read that one about ...?

Objective

To practise talking about books and reading for specific information.

Introduction

In this activity, you are going to look at a bestseller list and then talk about which books you would like to read.

What to do

1 Work in pairs. Your teacher will give each of you some questions and a bestseller list. Take it in turns to ask your partner the questions about his/her bestseller lists and then answer his/her questions about your bestseller list.

2 Tell your partner what kind of books you like and he/she will make some recommendations to you by referring to other books on your bestseller list.

Input

Student A

Questions about Non-fiction hardbacks
1 Who wrote *Grumpy Old Women*?
2 Which book is about French cooking?
3 Which book might help you with your English?
4 How many weeks has *Rock Me Gently* been on the list?
5 What did Jane Elliot write?

	TOP 10 FICTION HARDBACKS	LAST WEEK	WEEKS ON LIST
1	**Saturday** *Ian McEwan* (*Cape £17.99*) Brain surgeon reflects on his life as war looms 5,630 (38,267)	1	**5**
2	**The Broker** *John Grisham* (*Century £17.99*) Secret services vie to eliminate ex-con 4,607 (73,232)	2	**7**
3	**The Journey** *Josephine Cox* (*HarperCollins £16.99*) Chance meeting unlocks secrets of the past 4,362 (10,773)	4	**2**
4	**Honeymoon** *James Patterson and Howard Roughan* (*Headline £17.99*) Beware the black widow 4,143 (33,461)	3	**5**
5	**Always and Forever** *Cathy Kelly* (*HarperCollins £12.99*) Magic moments in the hills of Ireland 2,149 (2,267)	-	**1**
6	**Emperor: The Field of Swords** *Conn Iggulden* (*HarperCollins £12.99*) Caesar returns to Rome 1,826 (37,520)	5	**8**
7	**The Da Vinci Code: The Illustrated Edition** *Dan Brown* (*Bantam Press £20*) With the clues in pictures. Super 1,264 (74,534)	6	**13**
8	**Body Double** *Tess Gerritsen* (*Bantam Press £12.99*) Maura Isles discovers identical, but dead, twin 1,182 (11,173)	8	**6**
9	**The Wives of Bath** *Wendy Holden* (*Headline £12.99*) Parenthood and wives 1,106 (25,570)	7	**8**
10	**Chainfire** *Terry Goodkind* (*Voyager £18.99*) Wizard wields his Sword of Truth for the 10th time 948 (6,326)	9	**4**

Student B

Questions about Fiction hardbacks
1 How many weeks has Chainfire been on the list?
2 Which book is about ancient Rome?
3 Which book is about Ireland?
4 Who wrote *The Wives of Bath*?
5 What did Josephine Cox write?

	TOP 10 NON-FICTION HARDBACKS	LAST WEEK	WEEKS ON LIST
1	**The Little Prisoner** *Jane Elliott* (*Element £12.99*) Enduring 17 years of a stepfather's cruelty 3,945 (28,899)	1	**6**
2	**Grumpy Old Women** *Judith Holder* (*BBC £9.99*) Germaine Greer et al mouth off. More hot air, vicar? 3,042 (5,026)	12	**1**
3	**A Brother's Journey** *Richard B Pelzer* (*Time Warner £14.99*) Dave's kid brother on abuse 2,992 (19,062)	2	**5**
4	**Rock Me Gently** *Judith Kelly* (*Bloomsbury £16.99*) Hurt at the hands of nuns 2,755 (9,549)	6	**2**
5	**French Women Don't Get Fat** *Mireille Guiliano* (*Chatto £12*) Been to the Ardeche recently? 2,347 (33,069)	5	**8**
6	**Auschwitz** *Laurence Rees* (*BBC £20*) Looking back 60 years after the camp's liberation 2,101 (27,719)	4	**7**
7	**Red Herrings and White Elephants** *Albert Jack* (*Metro Books £9.99*) The etymology of everyday phrases 2,037 (95,524)	7	**10**
8	**Moving On** *Kevin Lewis* (*M Joseph £16.99*) Part two of the story of the Kid 1,926 (5,013)	11	**1**
9	**Eats, Shoots and Leaves** *Lynne Truss* (*Profile £9.99*) Observation of the otiose 1,834 (946,816)	8	**63**
10	**EastEnders: 20 Years in Albert Square** *Rupert Smith* (*BBC £14.99*) Why people flee to the country 1,772 (5,362)	9	**2**

22 If I were you ...

Objective
To practise using conditionals.

Introduction
In this activity, you are going to play a game where you have to respond to a number of situations using a range of different conditionals.

What to do
1 Imagine that Miranda Derry is a colleague of yours. Unfortunately, she always seems to have problems and makes a lot of mistakes.
2 Work in groups of three or four. Your teacher will give you a set of cards with functions for conditionals. Read these and put them face down. Look at the sentences about Miranda on the board.

3 Take it in turns to roll a die. Move the number of spaces on the board and pick up a conditional card.
4 Then respond to the situation using a conditional with that function, as if you are talking to Miranda. For example:
She didn't get her promotion. + Criticism
If you had worked harder, you would have got your promotion.
5 If you make a mistake with the sentence, you do not move forward and remain in the original position.
6 If you can't make a sentence, put the conditional card at the bottom of the pile and pick up another.
7 The winner is the first person to reach the Finish.

Input

Conditionals

✂- - - - - - - - - - - - - -
| Regret |
| Criticism |
| Offer to help |
| Threat |
| Advice |
| Your choice |

START ▶	She didn't get her promotion.	She wants to spend more time with her family.	She wants to do more exercise. ▼
She didn't write an important report at the weekend. ◀	She can't decide where to go on holiday this year. ◀	She has an important deadline coming up. ◀	She doesn't have much of a social life.
▼ She can't speak any foreign languages.	She forgot about a meeting. ▶	She overslept this morning. ▶	She shouted at a customer. ▶ ▼
FINISH ◀	Your own idea	She has too much filing to do. ◀	She wants to become more efficient at work. ◀	She is very stressed at work.

23 Big hair

Objective
To discuss ways of raising money for charity.

Introduction
In this activity, you are going to look at a short text that describes an unusual way of making money and then discuss other possible ways of raising money.

What to do
1 Read the article and answer these questions:
  • What is the objective of Comic Relief?
  • What do people have to do to raise money?
  • What does the BBC want people to do?
2 In groups, discuss your answers to the questions which follow the text.
3 Then choose one way of raising money and present it to your group, explaining the benefits.

Input

Big Hair, Big Dosh!
Ever needed an excuse to do something daft, experiment with your appearance or just do something out of the ordinary? Comic Relief provides you with the perfect reason as it is all about raising money in weird and wonderful ways for charity! This year, the Red Nose Day theme is Big Hair and Beyond, with the aim of getting as many people as possible to change the way they look on Friday 11 March. Don't forget to get sponsored for doing so though! Of course, there are many other ways you can raise money for Comic Relief too. The BBC wants to hear from you about your plans to raise money for Red Nose Day. Tell us about your event or how you have raised money and we will publish the details.

Discussion questions
1 Would you like to get involved with something like Red Nose Day? Why? Why not?
2 How would you change the way you look for Red Nose Day?
3 How would you suggest making money for a charity?
4 How many different ways of raising money can you think of?
5 Which charities do you donate to? Why?

24 It's my life

Objective
To practise talking about your education and career so far.

Introduction
In this activity, you are going to talk to a partner about your education and career.

What to do
1 Working individually, look at the table below and complete the information about yourself.
2 Then work in pairs and ask your partner questions about his/her education and career. For example:
   What school did you go to?
   Write notes on his/her answers.
3 Try to develop the conversation and ask follow-up questions.
4 Be prepared to present your partner to other students.

Input

	You	Your partner
School		
Further education		
Part-time jobs		
Qualifications		
Career		
Career development		
Training		

25 | will

Objective
To practise using future forms.

Introduction
In the first part of this activity, you will play a game that will encourage you to use a range of different future forms. Then you will practise using these forms in a conversation.

What to do
1 Work in groups of three or four. Your teacher will give you a set of cards with future forms on them. Put them face down in the middle.
2 Take it in turns to pick up a card and read out the future form to the rest of the group. The students in the group should try to make a sentence using the appropriate future form as quickly as possible. The sentence should be true for them.

Input

For example:
A fixed future arrangement, especially for personal travel and meetings → *I'm catching a train tomorrow at 5.*

3 The first person to say a correct sentence in the appropriate future form gets a point. The person with the most points at the end of the round is the winner.
4 Play the game again so that everyone can have the opportunity to make as many different sentences as possible.
5 Then talk about the week ahead with the other students in your group. Try to use each future form in as natural a context as possible.

Future forms

An activity in progress at a specific point in the future

A future intention, decision or plan

A fixed future arrangement, especially for personal travel and meetings

A future arrangement

A future event which is part of a timetable

A future action decided at the moment of speaking

Objective

To practise summarising recommendations and closing a meeting.

Introduction

In this activity, you are going to role-play a union meeting.

What to do

1 Work in groups of three. Your teacher will give you an item on the agenda of the union meeting.
2 Take it in turns to be chairperson. Read out your item, introduce the issue and lead a discussion on the item and try to agree on a recommendation. Discuss what should be done in each situation for three minutes.
3 Then summarise the recommendation(s) and bring the meeting to a close.
4 If possible, each student should lead two discussions.

Input

Items on the agenda

Parking The car parks are overcrowded.

Time worked Many staff are working longer than their contracted hours.

Staff development Many manual staff do not have access to staff development and training.

Pay There is an increasing gap between the rates of pay for male and female members of staff.

Disability access You are worried that the access to buildings and equipment might not meet new government standards.

Health and safety You are worried that there will be a health and safety audit soon.

27 The money doctor

Objective
To practise talking about personal finance.

Introduction
In this activity, you are going to role-play a discussion between a financial adviser and someone who has a few financial problems.

What to do
1 Work in pairs. Student A is a financial adviser who is doing a complete financial health check on Student B.
2 Your teacher will give you each a role card. Read it and plan what you are going to say. Try to include your own ideas.
3 When you have finished, compare the advice given with the rest of the class.

Did you know?
The amount of money Britons owe on credit cards, loans and mortgages is over £1,000,000,000,000 – £1 trillion. This is equivalent to £17,000 of debt for every man, woman and child.

Source: GM TV

Input

Student A

You are a financial adviser. Student B comes to you to discuss how to improve his/her financial situation. Ask him/her questions to get a clear idea before you make any recommendations. Ask questions about:
• Salary
• Monthly outgoings
• Mortgage
• Credit cards
• Savings
• Spending habits

You can recommend the following:
• Consolidate your loans – you can offer a loan with a rate of 7%
• Don't use your credit card – withdraw cash from ATMs – or switch to a credit card with 0% interest
• Invest in a savings scheme with a guaranteed return
• Get a mortgage with a fixed interest rate
• Make a monthly budget
• *Include some of your own ideas*

Student B

You have some financial worries so you are going to see a financial adviser to ask for some advice.

This is your situation:
• You have a credit card with over £3,000 on it – the interest rate is 22%
• You have an overdraft at the bank, but you don't know how much it is
• You have a savings scheme linked to the stock market – this has not increased very much recently
• The mortgage on your house is at a variable rate – interest rates have gone up quite sharply recently so you are having to pay a lot more every month
• You have no idea how much money is in your bank account
• Your salary is £3,000 a month
• You have a car loan with an interest rate of 15%
• You never use cash, always your credit card
• *Add some ideas of your own*

Objective

To practise using reported speech.

Introduction

In this activity, you will practise asking and answering questions about jobs and organisations.

What to do

1 Work in groups of three. Look at the table below. First, make notes about your organisation and your job.
2 Then think about what questions you could ask one of your partners to complete their profile.
3 Student A should interview Student B about his/her job, but should not do this directly. Imagine that you have fallen out and are not talking to each other! All questions should go through Student C who will report what each person said. For example:

Student A: *What do you do?*
Student C: *She asked you what you do.*
Student B: *I'm an engineer.*
Student C: *He said he's an engineer.*

4 Student A should note down Student B's answers.
5 Then continue with Student B interviewing Student C, with Student A as the reporter, and so on, so that each person has a turn at reporting.

Input

	You	Your partner
The organisation		
Job		
Your first day at your organisation		
Your most memorable day		
Your worst day		

29 Business and the law

Objective
To discuss legal problems in business.

Introduction
In this activity, you are going to read and summarise some news stories about companies that had legal problems. Then you are going to discuss the issues and decide what the companies should or shouldn't have done.

What to do
1 Work in groups of four. Your teacher will give you each a news story. Read it and prepare to summarise the main points to your group.
2 Take it in turns to summarise the story and lead a short discussion on the main points. Use these questions to help you:
   - *What did the company do wrong?*
   - *What should they have done?*
   - *What shouldn't they have done?*
   - *Do you know of any companies that have faced similar legal problems?*

Input

Multinational collapse
An American bank sued a multinational company after it collapsed. The bank claims that it lost millions of dollars as a result of the collapse and was a victim of the fraud that went on there and that the company lied about its true financial position. The administrators of the multinational had already filed a lawsuit against the bank claiming that it knew about the financial situation and helped to mislead investors. The bank alleges that the multinational forged documents and invented sales and that it would never have done business with the company if it had known.

A seizure
The state seized the assets of a large multinational company as part of a plan to recover millions of euros in unpaid back taxes. The company claimed that it would go bust if this happened and a court ruled that the move was illegal. Shares in the company surged and slumped as news of the seizure spread, and soon after this the shares were suspended by the stock exchange because they had fallen too far.

Search engine
An internet search engine lost its appeal against a court ruling over trademark infringement brought about by two travel companies, and so had to pay damages. A lawsuit was filed after users searching for the two companies found themselves directed instead to rival sponsored links. The search engine was told to stop displaying rival sponsored links but did not do this quickly enough. Companies usually pay to have their website linked to a search engine and if another advertiser uses a trademarked term the words should be taken out of the campaign.

Fair pay
Union officials claimed an equal pay settlement could mean more than 1,500 female workers sharing a £300m payout. The union said the women could receive between £35,000 and £200,000 each, after an eight-year legal battle. Union officials acted on behalf of staff and the organisation involved confirmed that a settlement had been reached. The union compared the pay of female staff with that of male workers and as a result some women are likely to receive up to 14 years' difference in pay.

30 I need to talk to you

Objective
To practise getting important messages across.

Introduction
In this activity, you are going to role-play a situation in which an important message has to be communicated.

What to do
1 Work in pairs. Student A and Student B work for the same organisation and have just been to a meeting with some important, longstanding clients.
2 Your teacher will give you each a role card. Read it and decide what you are going to say in the situation. You can add extra information if you like.
3 Try to use the language for getting an important message across.
4 After the role-play, think of a situation in your working or personal life where you might have to get an important message across.
5 Prepare this situation as a role-play with your partner and then perform it for other students.

Input

Student A

You have been with your organisation for a long time and know the clients well. You realise how important it is that you always appear professional and organised. Unfortunately, you noticed that one of your newer colleagues was late and didn't give the right impression during the meeting. You feel that you should talk to him/her to explain the importance of being on time and creating a good impression. Try to find a time to talk and explain what you think.

Student B

You have been with your organisation for only a few months. You work very hard, but you believe that as long as you get the job done it doesn't matter very much how you look or if you are slightly late. You have noticed that some of your colleagues who have been with the organisation for a long time are a little too worried about such things, in your opinion. You think that they should learn to relax.